Sisters in the Statehouse

Sisters in the Statehouse

Black Women and Legislative Decision Making

Nadia E. Brown

OXFORD
UNIVERSITY PRESS

OXFORD
UNIVERSITY PRESS

Oxford University Press is a department of the University of Oxford.
It furthers the University's objective of excellence in research, scholarship,
and education by publishing worldwide.

Oxford New York
Auckland Cape Town Dar es Salaam Hong Kong Karachi
Kuala Lumpur Madrid Melbourne Mexico City Nairobi
New Delhi Shanghai Taipei Toronto

With offices in
Argentina Austria Brazil Chile Czech Republic France Greece
Guatemala Hungary Italy Japan Poland Portugal Singapore
South Korea Switzerland Thailand Turkey Ukraine Vietnam

Oxford is a registered trade mark of Oxford University Press
in the UK and certain other countries.

Published in the United States of America by
Oxford University Press
198 Madison Avenue, New York, NY 10016

© Oxford University Press 2014

[Cataloging-in-Publication Data on file with the Library of Congress.]

9780199352432

For Eleanor Owens, in memory

The unwavering support encouragement from my maternal grandmother, Eleanor Owens, is what helped me to accomplish my goals. When I felt as if I did not belong in my first graduate seminar, she reminded me that I had a specialized knowledge that was needed in that classroom. She has been my biggest cheerleader— even if she did not fully understand what I do as a political scientist. She taught me to be unabashedly proud of who I was even if others sought to belittle me and my academic contributions. This book is dedicated to her. Furthermore, I thank God for allowing me the fortunate opportunity to develop a special bond with her during her twilight years. I am honored to carry on her legacy.

CONTENTS

ACKNOWLEDGMENTS

First, I would like to thank my Lord and Savior Jesus Christ for leading me, guiding me, and providing for me everything that I need to do that which He has called me to do. Apart from Him I can do nothing and am nothing.

Next, the completion of this book was made possible by the love and support of my family. I am constantly reminded of the sacrifices that my parents, Nadine Medley and Joseph Brown, made so that I could achieve my dreams, often times setting aside their own needs and wants to provide for me. In addition, this book is in honor of my grandparents who were unable to achieve college degrees because of structural and institutional racism that prevented them from obtaining a formal education. My maternal grandfather, Louis Owens (Poppo), instilled in all his grandchildren that education was something more valuable than gold. Specifically, it was something that Whites could never take away. In his view, education would level the playing field between the races. When I was eight years old, he made my brother and me watch David Dinkins inaugural address as the first Black mayor of New York City. My Poppo explained that we were watching history being made and the importance of using politics as an avenue to improve the lives of African Americans. I was hooked; politics soon became my first love. In his memory, I am constantly reminded that I am the hope and the dreams of the ancestors who toiled before me. Furthermore, my entire family has been extremely supportive of my academic endeavors. I would especially like to thank my siblings Nicholas and Lindsey, along with the Hudsons—particularly Edward and Christine Hudson, and the entire Brown family. I am also deeply edited to my paternal grandmother, Janie Barham for her constant love and support during this process. Thank you to my family for helping me keep it all in perspective.

I am deeply indebted to my friends and loved ones that have supported and nurtured me throughout this project. This work is a reflection of their collective love, encouragement, and assistance. Thank you to Brian Lawrence, Cotilya Brown, Kyla Day Fletcher, Nicole Files Thompson, Teeonna Richardson Jones, and my friends from Howard University for continuing to provide moral and emotional support. I have genuinely appreciated your friendship. A special thank you to Vernee Peacock for providing the initial design for the cover of this monograph as well as being my friend. I am grateful to F.A.T.E. 38 and my sorors of North Jersey Alumnae Chapter of Delta Sigma Theta Sorority, Inc. for their unwavering love and dedication to me and this project. I am truly indebted to for their invaluable support over this journey. I am also thankful for my soror-sistah-friends who are as close to me as my biological sister. Special thanks are owed to Lavette Bobbitt, Charisse Cisco, Lusharn Colvin, Tainesa Davis, and Kyrra Mosley.

I would also like to express my gratitude to the American Political Science Association Ralph Bunche Summer Institute where I benefited from the mentorship of Paula McClain. Without this program, it is doubtful that I would have entered a graduate program in political science. I am thankful for APSA's dedication to cultivating a pipeline for minority scholars. In a similar vein, I am blessed to have matriculated through Howard University. I am certain that the foundation I received at my alma mater provided the basis for my academic successes. My experiences at Howard University exposed me to Black politics, its theoretical underpinning, contributions to the field of American politics, and its shortcomings. I am grateful to my mentors Lorenzo Morris, Jane Flax, and Julia Jordan Zachery who allowed me to challenge exclusionary practices in Black politics that would later lead to my research interests. While at Howard University, I was afforded the opportunity to serve as a research assistant for Dianne Pinderhughes. This invaluable experience also expanded my horizons of Black politics and allowed me to learn from and be mentored by a pioneer in the field.

I am thankful and appreciative of the guidance of my dissertation committee: Jane Junn, Susan Carroll, Nikol Alexander-Floyd, Leela Fernandes, and Wendy Smooth. I have benefited immensely from studying under them. I am extremely fortunate to have such dynamic women of color advisors who provided invaluable insight to this project. Their comments shaped this project into a more theoretically, methodologically, and socially responsible manuscript.

Next, I am sincerely grateful for my Rutgers University women and politics family. These gender scholars pushed me to ask critical questions and develop a more nuanced analysis that allowed me to grow as a feminist scholar. I am indebted to my peers, Adryan Wallace, Aiisha Harden Russell, Anna Mitchell Mahoney, Dana Brown, Nimu Njoya, and Sara Angevine who read various drafts of the dissertation and book manuscript, provided insightful comments, and were a true support network. I am also thankful for my friend and sistah-scholar Danielle Taylor Phillips who has laughed, cried, and helped me in more ways than I am able to count during this process. Now that we are both assistant professors I am so grateful that we can look back to our days at Rutgers with fond memories.

I would like to extend my appreciation to the University of Hartford and the Jackie McLean Fellowship that enabled me to complete my dissertation. Additionally, I am thankful for the support of the Politics and Government Department, Hillyer College, and the Sociology Department/African American Studies Program. I was fortunate to develop valuable professional networks and friendships during my fellowship at the University of Hartford. This project was made better because of the mentorship, support, and feedback on my dissertation chapters from Ashley Woody Doane, Bilal Sekou, Karen Tejada, Laurel Clark, and Jilda Aliotta.

This book would not have been possible without the support of scores of people, including my mentors and colleagues in the St. Louis area. First, I must thank my former colleagues from St. Louis University. I am appreciative of Amber Knight, Christopher Witko, Emily Lutenski, Jason Windett, J.D. Bowen, Penny Weiss, Robert Strikwerda, and Wynne Moskop for reading drafts and helping me to conceptualize aspects of this project. Next, my sistah-scholars group in the St. Louis region provided encouragement, offered critical feedback on this project, and were a source of much needed friendship. Many thanks to Ashley Evans Taylor, Kira Hudson Banks, Maki Motapanyane, Olubukola Gbadegesin, Sowandè Mustakeem, and Treva Lindsey. Words cannot express my love and appreciation for these women. I am honored and blessed by their friendship and to be part of this cohort of dynamic women. These women were an integral part of my support system during a particularly trying period of my academic career. I am grateful to Jonathan Smith for his guidance and mentorship. My time at St. Louis University was greatly enriched because of Jonathan; I am proud to call him my friend. I also appreciate the support of Farida Jalalzi and Dayna Stock for inviting me to share my research at the University of Missouri–St. Louis and embracing me as part of the women and politics community in St. Louis. Lastly, I am thankful to my church family at St. John's United Church of Christ in St. Louis. At St. John's I was able to both grow spiritually and mature as a Christian. My church family afforded me the opportunity to ask questions, deeply grapple with religious practices and doctrine, and become a disciple in a beloved community. Big thanks to Rev. Starsky Wilson for leading me along this Christian journey, the women's ministry, and those who participated in Wednesday night bible study who truly became my family in St. Louis.

Furthermore, I remain very thankful to the network of stellar scholars who I count among my mentors and friends. My colleagues, Andra

Gillespie, Atiya Stokes-Brown, Byron D'Andra Orey, Christopher Whitt, Lakeyta Bonnette, Jennifer Oser, Joan Furey, Justin Hansford, Michael Minta, Sarah Allen Gershon, Shayla Nunally, Stephanie Kerschbaum, Tiffany Willoughby-Herard, Tyson King-Meadows and Zenzele Isoke have been consistent sources of support. This community of scholars have read and commented on this work, provided invaluable support and advice, and supported me during this process. This book was also directly improved by their active involvement in its development. I am also appreciative to my research assistants at both St Louis University and Purdue University for helping me during the writing process. A very special shout-out to Christina Greer who pushed me to submit my manuscript to Oxford and supported me through countless emails and phone calls throughout this process. I am happy to join her, Marcus Anthony Hunter, and Dorian Warren as members of the B.O.C. as their #3. Without the continued encouragement and support of Alvin Tillery, I would have not been able to bring my work to a successful completion. Next, I want to thank my new colleagues at Purdue University and their encouragement and support of this project. I am sincerely grateful to have found a home in a nurturing academic environment. I am profoundly appreciative of the support of Rosalee Clawson, political science department head and Venetria Patton, chair of the African American Studies and Research Center at Purdue University.

This research has been supported by numerous fellowships. I express gratitude to the Political Science Department at Purdue University for the summer research grant in the summer of 2013, which enabled me to prepare the manuscript for final submission. The WELFund Grant and Dean's Discretionary Funds Award from the University of Hartford, the Mellon Grant, and the Beaumont Faculty Development Fund Award from the St. Louis University, and the SUN Scholarship and Travel Grant from the Central European University have all supported this work.

Perhaps it is hardest to adequately thank is my dissertation co-chair, mentor, and my strongest advocate, Jane Junn. On the days that I didn't think that I could continue along this academic journey, Jane has been my constant source of support and strength. She believed in me when no one else did—including myself. Jane saw my potential as a scholar and has predicted every one of my achievements before they occurred. Over a margarita (or two) we'd discuss everything from shoes to trashy reality television and strategize on how to navigate our discipline as women of color. While I am deeply indebted for all that she has done for me, I am even more grateful for what she has done for the discipline of political science. Jane uses her influence and status in the profession to build up others and draw attention to injustice; she serves as a powerful ally to those who are marginalized and mistreated in the academy. I strive to have the courage, internal fortitude, selflessness, and fearlessness that she has.

I am extremely thankful to the Maryland state legislators who gave of their time and allowed me to interview them for this project. Without them, this book would not exist. Despite all of the support and assistance from all the aforementioned, any errors that have found their way into this manuscript, are the sole responsibility of the author.

Sisters in the Statehouse

Introduction

It is very different for African American woman to legislate in Annapolis because by the very nature of our culture we become extremely concerned about those issues that make people whole. . . . There is something about African American women that portrays a sensitivity that is deep rooted. It has to do with our culture, history, and our upbringing. We come down here to try to carry forth the beliefs and philosophies of the women of shoulders I stand on—my grandmother, a strong Black woman, and my mother.
　　　　　　　　—Maryland State Senator Yvonne Scott

Delegate Scott's 2009 comments sparked my interest in delving deeper into Black women's culture, history, and upbringings to better understand how African American women elected to public office employ identity in the legislative decision-making process.[1] As Barbara Smith has observed, "Black women, whose experience is unique, are seldom recognized as a particular social-cultural entity and are seldom thought to be important enough for serious scholarly consideration" (1976, 4). With that in mind, I sought to examine how Black women's unique experiences influenced their political behavior. What began as a project that compared Black women to Black men, White men and women, Asian American women, and Latino/as to explain what caused Black female legislators to advocate for both Black interests and feminist interests turned into a study that wholly focused on Black women. Barbara Smith's call for more research on Black women and Senator Scott's articulation of why identity matters in the statehouse led me to examine how, in combination, racial and gender identities affect how African American women legislate. I wanted to both theoretically and empirically capture the spirit of Delegate Scott's words (cited above), in which she reveals that she believes that being a Black woman influences how she legislates.

Delegate Scott's office décor illustrates the deep influence of Black women's culture on her political behavior. Pictures of the Obamas, quotes by Maya Angelou, biblical scriptures, family portraits, awards from various community and civic associations, and school children's paintings adorned the walls. Her office seemed to encapsulate her very essence—it captured the hope of her ancestors, the recognition of her hard work as public servant, her spiritual center, the gratitude of her former students and the dreams of current schoolchildren, and, implicitly, an acknowledgment of a shared experience with other Black women. I began to recognize the importance of sharing the heart, spirit, and lifeblood of Delegate Scott's actions as a state legislator. This inspired me to draw from the wholeness of African American women's identities and experiences to capture more fully the complexity and dynamism of Black women state legislators and its influence on their political behavior.

As both a researcher and a Black woman, I had come to the conclusion that there was a quiet yet strong-willed fortitude—a chutzpah—that causes African American women to view political representation as an extension of a unique culture, history, and upbringing that harnesses the sacrifices, dignity, and powerfulness of our foremothers. This intrinsic Black feminist principle of standing on the shoulders of giants—while standing shoulder to shoulder with others who are concerned with improving the lot of the least fortunate—is not easily captured in political science scholarship on representation. And while none of the women in this study used the words "feminist" or "womanist" to describe themselves, their actions and words could readily be described as Black feminism.

REPRESENTATIONAL IDENTITY THEORY

As legislators, and in their other duties as community activists, mothers, union leaders, lawyers, teachers, church leaders, caregivers, and entrepreneurs, the women in my study (re)define and shape society's images of Black women political elites. Because they all cite culture, history, and socialization as influential in their lives and in the legislation they choose to support, the women in this study are united in a particular and unique way. However, neither the idea of linked fate—recognition that one's individual life chances are intimately tied to one's race as a whole (Dawson 1994)—nor a Black feminist consciousness—the recognition that African American women are marginalized because of their race and gender (Simien 2006)—can adequately represent African American women state legislators' decision-making process. In this study I examine the differences within this population to highlight the complexity of intragroup identity politics, the process by which the women in my study draw on a shared race and gender identity, leading them by turns to similar policy preferences and legislative behavior or to divergent policy positions and representational beliefs makes for a compelling story.

In 2013, out of 7,776 female state legislators serving nationwide, 364 are women of color; of these 239 are African American women. Currently, women of color only comprise 4.9 percent of all state legislators (CAWP Fact Sheet, 2013). Although numbers of Black female elected officials are disproportionately low relative to the percentage of Black women in general, their presence in state legislatures is growing. In fact, Bositis (2001) finds that the increase in the number of Black elected officials can be attributed to Black women. While the election of women to state legislatures has begun to languish overall, African American women have steadily increased their numbers in state legislatures (Sanbonmatsu 2005; Scola 2006; Smooth 2006). Since 1990, Black women have outpaced Black men in election to public office (Orey, Smooth, Adams, and Harris-Clark 2006). However, little is known about the impact of Black women's identity on their legislative decision making. I seek to give voice to the experiences of Black women in politics who are often only presented as numbers within a linear model. Table 1.1 presents information on the increasing number of diverse bodies in American State legislators since 1964.

Maryland is a particularly appropriate case study for my research, owing to the fact that it is home to a large number of Black women legislators. Its

Table 1.1. GROWTH OF MINORITY REPRESENTATION
IN STATE LEGISLATURES SINCE 1964

	1964	2009	% Change
African American	94	628	668
Asian American	55[11]	85	157
Latino	90	242	269
Native American		77	
Women	35	1,797	512
Women of Color	<5[12]	350	7000

Sources: National Association of Latino Elected Officials and the National Conference of State Legislatures, National Caucus of Native American State Legislators, Women's Legislative Network, National Black Caucus of State Legislatures, UCLA Asian American Studies Center, Center for American Women and Politics.

legislature is a highly organized and regimented body, and legislators enjoy a sense of legislative autonomy even within a system that promotes strong partisanship. In addition, the state is racially diverse, which allows for greater control in analyzing how race and gender play out in political representation. As prototypically intersectional subjects—doubly marginalized by race and gender—Black women's narratives expose how undertheorized identity truly is (Nash 2008).[2] The stories of Maryland's Black women legislators, in fact, merit careful attention because they illustrate how a unique population of women experiences, manages, and synthesizes race and gender as social processes.

In *Sisters in the Statehouse*, I undertake an examination, in a specific historical moment, of how identity and lived experience influence the decision-making processes of Black women legislators (Chang and Culp 2002). This project does not contend that all African American women experience race and gender in the same way; instead, I highlight differences and experiential diversity among the women, including and especially those differences attributable to generational affiliation, religiosity, class, sexual orientation, profession, and motherhood status. In the process, I examine how Black women legislators use their own identity to mediate representation, as narrated by their policy preferences.[3] To fully establish a link between who these legislators are and what they do, I first investigate and contextualize the women's status as group members and, in a larger sense, the processes and conditions by which aspects of their identities are primed. Then, to understand more fully how different aspects of identity intersect in the legislative decision-making process, I theorize larger group dynamics while illuminating the various ways in which an African American woman state legislator might perceive her identity as an influence on her political behavior.

Viewing politics as either "gender politics" or "racial politics" ignores the intersectional space Black women occupy in American politics. Smooth (2006) contends that studying Black women in electoral politics is "messy" because it requires a perspective that combines both gender and racial politics, but I assert that this intersectional perspective can—and should—be further muddied. The "messiness" of Black women's studies necessitates that certain categories of identity coexist in relation to others and that identity is formed and maintained in a dynamic and historically contingent process. Employing an intersectional lens may complicate matters, but paying attention to how both race and gender identities influence Black women's politics is a "mess worth making" (Smooth 2006). It is important to note that intersectional identities create both oppression and opportunity; they reflect the social stratification that points to the operation of power relations among groups within a given identity category (Baca Zinn and Dill Thornton 1996). Thus, it is worthwhile and necessary to interrogate the complexity of Black women's identities, which cannot be neatly ordered and do not exist discretely in the categories of race, gender, or class.

Examining Black women's identities requires a marked departure from traditional hegemonic and exclusive practices of social and behavioral research and going beyond feminist or Afrocentric sensibilities. Scholars of Black women's studies recognize the mutually constitutive racial and gender identities of Black women and the hegemonic and restrictive systems and social structures that impact these women's lives. With this in mind, I approach the Maryland state legislature as a case study to show that race and gender identities combine to play a defining role in how Black women make key legislative decisions. Furthermore, rather than simply making comparisons between racial and gendered groups of legislators, I consider the diversity of experience and, consequently, the political behavior of Black women. By using an intersectional approach to identity and study a focused population, I am able to offer new insights about how identity mediates both representation and the role of intragroup differences among African American women elected to public office.

Using intragroup analysis, I develop the concept of *representational identity theory* to examine when and why Black women state legislators behave similarly or have divergent policy preferences. Representational identity theory helps me show that Black women are connected, defined, and intertwined in culture because they live in a country that uses race and racism, gender, sexism, and patriarchy as cultural, political, and economic controls in its exercise of power. Rooted in Black feminist theory, which asserts that African American women are simultaneously subordinated by the larger society because of their race and their gender, my conceptualization of a representational identity theory contends that Black women's relationships to linked fate are shaped by *collective* race and gender identities and their *individual* experiences as Black women. This conceptualization enables a clearer understanding of the relationships among systems of oppression (Collins 1990).

Due in part to common experiences with racism and sexism, Black women in the Maryland state legislature have developed mechanisms for deciding when collective interests should become stronger or weaker than their individual interests. In political contexts where race and gender intersect, African American women are likely to cite their racial and gender identities as factors in their legislative decision making. I have found that Black women form a cohesive bloc in the legislature when policies specifically impact African American women and that at other times they employ divergent legislative strategies and policy prescriptions to address issues that matter to them individually.

Throughout this book, I use representational identity theory to render a more detailed description of the ways in which Black women state legislators' identities influence policy creation. By employing this theory I am able to better analyze the complexities within Black women's identity and, in turn, identity's impact on her political decisions. The shared social identity among Black women characterized by experiences and attributes in common necessitates a more nuanced understanding of group formation as a type of social identification—a person's sense of who they are based on their group membership—rather than simply one of group cohesion, which determines how well a group holds together. Black women legislators use their knowledge of social identity to understand the negative material effects of a race-only or gender-only approach to public policy and other identity-based legislation. Their behavior is clearly mediated by how they experience the intersection of race and gender and other politically salient identities. Yet, because racialized and gender identities are not static, the interaction and interplay between these identities produces different outcomes for different women based on their life experiences and other significant facets of identity—class status or generational affiliation, for example. Consequently, not all Black women lawmakers make decisions in uniform ways or view legislation similarly. Therefore, representational identity theory allows for the possibility of intragroup variation among Black women while still considering what they have in common.

Because representational identity theory makes room to consider how legislators prioritize different aspects of their identities when they engage in legislative decision making, it also helps render clear how Black women's racial, gender, and other politically significant aspects of identity come to bear on their legislative decision-making processes. As a result, I expand on Kingdon's (1989) finding that most "field of forces"—actors whose opinion and influence the member actually values and any personal policy preferences the member has, including interest groups, party leaders, constituents, colleagues and personal preferences—are instrumental in creating the legislator's position. I also build upon Mansbridge's (1999) theory that legislators look to their own experiences and policy ideas to legislate. While legislative actions are not solely determined by a legislator's identity, Black women's legislative choices within the Maryland statehouse are often influenced by the intersection of their multiple identity characteristics. It is impossible to reduce identity to just one factor. My solution proffers a richer theoretical space for exploring the ways that Black women's identities aid in and influence the execution of their legislative duties. Her personal background, identity, and experiences as a Black person in America all influence a Black woman's policy preferences. However, because these elements vary from person to person, Black women cannot reasonably be expected to consistently take similar legislative positions.

Grounded in an analytical framework constructed with a focus on intersectionality, I use representational identity theory to analyze the legislators' experiences and the influence of such experiences on identity formation. I reject a single-axis approach that is common in antiracist and feminist scholarship; instead I use representational identity theory to evaluate how the multiple identities of Black women state legislators influence the manifold dimensions of their experiences in relation to their capacity to provide descriptive and substantive representation to their constituents. Beyond illustrating how race-gender identities inform both Black women legislators' policy preferences and legislative decision making in general, this theory demonstrates that identity is not static. It shows that legislators prioritize elements of their identity differentially depending on political context.

My theorization of representational identity improves upon existing beliefs about Black women's electoral behavior because it considers the diversity and dynamism that is a part of collective identity but that is largely unexplored in extant literature, which views Black women as a unified political group. As a countermeasure, and to demonstrate the possibilities of representational identity theory, I analyze the narratives and the policy preferences of Black women in the Maryland state legislature to illuminate the nuances of how and when African American women are likely to behave as a cohesive political block and when they are more likely behave as individuals. In sum, representational identity theory takes into account the collective nature of identity and emphasizes that Black women legislators use their intersectional identities and individual experiences as Black women to influence their legislative behavior.

IDENTITY POLITICS: PLACING BLACK WOMEN'S REPRESENTATION IN A RACE/GENDER CONTEXT

Descriptive representation occurs when an elected representative belongs to the same social or demographic group as his or her constituents. *Substantive representation* applies when a representative responds to the interests of his or her constituents (Pitkin 1967). Pitkin's influential book, *The Concept of Representation*, outlines the four dimensions of political representation: formalistic, descriptive, symbolic, and substantive. Of these, descriptive representation is perhaps the most problematic form of representation. Pitkin finds that the mirror-image function of descriptive legislators cannot guarantee that a representative will act independently, with discretion and judgment (209–210). However, because Pitkin approaches marginalized groups (i.e., racial, ethnic, or gender groups) as she does all other legislators, who she presumes are male and White, her work cannot address the constitutive roles of racial and ethnic minorities, or those of women and women of color, when it comes to providing representation for the interests of marginalized communities and constituents (Pateman 1988). Some political representation scholars have insisted that marginalized groups should be able to elect representatives from their respective communities. These representatives would then be expected to defend the minority's political interests, thus substantively representing the interests of marginalized groups (Beltran 2010; Dovi 2002; Guinier and Torres 2003; Htun 2004; Phillips 1995, 1998, 1999; Williams 1998; Young 1997).

Despite the growing racial, ethnic, and gender diversity within American legislatures, scholars still do not have a clear understanding of the power of Black women legislators when it comes to advancing the interests of African American women (Gay 2001, 2002; Swain 1993; Tate 2003). Theories proposing that descriptive representation can enhance substantive representation are based on the notion that shared experiences result in common interests. Using the Black women Maryland state legislators as a case study, I tease out linkages between descriptive and substantive representation. To deepen our understanding of political representation, I argue that the cumulative effects of embodying multiple identities, along with her lived experiences, significantly influence how a legislator will respond to political issues. In the process we see how Black women navigate the legislative decision-making process as members of racial and gender groups and as individuals.

The underlying assumption of theories on representation is that group members share similar interests based on a shared background. This belief leaves little room for individual differences among group members. It also supposes that group members will give some ground on their individual interests if the larger needs of the group are met (Dawson 1994). However, belonging to a marginalized group does not mean that a representative will necessarily have the same substantive interests; therefore, descriptive representation is not always preferable. In this vein, Mansbridge (1999) and Dovi (2002) advance our scholarly understanding of what makes an effective representative. Suzanne Dovi contends that descriptive representatives who have strong mutual relationships with historically disadvantaged groups are desirable. For example, Dovi highlights the unwillingness of some African American legislators to support HIV/AIDS prevention and awareness measures in Black communities to illustrate that being a member of a historically disadvantaged group does not automatically entail that a representative will champion the needs of all racial group members. It follows that some Black legislators do not have a strong relationship with members of the Black community who are affected with HIV/AIDS, the lesbian, gay, bisexual, transgender, and queer (LGBTQ) community, or supporters of prevention and awareness programs. Thus, sharing a racial group does automatically translate into adequate representation for all racial group members.

Mansbridge's discussion of gyroscopic representation—the idea that "representatives look within for guidance" (2003, 520)—is closest to the idea that descriptive characteristics, above and beyond party identification, can predict what legislation a legislator will prioritize. This theory of representation supposes that legislators include a sense of their own identity in the representation of their constituents to arrive at commonalities of interest and the principles that will serve as the basis for their actions. In this line of reasoning, a representative does not necessarily need a strong mutual relationship with historically marginalized groups to be an effective legislator. In the absence of a strong mutual relationship, legislators can draw from their own personal identity—from other identities that are structurally and historically disadvantaged—to better understand how a particular legislative decision will affect a marginalized group. For example, several of the younger Black women state legislators in this study draw from their own marginalization as African Americans to empathize with their LBGTQ constituents. While the majority of legislators in the study are neither queer-identified nor have traditionally had strong mutual relationships with the LBGTQ community, they were ardent supporters of marriage equality because of their race-based experiences of exclusion. Indeed, several of the young Black women in this study cited *Loving v. Virginia*—the Supreme Court case that struck down antimiscegenation laws—as a deciding factor in their political position on same-sex marriage.

My intervention into the current theoretical framework of political representation allows for the possibility of legislators engaging in the substantive representation of groups of which they are not immediate members. To be clear, even using empathy and drawing on one's identity as a constituent of other marginalized identities does not imply that well-intentioned legislators can consistently and adequately represent the needs of historically marginalized groups that have largely been absent in the legislative process (e.g., transgender Black communities may be best represented by Black transgender legislators).

While I draw on the work of Dovi and Mansbridge to further our scholarly understanding of how legislators from marginalized identities continue to represent the interests and needs of disadvantaged groups, I take their work a step further by disentangling the interests and experiences of the group from that of the individual legislator. While both gender and race in this research are interpreted as social structures and as socially constructed categories of identity embedded in the institutional dimensions of our society, I also contend that these identities are individual and interactional. Thus an individual may resist and negotiate her raced/gendered identity depending on the existing alternatives, because identity is in a constant state of flux. For example, several of the Black women legislators are moved to political action because of their roles as mothers. When a community in Prince George's County sought to build a youth recreation center as a way to give neighborhood youth a place to congregate and engage in structured after-school programs, one Black woman legislator saw the center as a way to keep her child away from street violence and drug usage. This legislator's motherhood status became the primary identifying factor in her support of this initiative. In this particular context, the legislator presented herself as a concerned mother of a Black teenager, and she knew that other African Americans in the community also sought to protect their children and give them a free place to socialize. Thus, she prioritized her identity as mother, within the social context of a Black community seeking to deal with street violence and gang activity, illicit drug use, truancy, and high youth unemployment. This is an example of a Black woman state legislator using her identity as mother to comfortably interact with other members in her community, drawing from an identity that is highly valued in that context.

Identity foregrounds experience, leading legislators to develop their policy preferences alongside their principles and beliefs. However, even theories that explicitly focus on the role of identity tend to fix it in one location and therefore fail to fully appreciate the dynamism and nuances within it. Representational identity theory offers scholars a deeper engagement and the means to assess the actions of descriptive representatives. In sum, while all the legislators in this study act "as Black women, for Black women constituents," they do so in ways that reflect their individual understandings of what each legislator believes and perceives a Black woman to be, in the process both descriptively and substantively representing Black women. Black women legislators can and do find ways to use personal identity to challenge existing notions of group politics.

INTERSECTIONALITY AND HISTORY OF BLACK FEMINISM

Both racial and gender identities—which I henceforth refer to as *race-gender identity* to reflect an intersectional approach contending that marginalized identities such as race, gender, class, sexual orientation, and others are mutually constituted and are not additive—affect how Black women legislate. Considering African American women's experiences and social identities at the intersections of both race and gender—rather than arbitrarily fusing them—creates a qualitatively different theorization of how identity influences their legislative decision making. To fully consider the mutually constitutive character and acknowledge the complexity of Black women's identities we must employ an intersectional approach. Using an intersectional framework, I argue, ultimately, that it is only through diverse representation that all voices in the body politic can be heard.

First conceptualized in a little over twenty years ago, intersectionality theory has expanded into several different strands of thought and application. Originally coined by Crenshaw (1989, 1991), "intersectionality" is a term used to theorize Black women's experiences using lived experiences and encompassing the "multidimensionality of marginalized subjects" (1989, 139). Crenshaw, by conceiving of the idea of intersectionality, was critiquing the legal system's failure to recognize discrimination against African American women. Because the legal system focused on either race or sex but did not make room to consider both, she argued that it had created a legal compartmentalization of identities that had had disastrous consequences for Black women. Crenshaw (1995) would later build on this observation to advance the idea that political intersectionality erases the politics of women of color and therefore counters an either/or politics that targets particular constituencies without recognizing their connectedness. Presenting the example of the politicalization of domestic violence, Crenshaw finds that women of color are located within two marginalized groups that often pursue opposing political agendas, a problem that Black men and White women do not have to deal with. She criticizes, for example, how feminist and antiracist political agendas are often seen as mutually exclusive. Crenshaw's brand of political intersectionality therefore advances strategies that use the experiences of women of color to understand how public policy discriminates against doubly marginalized groups. Therefore, intersectionality is useful for this study precisely because it challenges the stableness of mutually exclusive race and gender categories, simultaneously making way to consider how both affect identity and potentially exposing intragroup differences.

Earlier Black feminist scholars have used other terms to theorize the multiple oppressions that structure Black women's lived realities (Davis 1981, 1989; Dill Thornton, 1979; Giddings 1984; hooks 1981, 1984, 1989; Lorde 1984). These scholars have helped advance the idea that both racism and sexism are factors that shape Black women's lives and structural and political realities. Crenshaw's use of the term intersectionality draws on a long trajectory of Black feminist activism and thought. It is linked historically to the Combahee River Collective, a group of Black feminist women who organized and formed a coalition to end the oppression of Black women based on race, class, gender, and sexual orientation. Their understanding of the multiple means of Black women's oppression challenged analyses emerging from Black and male-centered social movements as well as from mainstream White, middle-class, heterosexual feminists (Smith 1983), instead drawing on their knowledge of African American women's experiences.[4] Crenshaw, building on the Combahee River Collective's work as well as other Black feminist texts, theorizes intersectionality as historically and theoretically rooted in the lived and multivariate experiences of Black women. And it is important to note that while intersectionality has been institutionalized in academia in the interim, it first started out as a Black feminist "home truth" (Nash 2011).

The strength of an intersectional analysis lies in its ability to theorize complex identity formations and to destabilize reductive binaries such as Black/White, men/women, old/young. In my work, in-depth qualitative research illustrates how the overlapping and multiple sites of identity affect the "matrix of domination"—the interconnectedness of oppression based on race, class, and gender (Collins 1990)—for Black women state legislators. As a result, I confirm that Black women's experiences and social location within a racist and patriarchal society informs their intersectional race-gender identities, which in turn influences their legislative behavior.

Scholars' findings regarding the role of gender or race alone in legislative decision making are instructive but not sufficient for identifying the ways in which African American women represent their constituents. Black women's studies scholars, including Michele Wallace (1990, 60), contend that an analysis that treats race and gender as separate and mutually exclusive categories is based on a dominant culture that seeks to erase Black women. This erasure occurs when categories are constructed as static groupings, which leads scholars to attempt to find an independent effect of one category against another—the effect of race on gender or vice versa. This approach fails to acknowledge the complexity of categories for people who occupy multiple salient identities. I disaggregate the data by both race and gender to demonstrate that African American women participate in ways that are both different and similar to one another, much in the way that they participate in ways that are similar to and different from White women and Black men. I utilize humanistic inquiry to examine the connection between the descriptive and substantive representation conducted by Black women legislators on behalf of their constituents. Finally, I extend the arguments that ideas about descriptive representation influence the substantive representation of entire race and gender groups and that using an intersectional approach to identity politics can enhance our understanding how these processes work.

By investigating and challenging the complexities of categorical identities, I do not deny the importance of categories—material and discursive—that are produced and reproduced in everyday life (Fernandes 1997; Glenn 2002). Feminist poststructuralist critique is an important means toward "freeing individuals and social groups from the normative fix of a hegemonic order and to enable a politics that is at once more complex and inclusive" (McCall 2005, 1777). This critique acknowledges that there is inequality within marginalized groups, which are fluid, constantly changing, and socially constructed (1777). While Black women's identity has no inherent essence and is by definition consistently complicated, an intersectional approach coupled with poststructualist critique allows me to explore change within social relationships.

FRAMING BLACK POLITICAL IDENTITY

In this work I push back against empiricist Black politics scholars who propose to study only a singular Black identity that maintains a concise and monolithic Black political agenda. Instead, similar to theoreticians of Black politics, I contend that Black solidarity is in fact a tactical approach geared toward creating freedom and social equality for Blacks. This view tempers racial essentialism yet complicates the idea of racial solidarity "as a pragmatic engagement of politics" (Glaude 2007, 61). African Americans as a group have commonalities, but it is not a logical conclusion that Blacks have identical interests or will agree on a unified course of action. Narrow constructions of Black politics miss the complexity of intragroup identity. Instead, as Robert Gooding-Williams articulates, building on Kateb's take on Arendt, "Black politics is what some Blacks do together" (2009, 12). This viewpoint, however, sidesteps the problematic creation of a monolithic Black political identity rooted in patriarchy and heterosexism that polices individual identities.

Blackness, taken as a political identity, necessitates that group members articulate common unifying experiences linking them to other group members. Tommie Shelby (2005) notes that Black group identification is based on shared experiences with anti-Black racism and Blacks' commitment to ending it. To be sure, hegemonic structures—that make anti-Black racism and race-based discrimination an enduring American legacy—force African Americans to maintain their group identity, although some Blacks may have to be convinced of the depth and persistence of race-based inequalities. It is of note, however, that even in his argument detailing the benefits of Black political solidarity, Shelby urges scholars to imagine Black identity in a myriad of constructions. If the sole goal is to end racism, he argues, Blacks do not have to share a distinctive Black identity (236). To extend Shelby's assertion, I investigate multiple constructions of a Black political identity and how they influence African American women legislators' advocacy for groups that have been framed as "outside" the boundaries of Blackness (Cohen 1999).

Black politics is communal; historically rooted, group-based race politics situate African Americans' political preferences within the belief that "individual life chances are linked to the fate of the race" (Dawson 1994, 45). Because American racial stratification confers citizenship rights, legal status, and economic status based on racial group membership, African Americans hew to racial unity despite growing social and economic divisions. Historically, African Americans' prioritizations of collective racial interests led to the development of racialized ideologies that in turn have shaped political action (Dawson 2001). However, while there is room for multiple social and political identities in the idea of linked fate, Black racial identity has overwhelmed other salient identities (Dawson 1994). Indeed, race as a metalanguage affects both the construction and representation of gender, class, and sexuality (Higginbotham 1992, 252).

It follows that recent political science scholarship has critiqued the one-dimensional model of linked fate for failing to account for multiple memberships and intragroup difference (Beltran 2010; Greer 2013; Price 2009; Simien 2006). Intragroup policy priorities among racial groups have always been contentious due to the failure of interest groups, activists, and scholars to recognize diversity within these groups (Cohen 1999; Orey et al. 2006; Strolovitch 2007). To further trouble the narrow account of Black identity and political behavior, *Sisters in the Statehouse* elucidates the multiplicities of Black women's identities and the political action that they take based on identity. Emphasizing linked fate as a motivating factor, however, fails to clarify the reasons for agreement and disagreement within the Black community and among African American women as a distinct race/gender group or its link to Black women's legislative behavior. Melanye Price (2009) unravels a series of flaws in current linked fate and group behavior studies. She notes that the concept is not sufficiently problematized nor does the presence of linked fate always result in political action (5–6). The impact of group membership on individual behavior does not explain why African Americans are often politically out of sync. While cohesive political behavior points to the importance of racial group membership for African Americans, the concept of linked fate cannot define when and how racial group affiliation will impact Black women's legislative activities. Visions of a "Black community" are blurred by social and economic class, geographic region, experiences with racism, gender, and views on socially accepted behavior (Cohen 2010; Price 2009; Simien 2006; Simpson 1998). If scholars fail to examine the multiple dimensions of identity, focusing on "groupness" only allows for a reductive explanation of how an individual's connectedness to her racial group explains her individual political calculus.

Because Black political identity is a site of performativity and performance, it is also a place where theory meets practice and textuality meets corporeality. As such, this identity may be avoided or accepted depending on a legislator's social position and her geographical, cultural, psychological, and physical location. I therefore problematize the assumption of a monolithic Black political identity in my analysis of the legislative choices made by African American women elected to the Maryland state legislature.[5]

(Anti)Essentialism of Blackness—The Case of African American Women

Racial essentialism comes out of the belief that a unifying, "essential" Black experience can be isolated from gender, class, sexual orientation, and other realities of experience. This essentialism leads to the idea that a unified Black identity naturally forges a political agenda based on shared goals, values, and ideas. Essentialist Black political identity, akin to an interest group, was born in an anti-Black social environment because a strong, unified collective identity was needed for Blacks to assert claims to self-determination. Therefore, Black collective identity is based on race-based loyalty, identification, and shared interests (including bringing an end to racial injustices) and leads to collective action on issues that disproportionately affect African Americans. I view this form of Black political solidarity as a position that has the ability to create a host of unattractive byproducts, particularly for African American women who are marginalized in an overwhelmingly patriarchal society. For example, scholars have readily noted the likelihood that *advanced marginalization*—a phenomenon in which some members of a marginalized group gain access to upward mobility by monitoring and disciplining other members of that marginalized group (Cohen 1999; Strolovitch 2007)—occurs when there is only one perceived authentic collective Black (political) identity. As a result, Black political solidarity may not be the answer, but examining essentialist Black political identity is useful for understanding how some forms of social consciousness and political positioning cultivate bonds among some African American legislators.

I investigate the role of African American women lawmakers in challenging restrictive norms that characterize an essentialist Black political identity based on the narrow interests of an elite cadre of political actors who claim they represent a homogeneous group sentiment (Reed 2000). Notions of an authentic Black political identity are generally narrow and assume that the majority of African Americans hold one particular political viewpoint while asserting that abandoning these essentialist notions would severely challenge Black political representation. As Cathy Cohen finds, Black politicians and political elites have constructed a political agenda that characterizes the "lived condition of Black Americans is extremely monolithic" (1999, 15). Unfortunately, there has traditionally been little room to contest hierarchical power relations among Blacks because fewer resources are available to advanced marginalized groups. It follows that political representation for those who are deemed deviant because they fail to adhere to proscribed notions of Blackness has also been scarce. *Sisters in the Statehouse*, by exposing the diversity of political opinions and behaviors among Black women Maryland state legislators, shows that an essentialist Black political identity cannot plausibly represent the myriad of opinions, life positions, and diversity among African Americans.

An anti-essentialist Black political identity disputes the necessity of hewing to a common Black identity and instead holds that there is room for additional identities to be explored within Blackness, either simultaneously or intersectionality. This point of view is perhaps most clearly in evidence among Black feminists and womanists who challenged and resisted Black patriarchy in such high-profile examples as the Million Man March and the nomination hearings of Clarence Thomas to the Supreme Court (Alexander-Floyd 2007; Bell 2004; Guy-Sheftall 1991; Smooth and Tucker 1999). Black women have long grappled with the fact that Blackness has traditionally been constructed as a male-dominated space. As a result, activist Black women have bucked the idea of a cohesive Black political identity, challenging Black men who fail to acknowledge sexism and patriarchy. In the fight against (Black) male hegemony, activist Black women have articulated how Black politics must incorporate women's policy interests, including domestic violence, reproductive rights/health/freedom, access to leadership positions, and sexual harassment. This recognition that African American women are marginalized because of their race and gender forms a consciousness based on ideology rather than biology (Collins 2000; Dawson 2001; Simien 2006), which may also lead to group-based political behavior. However, by advancing the scholarly understanding of Black women's politics based on consideration of their race-gender group membership, *Sisters in the Statehouse* makes space to parse the legitimate political and personal concerns of Black women via an anti-essentialist approach to Black political identity, giving weight to factors such as class, generation, region, religion, ethnicity, and sexual orientation. Too often only certain voices are recognized, prioritized, or legitimized by elites determining the Black political agenda, who view divergent opinions as deviant because they perceive them as a distraction. A non-essentialist Black political identity, however, is open to discussions of diverse issues. It is not hierarchical and may not necessarily aim to achieve Black solidarity on all issues all the time. The role of Black political identity in group and individual political practices and decisions has to be recognized, and one means of doing this is by examining the relationship between group politics and individual choices to highlight how African American women state legislators navigate identity-based politics.

Challenging monolithic Black political identity is a radical critique of both Black identity and subjectivity. Taking an oppositional and perhaps libratory view of complexities within Black political identity confronts "essentialism on the part of many African-Americans [that] is rooted in the fear that it will cause folks to lose sight of the specific history and experience of African-Americans and the unique sensibilities and culture that arise from that experience" (hooks 1990, 4). As an alternative, I offer the idea that non-essentialist Black political identity can be both fixed and malleable, especially once other relevant identities are introduced. Allowing for flexibility challenges the boundaries of essentialist ideas about Blackness at times and at others is compatible with current ideas about Blackness. For example, the younger African American women state legislators in this study challenge an essentialist Black political identity in their support of marriage equality. Here, these women confront the strict constructions of Blackness. As an open Black lesbian, Delegate Leila Baker challenges her colleagues to support her right to marry the partner of her choosing, regardless of gender, as a necessary human and civil right. Using the language of rights, Delegate Baker illustrates the possibility of queer inclusivity within a Black political identity.

Black feminists actively challenge hegemonic politics of unity because they have experienced exclusion and silencing within different forms of community. They work to dismantle the hard lines that determine who is included and excluded from Black political identity in a way that echoes a Third World feminist critique of social group membership, which admonishes the "marginalized communities with whom they claim political affinity" for failing to incorporate all members (Beltran 2010, 61). Because Black politics also fails to incorporate all its constituents in an egalitarian way, Black feminists build coalitions with other groups to construct new experiences of belonging. Alarcon writes that women of color live "in resistance to competing notions for one's allegiance or self-identification" (1990, 364). Minority women are also "less likely to invest themselves completely in any single dimension and more likely to realize that their likeness to others is never complete" (Ferguson 1993, 161). Building on Alarcon and Ferguson's work, I contend that African American women legislators display a political subjectivity that, like their race-gender identities, is multivalent. Beltran (2010), in her transformative work on Latino politics, finds that there are serious problems with evaluating minority representatives based on an uncomplicated view of identity, a point of view borne out by my research about the policy-making decisions made by Black women elected to the Maryland state legislature. Therefore, instead of conflating identity with political agreement, I assert that, while there are shared beliefs among African American state legislators, there is also legitimate variation that highlights not only differences among Black legislators but also intragroup difference among the larger population of Black women.

METHODOLOGICAL APPROACH

This project employs qualitative techniques to focus on African American women who have held elected seats in the Maryland state legislature between 2009 and 2011. I utilize in-depth elite interviews, case studies of select legislation, feminist life histories, and participant observation to advance understandings of diversity among African American women state legislators. To gain insight about these legislators' social and political positions within the Maryland legislature and the larger society, I examine how legislators use their own multiple identities to interpret legislation dealing with same-sex marriage, antidomestic violence initiatives, minority business set-aside programs, and criminal laws addressing the financial exploitation of the elderly. In the process, *Sisters in the Statehouse* illustrates that identity influences political decision making in a myriad of ways in the work of Black women Maryland state legislators.

This project is unique because I conduct in-depth analysis of legislation to investigate the policy preferences of the Black women legislators who were respondents in the study. Unlike typical political science research that utilizes roll call data and disaggregates legislators by demographic group, *Sisters in the Statehouse* accounts for legislator-specific factors that influence representation. The data I collected during the 2009 legislative session via in-depth, semi-structured, open-ended interviews with all twenty of Maryland's Black women legislators show the extent to which the women use identity to mediate political representation. To give me a more nuanced perspective, I also conducted interviews with a number of White men, Black men, Latino(a)s, Asian American men, and Asian American women legislators and with LGBTQ representatives and religious groups, including Jews, Muslims, Protestants, and Catholics. Because all of the African American women state legislators are Democrats, the study avoids distortions caused by partisan politics that might undermine the reliability of comparisons made among racial/ethnic and gendered lines. Controlling for party identification also allows me to highlight differences within identity groups. Because the interview questions enabled open-ended answers, the legislators were able to express themselves and narrate their stories freely. During the interviews, I utilized the so-called soak and poke method (Fenno 1978, 2003). This method allows me to delve deeply into legislators' responses to provide a thick description of their views on identity and representation. It also provides an exhaustive way to test many suppositions and claims made by legislative studies scholars who rely heavily on roll call and national survey data.

Furthermore, during the summer of 2011, I conducted feminist life histories with eighteen of the twenty Black women Maryland state legislators. The feminist life histories challenged me to understand an individual's current attitudes and behavior and showed me how she might have been influenced by decisions made at other times and places (Bell and Nkomo 2003; Berger 2004; White 2009). Furthermore, the feminist life histories provided an important link to contemporary explorations because they provided clues about how legislators use identity to support, oppose, or champion legislation. I draw from the legislators' life histories and combine my findings with participant observation to correlate the legislators' narratives of identity. As a result, the feminist life histories enable me to place the legislators' verbal articulation of the legislative decision-making process into the broader context of identity politics and legislative political phenomena.

In addition to data collected through elite interviews, case studies, and feminist life histories, I also utilize discourse analysis and participant observation. I attended and, in a limited capacity, participated in committee meetings and hearings, caucus meetings, and delegation nights. Participant observation of legislators and their staffs enabled me to have a clearer understanding of the motives and meanings behind the behavior exhibited by interviewees. *Sisters in the Statehouse* therefore diverges from traditional quantitative methods in political science to pursue a methodology based largely on ethnographic research and interpretivist methods.

Context for Maryland as Research Locale

Maryland has remained a leader in women's representation, never ranking below sixteenth among the nation in statistics of proportional women's representation in the state legislature (CAWP Fact Sheet, Maryland State Legislature 2013). Table 1.2 illustrates the growth in numbers of African American women state legislators nationwide and provides a detailed break-down of the growth in numbers of Black women and men elected to the Maryland state legislature. In fact, the percentage of African American men in the Maryland state legislature has decreased since 1995 while Black women have increased their number of seats in this representative body.

The Maryland state legislature attracted my attention because of the comparatively high number of African American women state legislators during the 2009 legislative session (twenty: fifteen delegates and five senators). After the 2010 election, the number of African American women legislators remained stable, although there was some shifting within this group (still numbering twenty, but with fourteen delegates and six senators). In 2010, Delegate Yvonne Scott won her Senate bid by defeating a long-term incumbent. She was sworn into office on January 2011. Delegate Kenya Barnes gave up her seat in the House of Delegates in an unsuccessful bid for County Executive of Prince George's County. Delegate Estrella Henderson,

Table 1.2. GROWTH OF BLACK WOMEN STATE LEGISLATORS

	1995	2011	% Change
African American Women Nationwide	137	152	11
African American Women in Maryland	10	20	50
African American Men in Maryland	25	22	−1

Source: Joint Center for Economic Studies.

who served twenty-eight years in the legislature and was one of the longest-serving members of the House of Delegates, lost her seat in the 2010 election. Delegates Fatima Coleman and Leila Baker joined the legislature in 2010.[6]

According to the 2010 Census, of the 5,773,552 residents in Maryland, 29 percent are African American, 58 percent are White, 5 percent are Asian, and 8 percent are Hispanic. The African American women legislators represent districts with a majority or near majority of Black constituents, primarily districts in Baltimore City, Baltimore County, and Prince George's County (a suburb of Washington, DC). Maryland state legislators serve a term of four years in the lower chamber. Members of the Maryland Senate are elected every four years, in off-year elections in the middle of four-year terms for presidents of the United States. The Maryland General Assembly includes 47 senators and 141 delegates elected from forty-seven districts. The multimember districts are compised of four representatives—one senator and three delegates.[7] More women are elected in multimember systems than in single member districts (Clark and Caro 2013), which allows for women legislators to conduct descriptive and substantive representation on behalf of women's issues. While *Sisters in the Statehouse* does not focus on institutional features that facilitate Black women's representation per se, it is important to acknowledge the structural and institutional factors that contribute to women's substantive and descriptive representation. The multimember district structure is ideal for examining the effects of race and gender identity on Black women's legislative decision making, because a majority of the African American women represent the same constituency. As a result, I can differentiate between constituent wishes and internal factors, such as identity, that drive legislators' decision making. Furthermore, concerns about representation in urban areas often manifest in discussions of descriptive and substantive representation. Literature on political incorporation, especially studies based on city councils, finds that minority representation in urban political institutions facilitates group interests in the policy-making process (Browning et al. 1984). The symbiotic relationship of Black legislators and Maryland's African American constituents, largely found in Baltimore City, Baltimore County, and Prince George's County,[8] illustrates that Black legislators are elected by Black constituents. Indeed, the largest proportion of Black lawmakers represent these constituencies.[9]

Table 1.3 provides descriptive statistics for the racial and gendered groupings of legislators serving during the 2005 and 2011 session.[10] These data were obtained from the legislators' campaign Web sites, the official Maryland state legislature online directory, and from the members' legislative staffs.

Table 1.3. DEMOGRAPHIC CHARACTERISTICS OF SAMPLE % (RAW)

	Black Women	Black Men	White Women	White Men	Total (*n* = 187)
2005	10.7%	12.3%	23.5%	53.5%	(*n* = 179)
2011	(*n* = 20)	(*n* = 23)	(*n* = 44)	(*n* = 100)	
	11.2%	12.3%	17.9%	58.7%	
	(*n* = 20)	(*n* = 22)	(*n* = 32)	(*n* = 105)	
Republican	0	0	31.8% (14)	44.0% (44)	31.0% (58)
	0	0	37.5% (12)	40.0% (42)	30.2% (54)
Democratic	100% (20)	100% (23)	68.1% (30)	56.0% (56)	69.0% (129)
	100% (20)	100% (22)	62.5% (20)	60.0% (63)	69.8% (125)
Independent	0	0	0	0	0
Tenure					
0–3 years	20.0% (4)	30.4% (7)	27.3% (12)	35.0% (35)	30.9% (58)
	10.0% (2)	18.2% (4)	25.0% (8)	16.2% (17)	17.3% (31)
4–6	30.0% (6)	17.4% (4)	6.8% (3)	13.0% (13)	13.8% (26)
	25.0% (5)	22.7% (5)	9.4% (3)	26.7% (28)	22.9% (41)
7–10	15.0% (3)	26.1% (6)	31.8% (14)	15.0% (15)	19.2% (38)
	15.0% (3)	18.2% (4)	25.0% (7)	23.8% (25)	22.3% (40)
11 or more	35.0% (7)	26.1% (6)	34.2% (15)	37.0% (37)	34.6% (65)
	50.0% (10)	40.9% (9)	40.6% (13)	33.3% (35)	37.4% (67)
Age					
25–35	0	0	2.3% (1)	10.0% (10)	5.9% (11)
	5.0% (1)	0	6.3% (2)	10.6% (11)	7.9% (14)
36–45	15.0% (3)	21.7% (5)	9.3% (4)	15.0% (15)	14.4% (27)
	10.0% (2)	27.3% (6)	9.4% (3)	13.5% (14)	14.0% (25)
46–55	30.0% (6)	21.7% (5)	27.0% (12)	25.0% (25)	25.5% (48)
	30.0% (6)	27.3% (6)	25.0% (8)	31.7% (33)	29.8% (53)
56–65	20.0% (4)	39.1% (9)	32.6% (14)	33.0% (33)	31.9% (60)
	30.0% (6)	27.3% (6)	37.5% (12)	27.9% (29)	29.8% (53)
66–75	25.0% (5)	17.4% (4)	20.9% (9)	14.0% (14)	17.0% (32)
	20.0% (4)	13.6% (3)	15.6% (5)	13.5% (14)	14.6% (26)
Over 75	5.0% (1)	0	6.8% (3)	0	2.1% (4)
	5.0% (1)	4.5% (1)	6.3% (2)	2.9% (3)	3.9% (7)
Education					
No High School	0	0	2.3% (1)	3.0% (3)	2.1% (4)
	0	0	3.1% (1)	3.8% (4)	2.8% (5)
Some College	15.0% (3)	13.0% (3)	13.6% (6)	13.0% (13)	13.3% (25)
	15.0% (3)	9.1% (2)	9.4% (3)	8.6% (9)	9.5% (17)
Associates	0	4.3% (1)	9.1% (4)	4.0% (4)	4.8% (9)
	0	0	3.1% (1)	2.9% (3)	2.2.% (4)
Undergraduate	25.0% (5)	21.7% (5)	34.1% (15)	33.0% (33)	31.2% (58)
	15.0% (3)	45.5% (10)	43.8% (14)	27.6% (29)	31.3% (56)

Table 1.3. (CONTINUED)

	Black Women	Black Men	White Women	WhiteMen	Total (n = 187)
Professional	55.5% (11)	47.8% (11)	40.9% (18)	46.0% (46)	46.2% (86)
	60.0% (12)	31.8% (7)	40.6% (13)	54.3% (57)	49.7% (89)
Doctorate	5.0% (1)	8.7% (2)	0	1.0% (1)	2.2% (4)
	10.0% (2)	13.6% (3)	0	2.9% (3)	4.5% (8)
HBCU					
Yes	45.0% (9)	60.9% (14)	0	0	12.2% (23)
	50% (10)	81.8% (18)	0	0	16.6% (29)
No	55.0% (11)	34.8% (8)	100% (44)	100% (100)	87.6% (163)
	50.0% (10)	18.2% (4)	100% (32)	100% (105)	83.8%(150)

Note: HBCU = historically Black colleges and universities

The data indicate that the Democratic Party controls the state legislature and that only White women and men identified as Republican. The data show that the majority of legislators in each racial and gender group have served eleven or more years in the statehouse and are between the ages of forty-six and sixty-five. White men had the greatest percentage of legislators in the youngest age cohort, and White women had the greatest percentage in the oldest age group, seventy-five or older. Turning our attention to Black women, we find that, compared to other groups, this group holds the highest percentage of professional degrees.

SUMMARY AND CHAPTER OUTLINE

Sisters in the Statehouse is an interdisciplinary project; it draws theory and methodology from the disciplines of political science, women's studies, and Black studies. It is wholly situated in the tradition of Black women's studies, which focuses on the voices, lives, and experiences of Black women. Indeed, scholars who investigate the complexity of Black womanhood from that perspective themselves offer a valuable conceptual framework at the intersection of African American studies and women's studies (e.g., Guy-Sheftall 1992; hooks 1984; Jordan-Zachery 2012). The challenge of examining the intersections of race, gender, and class have led these scholars to reject the separation of both analytical and identity categories (e.g., Crenshaw 1989; Davis 1981; hooks 1984; Smith 1983). My work builds on their work, and I find that the complexity and diversity of the Black female experience cannot be solely housed within a framework that neglects to address the relational dimensions of multiple social identities.

In contrast to utilizing primarily White women's or Black men's experiences as the basis for examining the benefits of descriptive representation, I focus on African American women state legislators' experiences to examine how, in combination, race-gender identities influence representation. Ultimately, this project contributes to a fuller scholarly understanding of the importance of diversity among elected representatives. Intersectional identity provides these women with a unique worldview that differs from that of their racial and gender counterparts. However, it is also necessary to further explore differences *among* Black women. We must consider the specificity of African American women's common group identity along with the complexity of the diversity within that group. It is important to recognize that intersectionality is not only a recognition of the confluences of Blackness and femaleness but also other categories of identity and experience. It is this view, informed by representational identity theory approach, that makes this book an important intervention into the disciplines of political science, Black studies, women's studies, and Black women's studies.

Overview of the Book

Chapter 2 begins by providing detailed portraits of the Black women within the Maryland state legislature to addresses identity formation and its impact on the political behaviors of these particular women. This chapter serves as the foundation for explaining how identity influences legislative decision making, and in it I use feminist life histories to explicate how personal experiences, race, gender, class, and other identities determine how legislators behave. Next, I show how the theory works by examining specific policy. Chapter 3 utilizes elite interviews—with people who are chosen because of who they are or what position they occupy—to investigate how the intersection of race, class, and gender affects Black women legislators' decision-making processes. I evaluate the extent to which the data supports my theory that legislators' identities are a factor in the legislative decision making. In this chapter, I argue that the political context for a particular issue strongly influences the likelihood that a representative will use her identity as a means for understanding and articulating policy preferences. Using legislation on Maryland's Minority Business Enterprise program, I make a connection between Black women's descriptive representation and substantive representation. I illustrate that, overall, although Black women represent Black women, they arrive at policy positions in diverse ways.

Chapter 4 demonstrates how the approach of political intersectionality in legislation seeking to prevent domestic violence provides an important

analytical tool for understanding how African American women representatives navigate traditional feminist policies. The chapter illustrates that
Black women legislators in the Maryland state legislature mention domestic
violence as a policy priority whereas White women and, overwhelmingly,
White *and* Black male legislators do not. I find that Black women legislators
in this study are more likely to discuss the role that race plays in domestic
violence situations. Yet there is a marked difference in how younger African
American women vote on domestic violence legislation in comparison with
their older counterparts.

Chapter 5 examines how Black women state legislators employ forms of
Black political identity when representing their constituents, specifically
when it comes to groups that are constructed socially as deserving and undeserving. By exploring Black women's stances on marriage equality legislation, which, I contend, is a racialized issue for African Americans, I
demonstrate views of Black political identity from different perspectives.
As in the previous chapter, I incorporate a generational analysis to show
that the younger African American women state legislators are more progressive and push back against the tropes of Black culture that construct
same-sex marriage as deviant. However, viewing this bill solely along racial
or gender lines misses the complexity of how identity informs representation. While older Black men and women did not support same-sex marriage legislation, citing religious grounds—pointing to the continued
prominence of the Black church as a political and cultural institution—I
find a clear generational split between Black women legislators born before
and after 1960, the latter of whom are more likely to support same-sex
marriage. This intragroup difference between Black women legislators illustrates the benefits of incorporating a generational analysis when comparing intragroup policy preferences.

Chapter 6 examines whether and, if so, how race- and gender-consciousness
shapes Black women's legislative decision making. In this chapter I investigate Black women's views on the Financial Exploitation of the Elderly bill and
compare them with a selection of those of Black men and White women and
men. As a result, I am able to evaluate the effects of race and gender on representation in the case of legislation that is specifically classified as women's
interest. I argue that, because of the racialized and gendered nature of
caregiving, Black women have a more intimate and hands-on awareness of
the necessity for this legislation and are therefore stronger advocates for it.

The book concludes by reviewing the theoretical arguments and summa-
rizing the findings of the empirical chapters. In chapter 7 I point to the
benefit of using Black women's voices as starting points for the analysis of
their political behavior. Taken as a whole, Black women's identities play an

important role in debates within legislatures and within their own decision-making processes. I highlight the potential of employing intersectionality as an analytical tool for achieving a better understanding of the complexities of political representation carried out by African American women who are elected to office.

My goal is to help advance understandings of diversity among African American women state legislators. While I examine group-based differences marked by racial, gender, sexual orientation, socioeconomic status, generational affiliation, nationality, and motherhood status, my primary focus is on race-gender identities. These African American women state legislators differ from one another in their political experiences and personal backgrounds and from their African American male counterparts. The differences I uncover here caution us to be mindful of monolithic categorizations of Black political elites in general and Black women political elites in specific. However, there is commonality in the midst of difference, and intersectional inquiry allows me to examine both among African American women Maryland state legislators.

As the study of politics and political actors becomes more diverse, using representational identity theory as an analytical tool will provide a useful alternative to dominant discourses. For instance, as scholars become attuned to other significant categories of difference—such as nationality, sexual orientation, or (dis)ability status—that affect how American lawmakers legislate, representational identity theory's flexible model of considering intersectional and shifting identities will help show how multiple group memberships influence legislators' political behavior. In the future, a more diverse body of legislators will challenge aspects of how American legislatures are structured along identity lines. For example, the Black caucus may incorporate more voices from the African Diaspora or the women's caucus may include transwomen as members. These identity-based caucuses will eventually be forced to make space for other categories of difference within in their memberships. Scholars will also need a more inclusive means for investigating how identity affects legislation. As we will see in this study of Black women legislators in the Maryland state legislature, representational identity theory can provide that model.

CHAPTER 2
Formative Experiences

Sometimes, I feel discriminated against, but it does not make me angry. It merely astonishes me. How can any deny themselves the pleasure of my company? It's beyond me.

—Zora Neale Hurston

There's always someone asking you to underline one piece of yourself—whether it's Black, woman, mother, dyke, teacher, etc.—because that's the piece that they need to key in to. They want to dismiss everything else.

—Audre Lorde

The Black women in Maryland's state legislature may come from diverse and complex personal backgrounds, but there are also many similarities between them, including generational commonalities (i.e., cohort), the circumstances of their upbringings, and their experiences with racial and gender roles. While legislators' backgrounds are readily available via their campaign materials, legislative Web sites, and personal social-networking sites, scholars have yet to fully capture the relationship between who the legislators are and how they legislate. Aside from the brief introduction to a legislator's personal background that he or she provides during campaign speeches, interviews with journalists, and comments made during legislative sessions, scholars know very little about political elites' personal lives. In this chapter I examine the relationship between legislators' formative experiences and their political behavior. Because they often lack access to legislators' more personal experiences, scholars instead use race, gender, and class as heuristics for understanding how a Black woman legislator might vote on a particular piece of legislation. While these rubrics must be considered, I find that understanding a legislator's formative experiences and considering identity from an intersectional standpoint is essential to a well-rounded understanding of legislators' decision-making processes.

Barry Burden calls legislators' life experiences, interests, and expertise the "personal roots of representation" (2007, 5) and goes on to illustrate that personal factors can drive legislators' positions on certain issues (9). However, political representation is influenced in myriad ways. Institutional factors—such as district concerns, partisanship, committee systems, party leadership, lobbyists, administration, interest groups, and campaign activists—influence the ways legislators respond to policy. Typical legislative studies use roll call voting patterns, committee assignments, agenda setting, and legislators' behavior to draw conclusions about the influence of race or gender on legislators' policy preferences (Bratton and Haynie 1999; Bratton, Haynie, and Reingold 2006; Haynie 2001; Reingold 2000; Swers 2002; Tate 1994). When an explanatory variable—such as race, gender, or the rarely investigated intersection of race and gender identity, which I refer to as race-gender identity—is a statistically significant predictor, the researcher deduces that racial, gender, or race-gender identity causes legislators' behavior. While it has its merits, this method does not allow for rich or detailed portrayals of how legislators' identities influence their actions and therefore fails to capture the nuance and dynamism of identity. Conducting interviews and life histories with the majority of the Black women state legislators helped ground my study in a broad historical and cultural framework. As a result, I am able to represent the inherent subjectivity of women's experiences and to illuminate the meaning and significance of the policy preferences of Black women state legislators. Because my study examines the extent to which Black women's experiences, identities, and worldviews shape their policy-making decisions, it is the first to reveal the importance of Black women's personal identities in shaping their legislative decision-making processes.

To understand the role that race and gender have played in the legislators' life journeys, I conducted feminist life histories with eighteen out of twenty Black women Maryland state legislators during the summer of 2011. A feminist life history interview is an interview in which the participant narrates the story of her life: her past, present, and what she sees in her own future. I designed the format for my feminist life history study in a way that would yield insights about the social and material contexts in which the legislators learned about and enacted their social identities. In the initial data analysis, I discerned that Black women state legislators routinely used storytelling techniques to expand on or illustrate their arguments, opinions, or beliefs, telling stories with themes that corresponded to the points that they were trying to make. When I studied these stories, I observed patterns, namely, that the women in this sample had difficulty representing singular identities. In other words, no legislator spoke solely of being a woman or of being African American. Instead, the identities they incorporated into their narratives were overlapping, intersectional, and interconnected, and their experiences mediated by linked views of the salient parts of their identities.

In addition to the legislative decision-making processes that the women outlined, their feminist life histories enabled me to make connections that were invisible to previous scholars, who used race, gender, or class as proxies for identity. I was able to move past the fixed and static accounts of identity and conduct instead an intersectional analysis of how identity affects the legislative process within a broader context that included sexual orientation, religion, motherhood status, and marital status. Gathering feminist life histories enabled me to glean information about the Black women of the Maryland state legislature to incorporate in a more holistic picture of these women and how they came to be who they are as legislators.

I started by asking the legislators to share their memories about childhood and young adulthood. To move the conversation toward contemporary issues, I then asked about their legislative work and their current personal lives (see the appendix for information on my methods). Their answers helped me see how these women's experiences have shaped their identity. I culled their responses into eight broad themes: messages about race, experiences during segregation, direct experiences with discrimination, religious upbringing, socioeconomic background, community activism and interest in politics instilled by parents, gender roles, and current family life. Table 2.1 provides a concise overview of the women in this study. I readily acknowledge that these themes are overlapping; none exists in a vacuum. True to intersectionality theory, Black women's life stories, although shaped by the confluences of race, gender, and class, are also peppered with other interconnecting identities. In the process of their highlighting significant moments in their lives, the Black women in this study illustrate that identity is varied and fluid, in turn making it irresponsible for scholars to view Black women as a monolithic political group.

THEORETICAL FRAMEWORK

Black women who are political elites and activists, both historically and in the present day, have demonstrated a connectedness to both gender and racial identities. Black women's political socialization and orientation have been shaped by the unique history and experiences of Black women in

Table 2.1. AFRICAN AMERICAN WOMEN MARYLAND STATE LEGISLATORS 2009 AND 2011

Name	Age Cohort	Class Background	Region of Origin/ Childhood Home	Relationship Status	Motherhood Status	Occupation	Legislative Tenure (years)
Olivia Jenkins	50–55	Middle class	Baltimore	Divorced	Two children	County government program director	10 or more
Cassandra Ross	70–75	Middle class	Jamaica	Divorced	Three children; five grandchildren	Nurse; Entrepreneur	10 or more
Tanisha Harold	55–60	Middle class	DC/Prince George's County	Divorced	Two children	College coordinator	6–10
Fatima Coleman	30–35	Working class	DC/Prince George's County	Married	One child	Lawyer	5 or less
Abigail Watson	70–75	—	Florida	Married	Three children	Educator	10 or more
Julissa Moore	30–35	Middle class	DC/Prince George's County	Single	None	Lawyer	5 or less
Keira Miller	45–50	Working class	Montana	Divorced	Two children	Social worker	10 or more
Justine Anderson	60–65	Working class	DC/Prince George's County	Married	Four children; four grandchildren	Union leader	6–10
Angela James	70–75	Lower class	Alabama	Widowed	Four children	Author; Entrepreneur	5 or less
Naomi Young	40–45	Middle class	Baltimore	Single	None	Lawyer	6–10
Leila Baker	40–45	Middle class	Pennsylvania	Married	None	Professor, nonprofit director	5 or less
Ingrid Jefferson	50–55	Working class	Baltimore	Married	Five children; eight grandchildren	Consultant; Union leader	5 or less

Bella Campbell	80–85	Working class	North Carolina/Baltimore	Widowed		Educator	10 or more
Yasmin Wood	45–50	Middle class	DC/Prince George's County	Married	Five children	Freelance writer; Media relations	5 or less
Yvonne Scott	70–75	Middle class	Western Maryland	Widowed	None	Educator	10 or more
Brenda Perry	60–65	Working class	Virginia	Married	One child; two grandchildren	Government employee	10 or more
Bailey Smith	45–50	Middle class	Baltimore	Single	None	Lawyer	10 or more
Pamela Price	55–60	Middle class	Baltimore	Married	None	Entrepreneur	10 or more
Imani Hayes	75–80	——	Virginia	Married	Three children	Professor	10 or more
Raquel Simmons	60–65	Working class	Pennsylvania	Single	None	Entrepreneur	10 or more
Kenya Barnes	40–45	——	Illinois	——	——	Lobbyist, attorney	5 or less
Estrella Henderson	75–80	——	Baltimore	——	Six children	Teacher's aid	10 or more

Some information is supplemented for the legislator's biographies on the Maryland State Legislature Web site.
Tenure is calculated based on the 2011 legislative session.
Class status reflects the legislators' self-report on the class background of their family of origin.

America. The African American women in the Maryland state legislature have a strong sense of racial identity that is closely linked to Black political identity—a heuristic understanding of how Black cultural, historical, and political identities are fused to produce a seemingly monolithic Black political agenda. Nevertheless, this strong cultural and racial identity shows in the high likelihood that Black women Maryland state legislators will choose to serve as advocates for the needs of African Americans.

The Black women in the Maryland state legislature display a gender consciousness that stems from their experiences as women rather than from any commitment to feminism; none of them self-identify as feminists consistent with the majority of African American women who do not use this label (Anderson, Kanner, and Elsayegh 2009). It is unsurprising that members of racial and ethnic groups are less likely to identify as feminists; these groups often perceive feminism as reflecting only the concerns of and solutions for middle-class White American women. "Many black women view feminism as a movement that at best, is exclusively for women and, at worst, dedicated to attacking or eliminating men" (Collins 2000, 11). Black women have historically had an uneasy relationship with White women, feminist organizations, Black men, and Black Nationalist organizations. In fact, history details the tribulations of Black women such as Harriet Tubman, Maria Stewart, Sojourner Truth, Fannie Barrier Williams, Elaine Brown, Ella Baker, Fannie Lou Hamer and other Black women activists who suffered within the civil rights movement, Black power movement, and the women's movement (Giddings 1984; Higginbotham 1992).

Alice Walker (1983) famously noted that feminism does not fully include the perspectives of African American women. Black women practice a form of feminism that is clearly distinct from what is typically understood to be feminism and in the process disavow neither their status as women nor their race. Undeniably, the work of Black feminism is always conducted from the intersectional vantage point of being both Black and women and is a generally recognized phenomenon that derives from the experiences of African American women. Indeed, Black feminism grew from the "othering" that Black women perceived as coming from Black men and White women. Black women have not had the luxury of fighting oppression on just one front; therefore, Black feminism grew out Black "women's historical experiences, social positions, and indigenous efforts to build multiple movements within the Black community and between the Black community and many other communities" (Dawson 2001, 140). Alice Walker also coined the term *womanism*, which describes a phenomenon similar to Black feminism. Womanism recognizes that both the racist and classist aspects of (White) feminism and opposes separatist ideologies, viewing Black men as integral parts of Black women's lives—as their lovers, children, and family members. Both Black feminism and womanism describe the perspectives and experiences of Black women in a way that diverges from the White feminist movement.

However, Black feminism remains an important element in Black political theory (Dawson 2001; Simien 2006). It supports the struggle for Black liberation by pursuing social justice on all fronts, rather than dividing members into factions to fight economic exploitation, racial discrimination, gender discrimination, and heterosexism. Patricia Hill Collins (2001) asserts that modern Black feminism grew out of Black women's growing dissatisfaction with the civil rights and women's movements of the 1960s and 1970s. Given the history of U.S. racial segregation, many Black feminist activities also grew out of Black Nationalist projects. "Thus, Black women's path to 'feminist consciousness' often occurs within the context of antiracist social justice projects, many of them influenced by Black nationalist ideologies. . . . To look for Black Feminism by searching for U.S. Black women who self-identify as 'Black Feminists' misses the complexity of how Black feminist practices actually operate" (Collins 1993, 31).

In this study I challenge the existing belief that Black women choose a racially constructed identity that strongly affects their political attitudes rather than one based on gender (Gay and Tate 1998). Instead, I posit that Black women use an intersectional framework of identity that accounts for concealed inequalities or those excluded from conceptions of the model of identity found in traditional linked-fate methodological approaches (Dawson 1994), which are typically used to study Black women (e.g., Simien 2006).

Intertwined with race and gender, class is another component of Black women's identity. Social class refers to the degree of access one has to resources and to power (Lerner 1997). Class determines one's access to education, political power, land acquisition, technology, and important social networks (Bell and Nkomo 2003). Class is multilayered, relational, and interdependent with other social identities. Economic success and social privilege are on a continuum that positions society's members in culturally specific ways. While William Julius Wilson (1978) and Michael Dawson (1994) disagree on the economic status of African Americans, as readily seen in their glass "half empty, half full" debate, it is poignantly clear that there are two Black Americas—one middle class and the other lower class. Whereas it is important to note the differences in social strata, gender, sexual orientation, multiracialism, and deracialization among Blacks, African American women's identities are fundamentally constructed via race, class, and gender. Hall explains, "Race and gender are the modalities through which class is lived; disentangling them is impossible" (1989, 68). An intersectional approach helps me to capture the complex factors that shape the lives and legislative priorities of Black women and examine the influence of race-gender identities on Black women's policy priorities in the Maryland state legislature. Utilizing the legislators' personal narratives to create case studies of distinct public policies allows me to delve into the complexity of the relationships that define their social networks. From this perspective, intersectionality enables scholars to consider the full range of dimensions in a single-group analysis.

FACTORS THAT SHAPED THE LEGISLATORS' IDENTITIES

The majority of the Black women state legislators grew up in the neighborhoods that they represent. Only eight out of the eighteen legislators interviewed were raised outside of their district. These eight grew up in Georgia, Alabama, North Carolina, Virginia, Pennsylvania, Montana, Jamaica, or western Maryland. While the communities they grew up in differ, the legislators share some similarities in background. In particular, there are cohorts of legislators who attended segregated schools, grew up in middle-class neighborhoods, or lived in working-class communities during their formative years. These physical spaces shaped legislators' senses of identity and influenced their worldviews.

Messages about Race

All of the women in this sample report receiving positive messages from their parents about being Black. Psychology literature demonstrates that ethnic and racial minority parents help their children understand race or ethnicity within the larger sociopolitical structure, thereby ensuring their children's adaptive functioning. These methods include: "(a) cultural socialization (i.e., promoting cultural customs, values, and traditions); (b) minority socialization (i.e., promoting awareness of and preparation to cope with minority status); and (c) mainstream socialization (i.e., promoting goals and values of the dominate culture)" (Hughes and Chen 1997). Parents' messages to their children about race vary widely. For example, some parents may encourage their children to value their history and culture, others may emphasize racial barriers, and others may highlight cultural pluralism. Children's racial socialization influences how they think about group identity. For example, the African American children of mothers who believed that it was important to teach children about race are more likely to demonstrate preferences for African Americans when forced to choose between Blacks and Whites in specific racial group tasks (Spencer 1983). Conversely, children whose parents overemphasized racial barriers and discrimination were more likely to display maladaptive behaviors, such as distrust and anger toward mainstream institutions (Marshall 1995). Finally, parents' own experiences with racial socialization and race-related experiences also influenced their children's racial socialization (Belsky 1984; Ogbu 1985). While the way in which each woman was taught about her Blackness differs, each readily reported that she was proud to be African American.

When asked what messages they received, if any, about being Black in America, ten women responded that Blacks have to work harder than Whites to achieve the same things. Linda Williams contends that the old "adage that Black parents often tell their children, 'You've got to work twice as hard to get half as far,' seems to partially explain the puzzle of Black women's success in winning public office" (2001, 314). The legislators that grew up in predominately Black communities do not recall receiving special messages from their parents about what it meant to be Black. For these thirteen women, the diversity within their communities provided walking examples of Blackness. Three younger legislators who grew up in Prince George's County, Maryland, detailed that there were Black professionals in the community alongside unemployed and blue-collar Blacks. The range of African Americans in their communities made it difficult for these women to articulate what "Blackness" meant to them. Similarly, Delegate Yasmin Wood describes her race-related socialization growing up in Washington, DC, "I had an Afrocentric education in the DC public schools. So I had the opposite experience of those who did not learn Black culture in school. Instead, I didn't think that White people ever did anything special because I learned so much about Black people. Plus, my dad and stepmom were very educated. They made sure that I was educated. They didn't tolerate any 'ghetto stuff'" (Personal interview, July 6, 2011).

Although they grew up with positive Black examples around them, these legislators also received messages from their parents specifically about what it meant to be Black. Delegate Keira Miller received raced, classed, and gendered explanations of how she was supposed to carry herself as a Black woman. She stated, "My mother used to tell me to be a lady. I was taught etiquette. She also told me 'Don't let White people see you acting nigger-ish'" (Personal interview, July 29, 2011). Senator Raquel Simmons was told by her parents that being Black meant "a sense of entitlement; me and my siblings were expected to be a certain way, respectful" (Personal interview, June 16, 2011). In many ways, these legislators' quotes indicate the interconnectedness of race and class in American society. Discussions of Blackness carried messages both implicitly and explicitly laced with ideas about middle-class respectability.

One younger delegate grew up in Prince George's County in middle-class Black neighborhoods. Delegate Fatima Coleman attended elementary school in Seat Pleasant, Maryland, and then high school in Capitol Heights, Maryland, in the 1980s. She now considers her experience in Prince George's an anomaly. "Growing up in PG is different because there are a lot of professional Blacks. The schools I attended were predominately Black. The majority of my teachers were Black. So growing up in PG, I didn't realize that there were racial tensions because the majority of the people I encountered were Black. I didn't experience racial tension until I attended the University of Maryland for undergrad" (Personal interview, July 29, 2011). The delegate grew up in Prince George's County during a time when Blacks and other racial and ethnic minorities were settling into the suburbs surrounding Washington, DC (Frasure-Yokley, forthcoming). As a result, she had a plethora of Black role models. This delegate vividly remembers the 1986 election of Vivian M. Dodson as the first Black mayor of Capitol Heights. Delegate Coleman and her mother had paid close attention to this election. Although her mother would remind her that "Blacks have to strive harder than others to be treated equally," she remembers Prince George's County as a supportive place for African Americans, with little racial discrimination.

Indeed, Blackness is interpreted broadly by these women and their families. It is notable that, despite the fact that they all come from different regions, economic backgrounds, and generations, all interpret Blackness through middle-class norms. These middle-class norms are filtered through a phenomenon that is closely linked to African American womanhood: the politics of respectability, which also informs Black political identity in a guiding way. Manners and morality were means by which African Americans redefined themselves outside of the dominant racist discourses. And while the politics of respectability was used—particularly by African American women—as a form of resistance, it also implied full acceptance of mainstream social values (Higginbotham 1993). Gaining the respect of Whites was intertwined with racial uplift, and Blacks attempted to debunk White supremacist rhetoric by adhering to strict moral codes, attempting to personify White Victorian middle-class ideals vis-à-vis the politics of respectability. The Black "female talented tenth" and the upper crust of Black society were critical of members of their own race who they did not believe were upholding middle-class ideals (Higginbotham 1993). Thus, pointing to a complicated and polemical relationship that further illustrates the problematic nature of the idea of linked fate, Black Women's Club Movement participants were at odds with lower status African Americans (Giddings 1984).

Racial uplift initiatives were often led by educated, middle-class Blacks who sought to advance the social, economic, moral, and physical conditions of lower-income African Americans. Women such as Mary McCleod Bethune and Nannie Helen Burroughs were among the Black women who led and promoted middle-class Black women's involvement in racial uplift in the late 1800s and early 1900s. Perhaps racial justice promotes class injustice, however. Respectability politics excluded legions of Blacks who could not (or chose not to) conform to gender roles, economic activities, and public behaviors that were viewed as legitimate by Black elites. While Jim Crow and White supremacy prevented African Americans from achieving full citizenship, the Black bourgeoisie claimed moral superiority and special recognition within the nation's hierarchical racist structure by distancing themselves from the masses of unrespectable Blacks (Ferguson 2002). While early Black reformers conflated race and class in their pursuit of racial uplift (Ferguson 2002), scholars have found that the civil rights movement betrayed the interests of poor Blacks (Morris 1984; West 1984). Among Black women in particular, those who work as unskilled laborers, have found that their precarious economic status points to further marginalization within intraracial politics when gender and class are accounted for within a nationalistic context. In sum, "given a social condition that is also compounded by other oppressions, Black women have necessarily been concerned with effecting, at the very least, an amelioration of economic and gender discriminations" (King 1988, 57). It was middle-class Blacks who were best positioned to take advantage of affirmative action policies and electoral politics.

The consequences of class polarization associated with racial uplift in the Black community continues to impact all African Americans. The politics of respectability was fundamentally conservative in action but radical in its claims that Blacks could be as respectable as—or more respectable—than Whites. Following what was an essentialist Black political identity gave Blacks agency to redefine themselves, albeit in very heteropatriarchal terms. The need to (re)affirm Blacks' humanity, however, later created a discourse of respectability that only reified sexism, homophobia, elitism, and classism. However, the legislators' narratives above illustrate that class and the restrictive politics of respectability disrupts monistic race politics more forcibly than gender for some of the lawmakers. While gender is a mediating force in Delegate Keira Miller's narrative, the other legislators speak to the role that class plays in defining their Blackness.

Experiences During Segregation

A mid-Atlantic state, Maryland played an influential role in Jim Crow politics. Many key players in the fight for equality called Maryland home, including Frederick Douglass, Harriett Tubman, Thurgood Marshall, and Lillie May Jackson. These activists held the state accountable for its race-based discrimination (Smith 2008). As a border state, Maryland was unique in that segregation and integration existed simultaneously within its borders. Indeed, in some cities such as Cambridge, Maryland, Blacks were allowed to vote and hold political office during the late 1880s. Yet Maryland law permitted segregated schools and neighborhoods. Levy (2003) illustrates how Maryland's segregation embarrassed the Kennedy administration during the Cold War because African diplomats were forced to stay in segregated public accommodations. Challenges by integrationists ultimately forced the local and state governments to desegregate. In fact, several of the Black women legislators lived through Maryland's struggle to end both de facto and de jure Jim Crow segregation.

Six legislators attended segregated schools; however, only two of legislators attended primary school prior to *Brown v. Board of Education* (1954). One of these legislators was eighty-one at the time of her feminist life history interview. Growing up between her older sisters' houses in Baltimore and her father's house in Charlotte, North Carolina, Delegate Bella Campbell said, at first, "Segregation didn't bother me" (Personal interview, June 20, 2011). She lived primarily in segregated neighborhoods and went to segregated schools and segregated churches. This delegate explained that the first time she realized she was Black was when she questioned why she could play with the two White children who lived near her Baltimore neighborhood but could not attend the same schools. This encounter changed her perception of racial relations. "I realized that I then needed to adjust my expectations of the world. Even as kids, people knew that you couldn't go to school with Whites. I couldn't expect to go to school with them" (Personal interview, June 20, 2011). Delegate Campbell's story reflects the era of de jure segregation that shaped her life experiences. During her feminist life history interview she mentioned segregation in a matter-of-fact way—absent of emotion and as a natural artifact of American history. While she does not provide details about her experiences of segregated life, this delegate moves the conversation toward her work with

Baltimore public schools and her connection to her neighborhood institutions. This conversation flows organically. However, it is clear that her connections to her community and neighborhood schools are directly related to segregation because she grew up in an all-Black population. For her and others, the de jure death of Jim Crow did not signal the end of all Black institutions and communities in East Baltimore.

Also born pre-*Brown*, Senator Yvonne Scott attended segregated Maryland public schools. This senator fondly remembers her time in segregated schools. She explained the benefits of having Black teachers. "I was taught that being Black was a positive thing. Teachers told me that I was intelligent and always encouraged me. Prior to integration, everyone in the community encouraged the kids to do well. It was a community effect. The church and the school were the life blood of the community" (Personal interview, July 18, 2011). After *Brown*, Senator Scott attended an integrated school outside of her community. She remembers there being an "instant" gap between the Black children and the community school she attended. This senator is visibly moved when talking about the effects of integration. She recalls that the "absence of Black teachers [in integrated schools] left us with no one we could relate to" (Personal interview, July 18, 2011). This absence of Black teachers also implied that Black students lost parental figures within the schools "who always reminded us to behave and stay away from bad company" (Personal interview, July 18, 2011). While she mourns having missed the positive influences of Black teachers and other benefits of attending a segregated school, as an adult this senator helped to integrate Prince George's County public schools. She also worked to integrate the hotels and restaurants along U.S. Route 40 and U.S. Route 1. Her quest for full integration was activated by her involvement in the civil rights movement. Still, although she celebrates the accomplishments of ending de jure segregation in Maryland, Senator Scott laments the loss of the positive elements of segregation.

Born in 1954, Delegate Olivia Jenkins attended a segregated elementary school because "people ignored *Brown*" (Personal interview, July 25, 2011). She grew up in a Black suburb in Baltimore County, in the district she represents today. This delegate first attended an integrated school in the sixth grade. As one of three Black students who attended this middle school, she vividly remembers a White boy saying that "he wasn't allowed to play with me because I was Black" (Personal interview, July 25, 2011). It was during her middle-school years that Delegate Jenkins learned that, to succeed, Blacks had to be twice as good as Whites. This delegate enjoyed and excelled in math and science in middle and high school. But "girls weren't pushed into the sciences back then" so instead she became a psychology major in college instead of majoring in a science, technology, engineering, or math field. Her high school guidance counselors highly encouraged her to attend Morgan State University, a historically Black university located in northeastern Baltimore. Delegate Jenkins explained that guidance counselors had assumed that the college-bound African American students would naturally attend Morgan. However, Delegate Jenkins enrolled in the newly created University of Maryland, Baltimore County. It is clear, however, that the delegate's experiences in the integrated Baltimore County public school system were both gendered and racialized when she was told that Black women do not major in the hard sciences. These experiences would later inform her political activism on behalf of women and minorities.

Born in 1955, Senator Pamela Price grew up in segregated East Baltimore. Her father owned a boarding house where Morgan State University faculty and students resided during the academic year. She reports that during the early 1960s and late 1950s there were no hotels in the area that would accommodate African Americans. This senator's father was adamant that Blacks should be self-sufficient because the government and other people could not be depended upon. He owned a lot of property and businesses in the neighborhood and instilled in his daughter that Black people should take care of the needs of their community. Senator Price attended segregated primary and secondary schools, and the first time she experienced racism was during college at the University of Maryland, College Park. Her father's advice about being self-sufficient helped her to see past students' and professors' bigotry and remain enrolled in college, even when it was difficult and she considered dropping out. She was determined that discrimination and prejudice would not stop her from earning a college degree. While Senator Pamela Price did not detail what had happened to her at the University of Maryland, College Park, she did make a direct connection between her experience there and her father's teachings of self-sufficiency. Characteristics perhaps most readily seen in the tenets of Black Power, self-sufficiency, self-determination, and Black pride combined to help this legislator overcome a racist experience that threatened, presumably, to end her college career.

In sum, the legislators' narratives that I have shared in this section illustrate that their experiences with segregation profoundly shaped them as individuals. The majority of these women connected these experiences either to directly launching their political careers or helping to shape their political agenda. Each narrative demonstrates a mode of resistance to racial oppression, and because these women were either born before or grew up during the civil rights and Black Power movements, their opposition to racial inequality is shaped by their generational experiences.

Direct Experiences with Discrimination

Incidents of discrimination are often difficult to objectively determine, because they are defined in part by intention. The perception of discrimination may be largely influenced by one's interpretation of the intentions of others. Yet, because the intentions behind social acts are often unclear, it is difficult for minorities and women—and women of color in particular—to definitively attribute harmful acts to a person's intent to discriminate (Phinney, Madden, and Santos 1998). Because discrimination can be unclear, perspective is not an objective measure (Lazarus and Folkman 1984). Discrimination can occur even if it is not perceived by the person being discriminated against. Perceived discrimination, which is based on an individual's interpretation of events, is also discrimination. Unfortunately, a majority of the African American women have experienced identity-based discrimination. And while most of the stories the legislators recounted were rooted in race-based discrimination, their experiences were also informed by gender, nationality, generation, and location.

Born in 1938, Delegate Angela James grew up in southern Alabama and Columbus, Georgia. She retold a story of walking down a dirt road in Alabama with her great-grandmother, on their way to the store. She recalls walking past White people and vividly remembers "seeing hate in their eyes." Delegate James reports having "experienced discrimination at an early age . . . this was the first time that I saw hate in a person" (Personal interview, July 20, 2011). From her time living in Columbus, this delegate remembers stories of a little Black girl who was killed for attempting to socialize with White children in neighboring Phoenix City, Georgia. Her dead body was thrown across her family's lawn as a violent reminder that segregation, White supremacy, and African American subordination would be strictly enforced in that community. Delegate James explained that segregation meant that Blacks were always treated unjustly. Hers is not a romanticized vision of Black life prior to integration, with unified Black families, communities, and institutions. Instead, James's experiences with segregation were the most disturbing and violent of all the legislators' narratives.

In another racially motivated incident, Delegate Ingrid Jefferson remembers witnessing a Ku Klux Klan (KKK) demonstration in Baltimore. As a ninth-grade student at Western High, the oldest public all-girls school in the United States, Delegate Jefferson and her friends had decided to watch the local boys play basketball at Patterson Park after school. In 1966, Patterson Park was a place where "African Americans only went in large numbers" (Personal interview, July 21, 2011). Delegate

Jefferson forcefully noted that she was only in the primarily White neighborhood because she attended Western High. Once the basketball game ended, she and her friends decided to leave the park by walking down Baltimore Street. From this vantage point she saw a large number of Klan members dressed in regalia. She recalled the story: "Some members of the Klan yelled 'There go some niggers. Let's get 'em!' I said, 'Come on!' Then some of the older guys who were with us said, 'Run, y'all, run!' I'm like, "Why? Who we runnin' from? Them?' Someone grabbed my hand and said, 'Come on now! Run, y'all, run! If they get us, they gonna kill us!'" (Personal interview, July 21, 2011). Delegate Ingrid Jefferson reiterated that she did not want to run; she had wanted to fight. She describes how engaging in fights as a teenager was akin to playing a sport for her and added that she "didn't fight like a girl. I was good at fighting" (Personal interview, July 21, 2011). However, she ran from the Ku Klux Klan because was she urged to run away by her friends. Noting how this experience cannot fully be defined by either race or gender, Delegate Jefferson evokes the passion of a young Black girl who wanted to engage physically with members of the KKK. Urged to run, she was the only one "foolish enough to want to confront the Klan for calling us niggers" (Personal interview, July 21, 2011). It wasn't until returning home later that evening that she realized the magnitude of her encounter. While watching the evening news with her mother, the delegate shared that she had seen the KKK. Her mother was horrified by her daughter's experience and that her initial reaction had been to fight the Klan. She then explained the Klan and how this delegate had put herself in a dangerous position. Delegate Jefferson notes that she was "simply blown away because I had no idea who the Klan was at that time" (Personal interview, July 21, 2011).

A Jamaican immigrant to the United States, Delegate Cassandra Ross explained how she never fully fit into America's racial hierarchy. Having grown up in Jamaica and attended nursing school in Great Britain before immigrating to the United States, this delegate recalled that she had viewed America as a land of golden opportunities. But she quickly learned that these opportunities were often closed to Blacks. "No one ever tells you the dark side of America, only the positive things" (Personal interview, July 29, 2011). She met her former husband, an African American, in the United Kingdom while he was in the military. They married in England and returned to the States after she completed her degree. When she arrived in the United States in the 1960s, she quickly learned about racism and discrimination. Delegate Ross remembered that she had a difficult time relating to African Americans because she did not understand their conceptualizations of race, and they did not understand hers. Because she had not been socialized into race-based segregation, hierarchies, and prejudices, she did not understand why Blacks were discriminated against. She recalls that this cultural difference led to different understandings of who she was and who Black Americans were. "I never felt that I had to submit myself to race-based denigration. They didn't understand me and I didn't understand them" (Personal interview, July 29, 2011). Delegate Ross concluded by telling a story about traveling through the South with her husband in the 1960s and how she had only later fully absorbed that racism impacted every aspect of Black life during this time. Despite her status as a Jamaican national, Delegate Ross was treated as second-class citizen because of her African heritage. Her different nationality at first hindered her understanding of American race relations, but her experiences with Jim Crow helped her to comprehend how racism shaped the United States.

In an interesting arrangement, Delegate Tanisha Harold recounts how she and her White neighbor, a friend, had decided to "share an office job when our children were in elementary school" (Personal interview, July 28, 2011). These friends were both stay-at-home mothers in a small, predominately White Prince George's County town in the early 1980s. Because they both needed the extra income and their children were becoming more self-sufficient, this delegate and her neighbor had decided to seek part-time employment outside of the home. They both interviewed for a clerk/secretary position at a local firm. After sharing the details of their interview with one another, the friends decided to propose to the firm that they would accept a full-time position if the employer agreed to split their wages. They would be responsible for scheduling their hours (which would incorporate their children's schedules and needs). The friends reassured the employer that because the firm needed a full-time clerk/secretary, this would be the ideal situation. The firm agreed. Over some time, Delegate Harold realized that her neighbor was offered a promotion, more money, and benefits, although she was not. This enraged Delegate Harold because the neighbor had begun to cut back on both her hours and tasks at the firm to due to family responsibilities. Delegate Harold had picked up the slack for her friend, as per their initial agreement, but was livid when she was not offered the same promotion. She recounted that because she viewed this "oversight" as a form of discrimination, "I asked the office manager if I too would be eligible for the promotion since the agreement we had was between three entities—me, my neighbor, and the firm. The office manager was visibly shocked by my question, which let me know that they never intended to promote me. It was because I was a Black woman sharing a job with a White woman" (Personal interview, July 28, 2011). Delegate Harold discontinued her relationship with the firm after this encounter. She recalled that her neighbor had assumed that both women had been offered the promotion and was unaware of the underlying racial discrimination.

These four unique narratives illustrate the diversity of experiences with discrimination that Black women have faced. Implicit within these stories is the intersecting nature of identities that complicate these women's experiences with racial discrimination. Delegate Ingrid Jefferson's story incorporates gender; she actively challenged constructions of womanhood as docile and weak. As an immigrant, Delegate Cassandra Ross viewed American racism as an outsider but later realized that her nationality did not buffer her from experiencing race-based discrimination. Delegate Angela James's story is both generationally and geographically specific; she is one of the older members in the study and grew up in a location and time where brutal, explicit, and dehumanizing forms of racial discrimination were commonplace. Lastly, Delegate Tanisha Harold's motherhood status played a distinct role in the form of race-based discrimination that she faced. As a mother of young children, she established a job-sharing arrangement so that she could prioritize the needs of her children while earning income. Each of these instances shows how gender, nationality, motherhood status, generation, and location can affect how African American women experience racial discrimination.

Religious Upbringing

Another commonality among the women in my study is a strong religious upbringing. The majority of the women report that they grew up in historically Black Protestant churches.[1] Indeed, three of the eighteen women legislators had fathers who were ministers. Another's grandfather was a Baptist preacher. The Black church, throughout its history, has facilitated not only the political socialization and the dissemination of information to members but also their mobilization. Black churches inspire their congregants to engage in political action, galvanizing them to work toward the goal of political righteousness. "Religion's psychological dimensions could potentially empower individuals with a sense of competence and resilience, inspiring them to believe in their own ability, with the assistance of an acknowledged sacred force, to influence or affect governmental affairs, thus--in some instances--to act politically" (Harris, F. 1999, 82). Thus, it is not a coincidence that well over half of the legislators credit their religious upbringing with both encouraging their interest in politics and influencing their legislative behavior.

The daughter of a Baptist minister, Senator Yvonne Scott, explained that Christian principles are the backbone of her political agenda. She believes that her role in the legislature is to take care of "the least of these" (Personal interview, June 21, 2011). This is a reference to Matthew 25:40–46, in which Jesus shares a parable urging his disciples to treat lowly people the same way that one would treat the King. She who would treat the most marginalized and underprivileged citizens with disdain and contempt would have eternal punishment; she who would treat others as she would Christ would be rewarded with eternal life. Senator Scott learned these values from her religious upbringing. As the pastor of a small Black congregation in western Maryland, her father was active in the community. The family engaged in community uplift by helping to feed and clothe the needy and provide books and educational services to the tiny Black population of in the town. Senator Scott's father encouraged her to take an active interest in her community. As a result, she became extremely active in the civil rights movement. She participated in sit-ins, marches, and boycotts. She also led educational seminars about civil rights for the community. "My father told me that politics runs your entire life. So it was just a natural move for me to enter the political arena. I've done everything to help my community and this [serving as a state senator] is just an extension of that" (Personal interview, June 21, 2011). During her interview, Senator Scott often quoted scripture to illustrate her beliefs on certain legislation, especially on same-sex marriage.

Raised by her devout grandmother, Delegate Justine Anderson recalls spending several hours a day in church. Her grandmother was a "strong Baptist woman" who believed that "if you could party on Saturday night that you could get up early and praise the Lord on Sunday morning" (Personal interview, October 10, 2011). Delegate Anderson recalled going to church at least three days a week and remaining there for hours on end. Church was both a social and religious experience for this delegate. Her grandmother taught her to be a good Christian girl and "to stay away from boys. And of course that didn't work!" (Personal interview, October 10, 2011). She became pregnant during her first year of college and had a son in the late 1960s. Because "no one believed in abortion back then," she had to drop out of school and raise her son (Personal interview, October 10, 2011). She moved back to Maryland and took an entry-level position at Prince George's Hospital, which was segregated at the time. While her grandmother was disappointed that this delegate had not lived up to her religious beliefs about chastity, yet she agreed to watch the child so Delegate Anderson could go to work. "My grandmother told me not to depend [on] any man, work hard, manage my money, and take care of my son" (Personal interview, October 10, 2011). The delegate noticed how poor workers, especially Black employees, were treated in the hospital where she worked. In 1974 she organized her colleagues to form a union to advocate for better jobs and treatment. She became "the voice of people who were too afraid to speak. I had absolutely no fear" (Personal interview, October 10, 2011). Delegate Anderson credits her grandmother and her religious upbringing for instilling in her the values of hard work and sacrifice. She also learned the importance of treating all people with respect, humanity, and dignity—just as Jesus did. In the end, this message of valuing people and forfeiting personal gain for the good of the group led her to become a leader (and later president) of her local union affiliate of the Service Employees International Union. The skills she learned as union leader easily translated into electoral politics, and Delegate Anderson credits her union experiences with providing her a training ground for her role in electoral politics.

While many of the Black women interviewed here indicated that religion had played a major role in shaping their Black identity and was central to the communities in which they lived, another delegate found that her religious identity was something that distinguished her from other Black women. Delegate Leila Baker recounted one of the first times she realized that she was different from other African Americans. Growing up the eldest of six children in a Pennsylvania city, this delegate recounted how, one summer during her childhood, her family visited her grandparents in North Carolina and she first learned that her family was different from other Black families. Her grandparents were active in the Central Baptist Association. However, her mother, raised as a Central Baptist, had converted to Catholicism when she married the delegate's father.

According to the National Congress of Black Catholics, there are three million Black Catholics in the United States (National Black Catholic Congress 2013). Research from the Pew Research Center indicates that, among African Americans, Black Protestants account for 78 percent of the population and Black Catholics for 5 percent (www.pewforum.org). As a religious minority among African Americans, as a child, the delegate realized that her religious denomination made her different than her cousins. This was one of the first times that Delegate Baker says she realized that there was diversity among African Americans. Again, pointing to ways in which Blackness is often constructed in narrow monolithic terms, Delegate Baker's narrative illustrates that the portrayal of Blackness as one-dimensional misses the diversity within this community.

While she grew up a devout Catholic, this delegate now identifies as a Presbyterian. She sees herself as a Christian in "a humanistic way"—a person who emphasizes the humanity of Jesus and his social teachings, juxtaposed to the divinity of Jesus (Personal interview, June 16, 2011). On June 12, 2011, Delegate Baker preached a sermon at a local Unitarian Church about marriage, in which she spoke in favor of same-sex relationships. While Delegate Baker did not explicitly state that her conversion from Catholicism to becoming a humanistic Christian is directly related to the Catholic Church's stance on same-sex marriage, it can be surmised that, as an out lesbian, both her own sexual identity and the issue of same-sex marriage may have contributed to her decision to leave the Catholic Church. Delegate Baker is proud to be one of the two Black women state legislators nationwide who are out lesbians.[2] Her identity as a Black lesbian is paramount. She actively lobbied her colleagues to support Maryland's same-sex marriage legislation, which was signed into law by Governor O'Malley on March 10, 2012. The Catholic Church, which has 1.2 million parishioners in Maryland, openly opposed the bill. Unlike the two other legislators mentioned above, Delegate Baker does not indicate that she uses her faith to influence her legislative decision making. Instead, on the issue of same-sex marriage, this delegate markedly departs from her religious upbringing. Similar to the Black feminists who have long called into the question of a unitary "women's experience" or an "African American experience" (see, e.g., Truth 1851), Delegate Baker's use of religion to contest a Black political identity illustrates an anti-essentialist depiction of Black political identity.

Socioeconomic Background

In the eighteen life histories that I conducted, fourteen women explicitly discussed class. Six self-reported that they grew up in a middle-class household, while eight described the communities of their childhood as poor or working class. The importance of class in shaping the political decisions of African Americans has been well documented (Dawson 1994; Ferguson 2002; Hochschild 1995; Wilson 1978). Scholars are concerned that if the social networks that reinforce Black identity have eroded, it may mean that race is a less salient factor for these individuals (Cohen and Dawson 1993; Dawson 1994; Gillespie 2012; Marable 1983; Reed 2000; Wilson 1978). The divide between poor and affluent Blacks is readily seen in differences in public opinion among African Americans (Dawson 1994; Simpson 1998). More affluent Blacks are less likely to support redistributive economic policies and tend to adopt conservative positions similar to those of Whites in similar economic circumstances. Less well-off African Americans are more likely to favor the ideals of Black Nationalism, such as starting an all-Black political party and disengaging from mainstream America (Price 2009; Simpson 1998). Other scholars have noted that the intersection of race, gender, and class creates complex social locations for individuals that complicate a race-only approach to studying Black politics (Collins 1990; Crenshaw 1989; Higginbotham 1992).

The study of new Black politics complicates questions of class in relation to African American elected officials. Third-wave Black politicians—young Black politicians born after 1960—generally benefit from belonging to a privileged class status (Gillespie 2009). However, the privileged socioeconomic status of younger Black politicians may challenge the notion of linked fate with those in less well-off economic circumstances. Thus, policy preferences, party affiliation, governing approaches, and campaign management may be different than for third-wave Black politicians. As a result, Adolph Reed argues, "There is no unified Black agenda because of class differences among African Americans" (Reed 2000). Furthermore, Simpson convincingly argues that a weak group identity for some African Americans is typically combined with middle- or upper-socioeconomic status, which may produce a more traditional conservative ideology (Simpson1998, 26). The socioeconomic differences among the Black women state legislators may exacerbate problems of communication between the haves and have-nots of Black communities. However, in this selection of legislators, there is an almost even split in the number of younger Black women politicians who grew up in poor or working-class communities and those who grew up in middle-class neighborhoods. Thus, the new generation of Black women political elites may better represent the opinions of both poor and affluent African Americans.

Bailey Smith, a younger African American woman senator, describes her community as pleasant and congenial. "Well, it wasn't Mayberry exactly but it was very close. Very, very close" (Personal interview, June 30, 2011). Senator Smith grew up around the corner from Kurt Schmoke, the first Black mayor of Baltimore. The current mayor of Baltimore, Stephanie Rawlings-Blake, presently lives in that neighborhood. Senator Smith remarked on how unusual her childhood community was: "It was a strong middle-class Black neighborhood. I was intrigued because it was a covenant community. The covenant always said no Blacks, no dogs, and no Jews. And so my father always reminded me that we had a black dog—so we always had dogs and we always had Black people in the community in spite of the restrictive covenant" (Personal interview, June 20, 2011). She remembers her neighborhood as one in which every child grew up in a two-parent household, where all the adults were gainfully employed, and children played freely in the streets. Senator Smith attended Duke University for her undergraduate education and earned her law degree from the University of Maryland. As a promise to her dying father, she agreed to return home after law school to take care of her mother. As a result, she currently lives in her childhood home. "He asked me to take care of his wife, who was the love of his life. I will keep my promise to my dad." (Personal interview, June 20, 2011). Senator Smith routinely comes across her former classmates, teachers, and Sunday school teachers while running errands or walking her dog in her neighborhood. These encounters have led her to realize that "Black politicians particularly need to realize that the community is proud of you when you've done the right thing, and we need to continue to affirm our neighbors and we need to affirm all those people that helped us because they are proud of us" (Personal interview, June 20, 2011).

A legislator who grew up in the Ashburton community in Baltimore, Delegate Naomi Young's neighborhood comprised middle-class Blacks who were college educated and held professional jobs. Although she lived in a self-described "utopia community," she was well aware of the struggles that African Americans faced. Her father was a prominent civil rights activist in Maryland. As a result, her family was more concerned with "working to change the living conditions for people, over making sure that the daily chores were completed. Daily functions were never more important than the daily good" (Personal interview, June 16, 2011). Born in 1964, Delegate Young was deeply affected by the Black Power movement. She recalls growing up in the 1980s in this community, which displayed Black power and pride. The most pivotal moment in her life was the 1971 death of her father. His untimely death at the age of forty-eight turned her world upside down. However, she holds steadfast to her "vision of the world" of Ashburton from 1964–1971 as a stellar example of what African American communities can look like.

Senator Brenda Perry described her childhood Lancaster, Virginia, neighborhood as a predominately Black middle- to working-class neighborhood. She was born and lived in Baltimore until her fifth birthday, but her family eventually settled down in Virginia to be closer to relatives. They lived in a rural area with detached housing. After retiring from the military, her father was a waterman serving as a mate, and later a captain, on a commercial fishing ship. She remembers that her family ate a lot of fish when she was growing up. Her mother was a domestic worker and a cook for a local family. Senator Perry recalls many family discussions about discrimination. Her father would remind her that Blacks always had to work harder than Whites to get less than half of what Whites got. So, in turn, her parents preached the benefits of education and always encouraged her to do well in school. Namely, she remembers her father telling her that he had made $2.50 a week prior to enlisting in the military and that Black men made so little because Whites didn't want Blacks to have economic freedom. This story had a great impact on Senator Perry, and she uses it to explain why she is committed to economic and social justice issues.

As a self-described "military kid" and the fourth of five children, Delegate Keira Miller portrayed life on an Air Force base as difficult, therefore forcing her family to become tightly knit. "We didn't have a lot of money to do things outside of the home," so the family would sing and play instruments as a pastime (Personal interview, June 29, 2011). Her parents each worked full-time and together raised five children. Her brother picked up extra work to help the family when their father was stationed in other places. She learned that things would "always be OK if you had family around" (Personal interview, June 29, 2011). Her parents were extremely religious; her mother was the daughter of a South Carolina preacher who could be described as a religious fundamentalist. Delegate Miller recalls a time when the family didn't have much but also that they were always helping others, donating food, clothing, and their time to the local food pantry. "My family was very big on helping others. That is the Christian thing to do" (Personal interview, June 29, 2011). This delegate lists her family as her greatest inspiration and support system. As a single parent of two teenaged boys, this delegate is grateful to her sister for helping her to raise her children and for facilitating her service in the legislature.

Born in the late 1930s in Alabama, Delegate Angela James faced many hardships. Her mother and father were not married at the time of her birth, and her mother later married a man who would eventually father her two stepsiblings. The delegate stated that being a "bastard child with dark skin and nappy hair meant that people never expected me to succeed in life" (Personal interview, July 6, 2011). She grew up extremely poor and recalled that her family lived on a dirt road diverging from a tar road where other poor Blacks lived. The Blacks who lived on the tar road were better-off than her family; her family lived in the poorest Black neighborhood. Delegate James noted, "We lived in shotgun homes. We didn't even have hot water and the commode was outside on the back porch. My sister and I would make dolls out of string and doll clothes out of rags" (Personal interview, July 6, 2011). In addition to her family's low income, Delegate James experienced physical abuse, sexual molestation, domestic violence, and mental anguish at the hands of her stepfather. Her mother was known as the town drunk. Delegate Angela James left her abusive home at the age of sixteen and became homeless. She later moved in with her grandmother in Columbus, Georgia, and finished high school. After completing her high school degree, Delegate James received a scholarship to a Baltimore-area university. However, she became pregnant and, as a single parent, had difficulty balancing motherhood and her studies. Today, Delegate James is a successful businesswoman and author. She has written numerous books and sees herself as a role model for women and girls in abusive situations. This legislator makes a direct connection between her upbringing and her perceived role in the state legislature. Delegate James believes she's in the legislature to advocate for the voiceless—a population she came from and is intimately connected to.

Delegate Ingrid Jefferson's father was a substance abuser who would also become physically and verbally abusive to the members in her household. Delegate Jefferson does not remembered her father ever working and recalled that he would frequently disappear. The family was forced to move several times, and, as a result, this delegate attended ten elementary schools growing up: "We moved around a lot. Running from the 'rent man,' so to speak" (Personal interview, June 20, 2011). Violence and lack of money contributed to her difficult childhood. Her family was on welfare and needed that assistance to eat. She remembers not knowing where some of her meals would come from. "I was from the wrong side of the tracks. I didn't go to school often because I didn't have money to buy the 'cool' clothes. I didn't have money to catch the bus so I had to walk three miles to school. I didn't have money to eat lunch so I didn't eat. So most times I was hungry. So you deal with all of that. And if someone says something to you or looks at you the wrong way—you know when you are hungry you would do anything to feed yourself and your outlook on life can be nothing but negative" (Personal interview, June 20, 2011). Delegate Jefferson later ran away from home to escape abuse. She was homeless at the age of thirteen and lived on the streets for one year—without the supervision of an adult—until she reunited with her mother after her father had permanently left the family home. Not surprisingly, Delegate Jefferson details that she was an angry teenager because of the abuse that she had experienced. After graduating from high school, she moved into her own apartment. She struggled to make ends meet on her own, and in her late teens, she lived in apartment without a refrigerator and a stove. She endured these hardships, however, because she was determined not to go back to her mother's house. Delegate Jefferson became a single parent at the age of nineteen. She speaks of having made bad decisions when she was younger and attributes these poor choices to the anger stemming from her childhood experiences.

The six lawmakers highlighted in this section hail from a mix of socioeconomic backgrounds. Senator Bailey Smith and Delegate Naomi Young grew up in middle-class neighborhoods with politically active African Americans. The African Americans from these communities were educated and held professional jobs. Indeed, these legislators presented their childhood neighborhoods as storybook-ideal. Senator Smith and Delegates Young and Miller are among the younger women in this study. However, only Delegate Young and Senator Smith reinforce Gillespie's (2009) finding that third-wave Black politicians have a privileged class status. Delegate Miller's family did not have much disposable income and relied heavily on family for both support and entertainment. Unlike Senator Smith and Delegate Young, Delegate Miller's family was not economically advantaged. Yet she was surrounded by love and a supportive community similar to the ones that Delegate Young and Senator Smith detailed.

Conversely, Delegates James and Jefferson grew up in poor communities and experienced several forms of abuse as children. These delegates faced severe challenges in childhood and early adulthood not only because they were low-income but also because they were women. Both Delegate James and Jefferson became unwed teenage mothers and experienced the financial difficulties of being a single parent. While she did not face the same vicious physical abuse and poverty as Delegates James and Jefferson, Senator Brenda Perry also grew up in a family with meager earnings. Similar to Delegate Miller, Senator Perry's family was close-knit, and love sustained the family in lean times. However, akin to Delegates James and Jefferson, Senator Perry also became a teenage mother. She married her son's father directly after graduating from high school and followed him to California for a short period of time. When it became clear that the young couple would divorce, she moved back to Maryland with her young son and enrolled in college. She sent her son to live with her parents in Virginia so he could grow up around a large, extended family.

While the primary focus of this section was to highlight the economic diversity of the legislators' formative years, it also illustrates the complexity of the women's early lives. These African American state legislators have had a myriad of experiences, from living in utopian communities to marginalized neighborhoods and hellish circumstances. The worldviews of these women are directly informed by class status. As a result, these women's class-based experiences influence how they perceive both themselves and others. In general, the interconnectedness of race and class for African Americans has been accented by "progress, relapse, and stagnation in the struggle for racial equality" (Simpson 1998, 11). Thus, while some women in the study have been privileged by their class status, the markers of socioeconomic status—occupation, education, and income—help to explain why younger generations of women who have been protected from some of the most abominable products of racism still discuss how race plays a role in shaping their middle-class identities.

Community Activism and Interest in Politics Instilled by Parents

Eleven of the eighteen African American women in the Maryland state legislature credit their parents with inculcating in them at an early age the importance of community activism and politics. A child becomes politically socialized by naturally "learning of social patterns corresponding to his societal positions as mediated through various agencies of society" (Hyman 1959, 18). Easton and Dennis find that children are taught to like the government before they are fully aware of what government is (1965, 56). From the beginning, political socialization studies have been concerned with subgroup differences of race, sex, age, class, and, more recently, gender (Dennis 1986; Greenberg 1970; Greenstein 1970). Yet the literature does not explain how the roles of identity and difference play in political socialization (Sapiro 1981). Walton (1985) concluded that, in the African American community, political socialization occurs in indigenous institutions, where resocialization and counter-socialization is a response to dominant attitudes. This leads to different views of politics, challenging the assumptions of previous political socialization studies.

Ruth Nicole Brown offers a framework to understand African American girls' political socialization. Building on Collins's Black feminist standpoint theory, she contends that "Black women and girls encounter a distinctive set of social practices that accompany our particular history within a unique matrix of domination characterized by intersecting oppressions" (Brown 2007, 124). To this point, racism, sexism, and other systems of domination shape a Black girl's lived reality. In her examination of what life is like for the urban Black community for the "average girl," Joyce Ladner finds that both cultural and familial relationships influence how girls grow up (1971, 12). By incorporating the role of human interactions in political socialization, the concept of democracy expands to include not only cognition but also the ways in which citizens mingle and interact (Taylor, Gilligan, and Sullivan 1995). Thus, the emphasis on participatory values for political behavior—along with a sense of political efficacy, partisanship, and cognitive and affective underpinnings—may be different for African American women than Black men and White men and women.

The eldest girl in a family of five girls and two boys, Senator Raquel Simmons was born in a small borough within Montgomery County, Pennsylvania, to working-class parents. Her parents instilled in their seven children the value of hard work and dedication. Although her parents did not have much money, she and her siblings were always well-groomed and nicely dressed—her mother worked hard to ensure that the family was always presentable. The senator recalls that her parents would always dress up to go to vote. On trips to the polling place, she recalls, the entire family would be tastefully clothed and scrupulously neat. She explained this family ritual as her parents' way of showing her the importance of voting. Getting dressed in their best outfits, for African Americans who were once disenfranchised, illustrated the significance of their taking part in an election. The magnitude of importance in being politically active was clear to this senator at an early age, and Senator Simmons describes her involvement in politics as stemming from a passion to make the world a better place. She notes that politics "is innately part of who I am. I want to improve people's lives. My legislative priorities are all to improve people's lives by meeting the specific needs of people" (Personal interview, July 12, 2011).

Delegate Yvonne Wood is biracial, but she reports that she has never thought of herself as half-White. Instead, "I just thought of myself as light skinned because I was raised culturally as Black" (Personal interview, July 6, 2011). Her parents, a Black man and White woman, married in Washington, DC, in the 1950s because their union was illegal in Virginia and Maryland at this time. She remembers being politically aware, even as a young child. The delegate was seven years old when Martin Luther King Jr. was assassinated. A local television news reporter interviewed students from her elementary school about King's death. She told the reporter that King meant a lot to her because "he got us a seat on the bus" (Personal interview, July 6, 2011). Later that evening she told her family that she would be on the local news. She remembers her family watching the news story and being impressed with her knowledge of King because "no one trained me to say this. I had no sort of preparation to speak to the news reporter" (Personal interview, July 6, 2011). Here, Delegate Wood reflected that she grew up in a political household, and so training was unnecessary. Discussions of current events, politics, and race relations were common among the adults in her household. It was only normal that she would pick this interest up. To be sure, race relations were "always a subtext for us" (Personal interview, July 6, 2011). Delegate Wood's mother was a liberal White woman who used subversive tactics to challenge the racial order of the 1950s and 1960s. For example, when her parents would drive to the South, her mother would stop at restaurants that did not serve African Americans. She would feign ignorance and ask the restaurant owner what did the "Whites Only" sign on the door mean. Then she would place a large to-go order and leave without paying as an act of defiance. Delegate Wood's mother shared with her daughter that she took the hamburgers from the segregated restaurant out to her Black husband who was asleep in the car. Additionally, Delegate Wood's mother would attend White Citizen Council (WCC) meetings pretending to be a White supremacist. She would take notes at the meetings and then make reports to the *Afro-American* newspaper, which would later print her stories. The WCC had no idea how the *Afro-American* had such intricate details of their organization's plans. The delegate fondly calls her mother "a rabble-rouser," whose sense of humor was key in her efforts to disrupt the racial hierarchy of the day.

Senator Bailey Smith recalls being active in a 1972 teachers' strike in Baltimore. Both her parents were teachers and active in the union. Remembering that her parents required that she and her brother attend school despite the strike, she notes, "We were the only children in school" (Personal interview, June 30, 2011). After school, she would join her parents on the picket line and they would protest as a family. Senator Smith believes that "politics might be in people's blood; it certainly is in mine" (Personal interview, June 30, 2011). She provided the example of her grandmother's grandfather, a member of the North Carolina House of Delegates in 1885. Edward "Ned" Rawls had been born into slavery. He attended Shaw University and then ran for public office in 1884 and won an election to the short session from January to March of 1885 (Ijames and Lanier 2009). Rawls lost a contested reelection due to Reconstruction-era voting trickery. He later represented Northampton County, North Carolina, as a legislator in 1887, 1889, and 1897. "He is one of 123 known Black Republicans to serve the Tar Heel State in this way during the Reconstruction period of 1868–1901. This period ended in 1901 with the "colored" people again losing the right to vote and with a political and social climate that had become increasingly hostile to African Americans" (Ijames and Lanier 2009, 4). Senator Smith became so intrigued by her family's oral history of Ned Rawls that, at the age of ten, she visited the National Archives to research her great-great grandfather. Because her parents were teachers, they encouraged her to explore her heritage by delving into archival materials. Several years later she would use census data, primary documents, and the oral histories of family members, to write her undergraduate honors paper about Ned Rawls. Senator Smith remarked that she, herself, is like Ned Rawls: "I work to represent Black people" (Personal interview, June 30, 2011). She is thankful to her ancestors for "being strong enough to withstand slavery and Jim Crow and segregation and all of the lost and missed opportunities that had been stolen from them. . . . I thank Ned Rawls for saying, 'You can be a politician, because I did it'" (Ijames and Lanier 2009, 6).

The stories here demonstrate the prominent roles of the women's parents in developing the political consciousness of their children. The legislators were politically socialized at an early age, and, as a result, political involvement was second nature for them. Senators Smith and Simmons and Delegate Wood, concluded their life histories by stating that their goals are to improve their communities and people's lives. Indeed, Senator Yvonne Simmons was running for mayor of Baltimore when her feminist life history was conducted. While her bid for mayor was unsuccessful, her desire to run for mayor was predicated on her wish to improve the lives of young people and other marginalized groups in Baltimore. Senator Simmons had noted that incumbent Mayor Rawlings-Blake did not fully understand the challenges faced by younger residents of the city and that she felt a responsibility to advocate for this seemingly silent and apolitical group.

Senator Smith and Delegate Wood also directly connect their race consciousness to their parents. These women both actively challenge race-based stereotypes and discrimination. Delegate Wood co-founded Mocha Moms, a supportive organization for stay-at-home mothers of color who seek to devote attention to both their families and communities. Founded in Prince George's County in 1997, the 501(c) (3) now has over one hundred chapters nationwide and makes an intersectional connection between race and gender to present positive and affirming messages of minority motherhood. The organization's mission statement acknowledges that African American women have historically been denied the option to devote the entirety of their time to their family and communities, a choice unavailable to many since it constitutes unpaid labor. Mocha Moms primarily advocates for the engagement of minority mothers as activists in their communities. Lastly, Senator Bailey Smith has been a stalwart agitator against Maryland's refusal to apologize for slavery and its treatment of African Americans. In 2011, she challenged Western Maryland's all-White Republican delegation to change the name of Negro Mountain to Nemesis Mountain, the name of a Black frontiersman who died defending White settlers from Native Americans. Illustrating that parental example matters, these women have continued in their footsteps of their parents to push for remedies to alleviate race-based injustices.

Gender Roles

American society is patriarchal, and gender roles are organized via a social order in which men hold the dominant positions of power and authority. Sylvia Walby (1990, 1994, 1997) contends that patriarchy is upheld by six major structures: work, relations in the state, modes of production, relations in cultural institutions, male violence, and relations in sexuality. In this system in which men dominate, oppress, and exploit women, relationships between men and women are inherently unequal and hierarchical. However, patriarchy is expressed in the political, economic, and social structures that have special meaning for African American survival (Lawrence-Webb, Littlefield, and Okundaye 2004). As patriarchy denies individuals' humanity, African Americans negotiate how gender privileges are bestowed. While patriarchy allots men special privileges and, in a racist society, assigns special privileges to White men, it also denies others opportunities and resources, including employment and education for women. The historical and current oppression experienced by Blacks has a tremendous effect on the construction of gender roles among African Americans. From the period of slavery to present day, Blacks' gender roles have been continuously socially reconstructed according to normative conceptions for men and women. As such, Blacks perform gender in culturally appropriate behaviors classified as either feminine or masculine. While gender varies across time, space, and racial/ethnic and social locations, it is an ongoing and evolving aspect of social interaction (Green 2005; Risman 1998). Rather than a set of behaviors, identities, and practices, gender can be envisioned as a project to be accomplished in varying ways depending on the social context (Connell 1995).

The majority of the Black women state legislators interviewed for this study self-reported being socialized in or as embodying traditional gender relations. Of the women in the study, Delegate Keira Miller had the strictest sense of gender roles growing up: "Politics was men's business. Because of that I had to grow into an assertive role as a person who now represents others" (Personal interview, June 29, 2011). This legislator's perception of gender roles may be more clearly defined than others' because she grew up with religiously conservative military parents. Out of the eighteen women in this selection, only three reported that their parents encouraged them to take on nontraditional gender roles. These three women are among the youngest legislators in this study, born respectively in 1962, 1964, and 1977. The youngest delegate reports that her mother grew up with very strict enforcement of gender norms and was determined that her children would not. As a result, she and her brother split household chores and, as teenagers, were held to the same expectations. Many of the legislators who report having grown up being taught traditional gender roles provide examples of household duties. For example, six legislators report that they were responsible for washing dishes, cooking, watching younger siblings, and doing the laundry, while their brothers had to mow the lawn, take out the trash, and shovel snow. However, even this division of labor was uniquely accompanied by parental messages that empowered female children. Many of the legislators who experienced these gendered chores were also taught that girls could grow up to do anything that they wanted and that gender should not stop them from accomplishing their goals. Indeed, it was the legislators' fathers who were their strongest proponents of non-gendered achievement. Seven legislators from this group explained that their fathers had played an important role in their lives and gendered socialization.

Beyond citing household chores as a proxy for traditional gender roles, a few legislators gave examples of explicitly gendered norms during their childhoods. In a story about a childhood fight, Senator Bailey Smith recalled how her parents responded to her method of defending herself and her older brother by both establishing and challenging traditional gender norms. The senator's older brother was a shy and quiet boy. Because he was bigger than the other children on the block, many people did not bother him. One day, however, a neighborhood boy began to bully Senator Smith's brother. She "got mad and chased him down the block with some hedge clippers!" (Personal interview, June 30, 2011). Once her parents learned of the "hedge clipper incident" from several neighbors on their way home from work, they were rightfully angry. Her father chastised her: "Young ladies don't do that" (Personal interview, June 30, 2011). However, that did not stop her from engaging in several other neighborhood fights. Her brother, on the contrary, was never involved in fight. Although her parents disciplined her for fighting, "they also sent the message that girls have to be girls, but by the same token they were like 'don't let them walk all over you.' And I think having a brother, I kind of knew gender roles too. My parents made it clear that [it] was unacceptable for me to allow other people to treat me badly. But I was not allowed to stomp all over my brother. To some extent, my parents were right. They gave me some good lessons on politics" (Personal interview, June 30, 2011). Senator Smith believes that she learned to know her place and work within the context she was given. "As the youngest kid in the house who was a girl, I knew that my father particularly would not have liked me to stomp all over my brother. So I knew my place, I couldn't stomp all over him but I could stomp around him, and I did. That's all. I just think you have to know how to use what you've got, to be better." (Personal interview, June 30, 2011). This senator learned at home how to act within the society's constructions of femininity by maneuvering around gender-oriented obstacles.

It was not until her junior year in college at the University of Maryland that Delegate Fatima Coleman developed a perspective on gender. She credits college with expanding her horizons and exposing her to different ideas. It was during a women's studies course that she met an out lesbian for the first time. She recalled not knowing what the word "gay" meant until college. She reports that when she grew up in a Black middle-class community in Prince George's county, sexual orientation and gender were not considered salient components of identity. Instead, Delegate Coleman noted that prior to college, she was more aware of race and socioeconomic status.

Delegate Leila Baker emphasizes her sexual identity as a lesbian in recalling gendered messages that she received from her family. This legislator remembers becoming aware of her sexual orientation at an early age, although she came out to her parents in high school. "My parents told me that they were disappointed in my sexuality . . . due to their middle-class values" (Personal interview, June 16, 2011). And although she would label her mother a feminist, her mother had not been pleased about her daughter's sexual orientation. This delegate remembers deriving a message about gender from her mother's comments when life was particularly hard for her family. Her father suffered from manic depression and could no longer work due to his mental health. When her father lost his "good job," she was nine years old, and the family consequently lost their middle-class comforts because they now relied solely on her mother's income to provide for the family of eight. Delegate Baker learned through watching her mother that "you still had to get up and go to work in spite of what's going on around you. You have to be able to see the big picture. One day when I was particularly sad and unmotivated, my mother told me 'you are a poor Black girl. You don't have the luxury of not getting up. You're not depressed!'" (Personal interview, July 16, 2011). While problematic in its failure to address mental health challenges in the Black community and by reifying the Black superwoman myth, this admonishment by Delegate Baker's mother inspired her to move beyond her particular situation. Heeding her mother's advice, this delegate picked herself up and focused on helping the less fortunate. She would later go onto form a progressive student alliance while in college. This organization brought together women, African Americans, and LGBTQ individuals.

For these legislators, gendered messages were mediated through a myriad of other social identities and relationships that included sexual orientation, race, class, family dynamics, and mental health. Illustrating that Black women's lives are complicated by other factors, the legislators in this study are similar to other African American women who negotiate gender in highly context-specific manners. Representative of my sample, Delegates Baker and Coleman and Senator Smith discussed gendered identity construction in relation to what they learned from others. Unlike stories of race consciousness, gendered identity construction was an individual and negotiated process through which the legislators evaluated themselves in relation to others. Interpersonal relationships with others, in fact, reinforced gendered expectations, behaviors, and differences.

The themes in this chapter show the intersectional nature of identity; however, legislators had difficulty identifying purely gendered themes in their early adulthoods and childhoods, finding it much easier to identify racialized messages and experiences. Indeed, many of them paused prior to responding to the question. This was the only noticeable gap in my conversations with the legislators in the course of conducting the life histories. Perhaps race acts as a metalanguage for these African American women state legislators (Higginbotham 1992) since it plays an encompassing and prominent role in Black women's lives. Or perhaps, in line with intersectionality theory, Black women cannot parse out parts of their identity and respond solely to one aspect of identity (Jordan-Zachery 2007).

Current Home Life

Traditional gender socialization remains an aspect of electoral politics (see Flammang 1997; Kahn 1996; Sanbonmatsu 2002), and gender stereotypes still affect the electoral process (Fox and Lawless 2004; Kahn 1994; Koch 2000). Being married and having children involves diverse responsibilities for men and women. For example, traditional gender norms dictate that women are primarily concerned with caretaking while men are the providers. As a result, the household division of labor is unequal for many women, which may make it more difficult for them to balance the demands of legislative duties. Studies are inconsistent about whether women's familial responsibilities hinder their participation in electoral politics. Some scholars have found that women's family roles influence their political ambitions and that women with young children are less likely to enter politics (Bledsoe and Herring 1990; Fox and Lawless 2004; Sapiro 1981). Other findings show that having children living at home does not influence whether a woman will consider running for office (Fox, Lawless, and Feeley 2001). In fact, little is known about the effects of family on African American women state legislators.

This group of female lawmakers reveals a broad range of current family situations. Thirteen women in this study have children, and seven are grandparents. Four of the women were unwed teenage mothers. Seven women are currently married,[3] four are single, three are widowed, four are divorced, and none identify as partnered. Of the seven married legislators, five are in their second marriages.

Delegate Justine Anderson remarked, "God sent me this wonderful man" (Personal interview, October 10, 2011). Her husband is retired and has the time to assist her in campaigning and attend constituent events. He often accompanies her to Annapolis. Delegate Anderson shared that her husband is extremely supportive. "He never let me quit. He always pushes me to accomplish my goal—to one day be a Maryland state senator" (Personal interview, October 10, 2011). Delegate Anderson added that she did not run for political office until her children were self-sufficient. The mother of four adult children and grandmother to four young grandchildren, she notes that politics is a family affair and that she is able to balance her legislative responsibilities and family life because her husband does most of the housework. Delegate Anderson's example speaks to the necessity of a supportive spouse if married women political elites want to maintain a successful marriage and political career.

Delegate Fatima Coleman also shared that her husband supports her in her career and legislative responsibilities. This legislator's husband is a political advisor and an attorney, and this delegate noted that it is hard work to maintain a marriage when one partner holds elected office. She acknowledged that she is able to balance her family, work responsibilities, and legislative duties because she has such a supportive family. "My husband is very hands-on and that helps a lot" (Personal interview, July 29, 2011). After six years of dating, Delegate Coleman married her husband directly before her new duties as a legislator were scheduled to begin. They had a small and informal wedding at the University of Maryland chapel on a December Sunday in 2010. They did not have a honeymoon and spent their first three days as husband and wife apart. Instead of a honeymoon, she joined her fellow freshman class of Maryland state legislators for a bus tour of the state. Delegate Fatima Coleman has an elementary school-aged daughter. "My mother, husband, and I have a system where we all share family responsibilities. My family takes care of my daughter when I'm in Annapolis. But it is a hard decision to make" (Personal interview, July 29, 2011). Delegate Coleman shared that being a working wife and mother is a difficult yet rewarding task. She explained that she has to set boundaries so that she can carve out time just for her husband and daughter and that the housework is often demanding. "I have to cook for the entire week to ensure that my family has wholesome food to eat. I cook all day on Sundays. Usually I do a lot of Crock Pot meals. Crock Pots are great! My Sundays are spent at the grocery store and in the kitchen" (Personal interview, July 29, 2011).

Echoing similar sentiments, Delegate Ingrid Jefferson said, "This life is hard. It's hard. It would be different if I were a male legislator and had a wife to take care of me and our family. So no, I don't have a traditional life and neither does my husband" (Personal interview, July 19, 2011). This statement mirrors feminist research, which finds that work and family balance is different for men and women. Milkie and Peltola (1999) detail that the more hours one works outside the home, the greater the perceived unfairness of sharing housework. This imbalance occurs for both men and women who are employed full time, and yet, for women, when young children are accompanied by these tradeoffs, martial unhappiness is often the result. Delegate Jefferson is currently raising one of her granddaughters, which she noted that she would be unable to do along with having a political career if she did not have the support of her husband. "It's important to be married to the right person. I wouldn't be a legislator if I was married to my first two husbands. My husband helps me. He helps me with my campaigns and he's my biggest advocate" (Personal interview, July 19, 2011).

Married for two years to her second husband, Senator Pamela Price emphasizes the importance of marrying a man who will complement and add to the quality of life. Because this legislator was first married at nineteen and divorced at twenty-five, she believes that she learned a lot about herself and what she wanted her next relationship to be like. She also learned that she needed to develop a work and life balance because she became physically sick and unhappy due to stress. Senator Price explained, "Black women need support bases. If we don't, we'll fall apart mentally, spiritually, and physically. We need to be sure that we take care of ourselves and have a balance" (Personal interview, June 21, 2011). Once this lawmaker "worked on" herself, she met her current husband. Her husband has been involved in electoral politics in the past and, as a college professor, is involved in community development. These attributes allow her husband to understand her legislative duties. Because of this, "he's very supportive. My husband is supportive and is great at communicating. He is trusting" (Personal interview, June 21, 2011). Senator Price noted that many of her colleagues do not understand how to balance their home lives and legislative responsibilities. "Well, the men colleagues just don't get it. They have women at home who take care of things. So they don't have the same levels of stress. And the unmarried women in the legislature want to be connected to men too, but they have to make sure that they end up with men who are supportive" (Personal interview, July 21, 2011). Senator Price ended our interview by stating that mental, spiritual, and emotional health is paramount and that a woman should only connect herself to others who are going to enrich her life, reiterating that women need to marry men who are encouraging, supportive, and cooperative.

The women who are currently married to men emphasize the importance of having a supportive husband. The divorced legislators note that their husbands' lack of support led to the dissolution of their marriages. Several of the unmarried and divorced legislators claimed that African American men may lack the self-assurance to be in a relationship with a powerful Black woman. Delegate Olivia Jenkins's narrative best illustrates the outcome of marrying an unsupportive and insecure man. She stated, "When I became speaker pro tempore I began to realize that my husband had a problem with this. People would call him Mr. Jenkins (the legislator's maiden name). It was a resentment factor; he didn't feel secure in his position as a man" (Personal interview, July 25, 2011). She noted that her husband wanted a traditional marriage. He was thirteen years older than she, which she believes may have contributed to his desire to have traditional gender roles within the marriage. Delegate Jenkins concluded that the demise of the relationship was caused because her new position as speaker pro tempore did not easily allow her to fulfill traditional gender roles. Although she had been active in both community and electoral politics when she married her second husband, the increased time commitment demanded of her as speaker pro tempore was the proverbial straw that broke the camel's back. "When we married in 1999 I wasn't speaker pro tempore but then when I took that position I had to come to every session. So the day that I was going to be sworn in at noon, he called at 10 A.M. and told me to get someone else to hold the Bible for me. The relationship was over. I had to call my brother. So my brother rushed down to Annapolis and held the Bible for my swearing-in ceremony" (Personal interview, July 25, 2011). One of her defining political moments also signified one her lowest personal moments; the end of her second marriage. Delegate Jenkins adds that she is extremely cautious about dating now.

Delegate Cassandra Ross detailed that she had been a single mother even when she was married. Her former husband did not help her with their three children, nor did he have regular employment. Delegate Ross worked full-time and went to school part-time to earn her nursing and business degrees. She also took care of the household responsibilities and the children. "My husband thought that I took on too many responsibilities. You know, children, school, and working full time. This led to the demise of my marriage. Sitting up late night doing homework and working with the kids, my marriage didn't survive" (Personal interview, July 29, 2011). In hindsight, Delegate Ross surmised that her husband had difficulty "feeling like a man. I was the breadwinner. And I was pursuing my dreams to become a registered nurse and business owner when he didn't aspire to do much of anything" (Personal interview, July 29, 2011).

Of the unpartnered heterosexual women, three explicitly stated that, as powerful women, they have difficulty dating Black men. The term "powerful woman" took on negative connotations for these women, who surmised that Black men would rather partner with a submissive woman with a lower-profile occupations than theirs. Delegate Naomi Young added that Black professional women are least likely to be married so "why would I be any different just because I'm in Annapolis. If anything, this is more reason to be single" (Personal interview, June 16, 2011). Delegate Tanisha Harold, who is divorced, noted that people react differently to her now that she's a state legislator. "Some of my friends started to call me 'Delegate Harold' instead of by my first name. They changed when I got elected. People see me differently now. So if people who knew me before Annapolis act that way, imagine how men, potential dates, would treat me now?" (Personal interview, July 28, 2011). Lastly, Delegate Keira Miller, who is also divorced, said, "I was married for seventeen years and divorced for seven years now. I'm not involved in a serious relationship now. Who wants to date a powerful woman? When you get into politics, in a man's game, you pick up male behavior. I communicate differently now. I picked up their behavior" (Personal interview, June 29, 2011). All three of these delegates express that is difficult to date. They attribute much of their inability to find and maintain relationships with men to their political stature.

Unlike the other legislators who narrate gender norms vis-à-vis hetero-sexual relationships, one legislator in this study is in a same-sex relation-ship. Delegate Leila Baker is one of eight openly gay and lesbian members of the Maryland state legislature. This delegate is estranged[4] from her wife, whom she married in Vermont, the first state to allow same-sex unions without being required to do so by a court order. She is now in a long-term, committed relationship with another woman who lives in Maryland. Delegate Baker notes that she does not have the desire to move in with her girlfriend and her girlfriend's children. She noted that politics is rough on families, especially those with young children, and she does not want her girlfriend's family to be forcibly immersed in her political life. Instead, Delegate Baker relishes the quiet time that she is able to spend with her girlfriend and her girlfriend's children outside of the public eye. While her girlfriend's identity is not a secret to the majority of Marylanders, Delegate Baker chooses to keep her personal life private and declined to elaborate further on her current relationship.

The majority of women legislators who are mothers entered electoral politics when their children were self-sufficient. Five women entered elec-toral politics when their children were teenagers. Delegate Keira Miller ex-plained, "Although my sons could basically look after themselves, I still had to be a present and attentive mom. I went to all—well, maybe except two—of my son's basketball games. My other son is in the school band. I attend his performances. If I can't, then I make sure that my sister goes. I want them to have family support" (Personal interview, July 29, 2011). Similarly, Delegate Fatima Coleman shared that she tries to make it to her child's events. But often she is forced to choose between attending her child's event and a civic association meeting. "My kid cares more than the civic association if I show up. So I really try to make my kid's event first. But sometimes there is something going on that is so important that I have to miss my kid's events. And then you have to tell her that I'm going to be late. Thankfully, my daughter is pretty understanding" (Personal interview, June 22, 2011).

Two legislators had young children when they decided to run for office. The mother of five boys, Delegate Yasmin Wood used her children to help her campaign. Her husband, a state's attorney for Prince George's County, did not want her to campaign door-to-door alone. He was concerned that someone would try to hurt her. So she devised a buddy system in which she would pair up with people and campaign. "So I went through a whole lot of volunteers. On a typical Saturday I could easily go through three shifts of people because I was going to start in the morning and door-knock until it got dark. No one else was going to do that. I would get three different people to be with me plus any extras I could get. It was a lot" (Personal interview, July 6, 2011). When Delegate Wood could not get any volunteers to canvass communities with her, she would take her children. "That's the thing about having children. They don't have a choice. If I got truly desperate I would take the two little ones and they would ride their bikes. They would just be on the street with me. If I got snatched they could scream. That would be my last-ditch effort" (Personal interview, July 6, 2011).

As a grandmother to young children, Delegate Tanisha Harold expressed that her legislative duties keep her from being as involved in her grandchildren's lives as she would like to be. When it is possible, she schedules political events for times that do not conflict with her family dinners. But she lamented that she "can't do anything with my family when I'm in session!" (Personal interview, July 28, 2011). As a result, she has found that she has had to adjust her life around her legislative duties, and so she schedules time with her extended family around the Christmas holiday. And Delegate Harold has found ways to merge some of her legislative responsibilities and her desire to spend time with her grandchildren. "The grandkids love campaigning with me. I put them in a little red wagon and pull them door-to-door with me when I campaign. But even more than that, they absolutely love attending parades with me. They get to be part of the parade since I usually have some sort of official capacity there. I pull them in the wagon and they get to wave and smile at the onlookers. They love that!" (Personal interview, July 28, 2011).

Eleven of the legislators in this sample are unpartnered, and seven are married. This represents national trends, which indicate that, as a group, Black women are the least likely to be married (Goldstein and Kennney 2001). Academic and public conversations around Black womanhood and marriage rates have lately reemerged in the public forums. Studies that illustrate the lower marriage rates of African Americans often conclude by pathologizing Black womanhood and Black motherhood. Yet the narratives shared by the women in this section also hold Black men accountable for the low marriage rates in the African American community. The narratives of delegates Naomi Young, Fatima Coleman, and Keira Miller illustrate that Black women are not solely to blame for why they are single, and Delegate Miller finds that her behavior has become masculinized as a result of serving in the state legislature, which she feels prevents men from wanting to date her. Delegate Olivia Jenkins's story, while still within this narrative, paints a more detailed picture, illustrating her perspective on why her marriage ended. It is significant that these three legislators all theorize that Black men lack the necessary self-confidence to marry a powerful woman.

The women in this study highly value their roles as mothers and grandmothers. They note that they take pleasure in caring for their families and are proud of their children's accomplishments. These women also go out of their way to mother other children in their churches, communities, and extended families. For example, Senator Yvonne Scott detailed that her biggest regret in life was not having children. She has taken a very active role in her the lives of her nieces and nephews, even paying for one of her nephews to attend college. Similarly, Senator Raquel Simmons does not have biological children but considers the children of Baltimore to be her family, so much so that she has dedicated her political career to advocating for the city's youth. However, Delegates Yasmin Wood, Fatima Coleman, and Tanisha Harold note that simultaneously being a legislator and a parent or grandparent to young children can be difficult. These women stated that they constantly work to strike a balance between their legislative duties and spending time with their families. Yet they all affirmed that their family comes first and that it is essential to their lives.

CONCLUSION

Akin to the findings of Cole and Stewart (1999), who found that Black women's lives, more than White women, are shaped by historical events, the women in this study indicate that they feel driven to participate in social movements and that historical events have helped shaped their relationship to politics. Collins (2000) detailed that Black women's advocacy begins with their support for African Americans and the poor. She later found that the experiences of being non-White and a woman increased Black women's desire to advocate for women, a pattern that is echoed in this scholarship which supports the findings that race and gender have a distinct impact on African American women's politics. Unlike previous studies, however, this chapter has presented an in-depth view of Black women's lives that may provide scholars with a better starting point for understanding the motivations behind their legislative behavior. As the following chapters will continue to illustrate, Black women's personal identities significantly inform their policy-making.

We assume that Black women political elites are privileged individuals who have benefited from education, financial security, and professional opportunity. Yet, as the feminist life histories in this work establish, African American women state legislators face numerous challenges that upend these assumptions. These women have shared as many similar as divergent life trajectories on their paths to the Maryland state legislature. The narratives that I have shared in this chapter point to the intersection of race, class, and gender in these women's lives. We see here both a homogeneity and heterogeneity of Black women's experiences as the state legislators reveal the complexities of their lives how that complexity influences what they do as lawmakers.

Perhaps most interesting are the common threads that weave throughout. Regardless of generational and socioeconomic difference, race and gender play a prevailing role. All the women prove the relationship of race to identity when they tell stories about their backgrounds and how they currently see themselves. Yet their racialized experiences are filtered through and mediated through other social identities. The Black women state legislators rarely explicitly spoke about womanhood in general but instead couched their discussions of self specifically in terms of being Black women. For these women, race and gender work in tandem when they explain how they view their formative years and who they are today. In addition, sexual orientation, motherhood status, marital status, professional identity, and nationality inform their lives.

I do not contend that the feminist life histories of these eighteen legislators are representative of Black women in general or African American women legislators nationwide. I acknowledge that everyone's life experiences influence his or her legislative behavior. Yet, this study illustrates the importance of incorporating race and gender to better understand the impact of identity on legislative behavior. Future studies that explore other groups of minority legislators (e.g., Black men, Latinas, Jewish women, etc.) are necessary for examining how a group's specific identity may or may not impact individuals' legislative decision making. Of course one limitation to this study is that the data collected are retrospective and that the legislators' recollections of past events are subject to problems inherent to memory.

While this chapter cannot fully capture the rich narratives of all of the women in this sample, the experiences detailed here are representative of the group. It was not a goal of this chapter to present each woman's complete life history but rather to highlight the diversity in this sample. Because this book is not a collaborative project, I cannot readily assume that the legislators would have self-selected to highlight some of their experiences and stories under these particular thematic headings. My findings are shaped by the women's words but rely on my interpretation, and I accept responsibility for the information and analysis presented.

While there are limitations to any study, detail-rich case studies obtained from personal interviews and feminist life histories provide readers with a multidimensional understanding of Black women state legislators' intersectional identities. Using the case-study approach with one state as the unit for analysis provides the necessary first step toward fully understanding the roles and motivations of Black women state legislators in the policy making process. Hopefully this study will elicit future studies on Black women's policy preferences in other states and provide a model for studying other minorities who are elected officials. The feminist life histories I present in this chapter serve as the anchor for the remainder of the book, and the following chapters go on to examine how Black women use multifaceted and nuanced understandings of identity to influence their legislative decision making.

CHAPTER 3

Black Women's Representation

The true worth of a race must be measured by the character of its womanhood.
—Mary McLeod Bethune

I have crossed over on the backs of Sojourner Truth, Harriet Tubman, Fannie Lou Hamer, and Madam C. J. Walker. Because of them I can now live the dream. I am the seed of the free, and I know it. I intend to bear great fruit.
—Oprah Winfrey

Scholarship about women and minority legislators consistently indicates that member characteristics and group identity influence legislative behavior (Fenno 2003; Mansbridge 1999; Rosenthal 2000; Smooth 2001; Swers 2002). However, this does not imply that there is a predetermined unity of vision based on group identity; there is variation in the political agendas of African American women who are elected officials. For example, while the overwhelming majority of Black women elected officials are Democrats, the 2010 elections saw Jennifer Carroll, a Black Republican, elected as the lieutenant governor of Florida. Prior to assuming the post of lieutenant governor, Trinidadian-born Carroll was the first Black woman Republican to serve in the Florida House of Representatives. Carroll represents a deviation from the liberal-leaning, identity-based politics that Black women legislators have traditionally partaken of. Perhaps the growing number of Black women political elites will highlight diversity within this population, leading scholars to pose new questions about what issues Black women will prioritize in office. Regardless, in the "Age of Obama," identity politics should be more cognizant of diversity within demographic groups. It remains yet to be seen whether diversity among Black women legislators will change the nature of policy making in any systematic way.

This question of diversity among Black women legislators hinges on how legislators perceive their own race-gender identity's effect on their legislative work. In seeking to identify the ways in which African American women represent their constituents, scholars' findings about gender or race, taken as mutually exclusive factors, are instructive but not sufficient. By expanding the scholarly understanding of factors such as race and gender in descriptive representation, I uncover differences in Black women's representation and their self-conceived ideas about substantive representation. Based on the assumption that gender, race, and class are social markers that play a major role in organizing U.S. society and its institutions hierarchically (Simien 2006), I argue that the political context for a particular issue strongly influences the likelihood that a representative will rely on her identity as a means for understanding and articulating policy preferences. I contend that although Black women legislators mobilize their identity differently from one another, they nevertheless arrive at the same policy solutions when it comes to legislation that uniquely impacts African American women.

Because each African American woman has different experiences that help to shape her worldview, her race and gender are instructive but not definitive characteristics of how she defines herself. Building upon self-categorization theory and using an intersectional and additive approach to understanding Black women state legislators' contribution to policy creation, I use representational identity theory to posit that African American women legislators share a social identity that influences both group and individual behavior. This shared identity in turn impacts how the women view their legislative work.

Yet political science scholarship neither fully addresses the formation of group identity nor entirely examines its relevance within the legislative arena. In order to fully establish a link between legislators as people and how they prioritize the legislation that they champion, we first must investigate legislators' personal identities as group members and consider the processes and conditions by which social identity is primed. In this chapter, I argue that Black women legislators connect descriptive and substantive representation—meaning that they look like their constituents and represent the policy interests of their racial and gender groups—to advance the policy priorities of Black women. However, this is not to say that Black women constitute a legislative bloc. In fact, Black women use their identity in the legislative decision-making process differently, depending on context. My findings point to the need to study Black women legislators both as individuals and as group members precisely because their identity mobilization affects their legislative work. I examine here the viability of the idea that African American women elected to office engage only in descriptive representation based solely on their mirroring the physical characteristics of their constituency.

IDENTITY FORMATION

Identity formation is a process shaped by political, economic, and cultural forces that come together in distinctive and dynamic yet mutually constitutive ways (Sánchez 2006, 35). Identity is therefore linked to social positioning. Sánchez finds that "positionality is always at variance with other positionalities, including one's own on other issues, as one's perspectives are always multiple, contradictory, and again, constantly in a state of flux, renegotiating themselves in the face of changing realities" (2006, 39). Consequently, identity formation is rooted in class/structural positioning and is connected to social conjunctures. I employ Sánchez's fluid definition of identity formation to examine and understand why individuals sharing a similar or even the same positioning do not *live* their situation in the same way (39). Legislators belonging to the same identity group may express policy preferences rooted in lived experiences that are germane to specific marginalized social groups. A critical realist theory of identity formation necessarily implies that "identity formation takes place at a conjuncture of external and internal, contingent and necessary, processes that interconnect and emerge with specific historical conditions that are in good measure not of our own making" (34). Identity is grounded in reality, specifically in its social structures and relations. As individuals, Black women legislators' identities are a combination of communal culture and of reflection and observation. The multiple identities that Black women legislators occupy add to the complexity of their own awareness. Thus, African American women legislators' articulations and understandings of identity are essential to this study of descriptive and substantive representation.

Black women's shared social identity is formed from distinctive shared experiences, linked fate, and other attributes. Examining group formation offers a deeper understanding of group cohesion based solely on shared characteristics. Social psychologists understand social identity as part of an individual's self-concept originating from her knowledge of her membership in a social group (or groups). Social identity is imbued with the value and emotional significance that is attached to group membership. (Tajfel 1974). Group members recognize that they are a distinguishable social entity comprising socially relevant characteristics that, in turn, produce self-awareness. Important for our purpose here is the development of social identity as a theory that recognizes that identity can be "switched on" or primed by certain situations. Tajfel found that social identity provides a basis for cognitively regulated behavior but was uncertain under which circumstances and environments it would manifest itself as social behavior. In response, Turner, Hogg, Oakes, Reicher, and Wetherell (1987) develop the self-categorization theory as the "cognitive elaboration" of Tajfel's (1974) earlier social theory that provides an explanation for how individuals come to identify and "act as a group" (Turner et al. 1987, 42). Turner et. al.'s self-categorization theory is helpful in explaining how people shift their self-perception from personal to social identity. This process of depersonalization is fundamental for understanding how group processes emerge from social identity. Thus, when social identity becomes salient and people define themselves in terms of shared identity, they tend to see themselves as alike due to the defining attributes of their shared identity rather than due to their personal characteristics. In sum, social identity can vary in highly situational or specific ways.

Haslam Turner, Oakes, McGarty, and Hayes stated that "salient self-categories are . . . intrinsically variable and fluid, not merely being passively 'activated' but actively constructed 'on the spot' to reflect contemporary properties of self and others" (1992, 5). From this we see that identities have the ability to vary over time as situations change or the social categories shift in importance. One of the key tenets of self-categorization theory is that individuals constantly shift back and forth between individual and social identities (Brewer and Weber 1994; Simon, 1979; Turner et al. 1987). The benefits of self-categorization theory for explaining Black women's legislative behavior are vast. Because they are united by the common characteristics of race and gender, Black women legislators have a common social identity. This common identity produces socially validated knowledge and shared beliefs about ways of perceiving, thinking, and behavior. The collective self then reflects the collective realities of the group. While acknowledging group membership but still allowing for individual behavior, self-categorization theory allows Black women state legislators' social identity to be contextualized as dynamic and context specific. Thus, self-categorization theory is a useful and practical theoretical tool for examining an individual's behavior in a range of contexts (Ashforth and Mael 1989).[1] It makes room for scholars to consider how a Black woman legislator acts as an individual whose cognitive connection to a group of other Black women is based on a shared fate but may be deployed under different situational contexts.

To increase our understanding of how group formation and social identity influences Black women's political behavior, I develop a theory of representational identity, which contends that Black women legislators' race-gender identities influence their individual political actions and beliefs that are tied to their awareness of race-gender group interests. Baxter and Lansing (1981) suggest that the dual discrimination of racism and sexism experienced by Black women for generations has produced heightened political awareness in this group. Because of these common experiences, I argue, Black women have developed a mechanism that enables them to specify the conditions under which African American women's group interests become stronger or weaker than their individual interests.

In political contexts where race and gender intersect, African American women are likely to use their race-gender identities in legislative decision making. Thus, at times, Black women form a cohesive bloc in the legislature when policies specifically impact African American women. At other times, Black women express divergent legislative strategies and policy prescriptions in addressing Black women's issues. My representational identity theory makes room for a Black woman legislator to act as an individual whose cognitive connection to a group of other Black women is based on a shared fate and which may be deployed under different situational contexts.

I employ an intersectional approach to help explain how Black women use social identity to understand the negative material effects of a race- or gender-only approach to public policy in state legislation. This approach supposes that relevant categories of difference are mutually constituted, both analytically and experientially, and that they shape political actors (Garcia Bedolla 2006; Hancock 2007; Hawkesworth 2003; Weldon 2008; Yuval-Davis 2006). It cannot be understood simply as adding race to gender in order to understand Black women's experiences. The additive model—one that posits that race and gender are mutually reinforcing—theorizes that two or more disadvantaged identities can be brought together if the subject experiences two or more distinct forms of discrimination in tandem (Gay and Tate 1998; King 1988). This approach, assumes that categories are static and constant. It is problematic because it may create or reinforce binaries between advantaged and disadvantaged groups by assuming that there are mutually exclusive categories of identity that privilege one identity over another.

Lastly, I assert that Black women state legislators use an intersectional approach to formulating public policy. Their social identity as Black women enables them to understand how "the multiple marginalization of race, class, gender, or sexual orientation at the individual and institutional levels create social and political stratification, requiring policy solutions that are attuned to the interactions of these categories" (Hancock 2007, 65). Public policy that treats race and gender as mutually exclusive categories is antithetical to Black women's lived experiences; thus, they may be better positioned to recognize the inherent problems of using an additive approach in the creation of public policy. As Hancock (2004) concludes in her influential work on the impact of race, class, and gender on the stereotypical and political motivations for welfare reform, an intersectional approach illuminates the relationships between categories to create effective public policy. I thus utilize an intersectional approach to examine how Black women state legislators understand public policy that is targeted to assist either racial or gendered groups and then go on to show that it actually serves to marginalize Black women. As a result, I find that Black women play an important role in providing descriptive representation for African American women.

IDENTITY MATTERS—RACE AND GENDER

The Black women in this study invoked identity in two distinctive ways to explain its role in the legislative process. For example, some legislators stated that they prioritized a particular part of their identity depending on the legislative context. Other Black women legislators asserted that they could not prioritize aspects of their identity. They were unable to parse the factors of their identity. Overall, the Black women state legislators acknowledge that identity affects their legislative work, and they all ultimately connect descriptive representation to their substantive work in Annapolis. While several disagreed on the importance and frequency with which their identity had an effect on their legislative work, the legislators all believed that their identity, as mediated through experiences, was beneficial to their activities as representatives.

Two of the African American women legislators purport to have an either/or approach to identity-based representation. For example, Delegate Miller, a divorced mother of two, claimed that there are times when parts of her identity influence how she interprets legislation: "It [identity] probably contributes to but is not the only factor in how I feel about legislation. It would be difficult for me to tease out which parts of me because I am a Black woman and I am from the Midwest, I'm a mother. So which part of me is it that?" (Personal interview, March 12, 2009). Delegate Keira Miller further discussed the importance of using her identity, when applicable, in the legislative process. She stated that she draws on different aspects of her identity to better recognize whom legislation may affect. For example, she explained that her entry into politics was motivated by her desire to create more recreational opportunities for her children. Delegate Miller's twenty-two-year old stepson was killed in 2001 after becoming involved in the distribution of illegal drugs. She reasoned that if her stepson, and other neighborhood children, were engaged in after-school activities, they would channel their energy into productive outlets. Indeed, when she questioned the neighborhood teenagers about why they were involved in gang-related activities, she learned that some teens did not feel that they had options for more constructive pursuits. She ran for the school board as an advocate for teenagers who wanted a community recreation center so they could channel their time and energy into positive behaviors. She believes that the recreation center would have helped to save her stepson's life, and that is how she became engaged in politics.

Delegate Keira Miller prioritized her identity as a mother in this situation. However, there are serious racial and class undertones to this story. "The Justice Department estimates that one out of every twenty-one Black men will be murdered, a death rate double that of U.S. soldiers in World War II" (Black Star Project 2010). Similarly, a young Black man is more likely to die from gunfire than any soldier in Vietnam was. This makes the homicide rate of Black males seven times higher than that of White males. Therefore, race was a factor in the death of Delegate Miller's stepson, and this fact surely has an effect on her legislative choices.

There are also class connotations. Delegate Miller's stepson was involved in drug dealing because he did not have steady employment. While it constitutes roughly only 13 percent of the total population, Black America represents nearly 30 percent of America's poor; 53 percent of Black men aged twenty-five to thirty-four are either unemployed or earn too little to lift a family of four from poverty. The share of young Black men without jobs has climbed relentlessly, with only a slight pause during the economic peak of the late 1990s. In 2000, 65 percent of Black male high-school dropouts in their twenties were jobless—that is, unable to find work—not including those who were not seeking it or were incarcerated. By 2004, the percentage had grown to 72 percent, compared with 34 percent of White and 19 percent of Hispanic dropouts. Even when high school graduates were included, half of the Black men in their twenties were jobless in 2004, up from 46 percent in 2000. While people of color make up 30 percent of the U.S. population, they account for 60 percent of those imprisoned. One in every five Black men and one in every thirty-six Latino men was incarcerated in 2012, compared with one in every 106 White men (National Association for the Advancement of Colored People 2009). These numbers show that African American men, compared to other demographic groups, are incarcerated in disproportionately high numbers.

Delegate Miller's stepson's murder, while partially a result of his bad decisions, was informed by his status as a Black male. She cites his death as the catalyst for her run for public office using the stand-alone framework of motherhood to explain the impetus. I contend that the circumstances around his death that were framed by race and class-based social structures, along with her citing motherhood as the impetus for her political involvement, are all powerful examples of how identity affects political decisions. However, this African American delegate singles out motherhood, one specific aspect of her identity, in her example of how identity impacts her political work. Thus, Delegate Miller's story illustrates an additive approach to identity politics.

In articulating the trilogy of race, class, and gender as social categories that inform her identity and her experiences, Delegate Julissa Moore, a lawyer who grew up in a middle-class Black neighborhood, reported that how she positions herself via-à-vis identity is dependent on context. She said, "I have a different experience. If I did not bring my experience here I don't think I would be doing a service to the entire state of Maryland. I don't make decisions based on my race and gender, I bring an understanding that's reflective of my race and gender. . . . [In certain situations] I feel my gender more here or my race more here or my class background there." (Personal interview, March 12, 2009). Delegate Moore indicated that she sees her experiences as filtered through her identity. She draws on these experiences in her legislative work. For example, she is a champion of worker's rights. This delegate acknowledges her own privilege; she grew up in a stable, middle-class family. Her upbringing, coupled with her identity as a middle-class African American woman, led her to sponsor a bill that would raise Maryland's minimum wage. While she feels fortunate to have had a privileged lifestyle, she also strongly believes that everyone should have their basic needs met. The 2011 Census Bureau Poverty Report recently found that the Blacks have been hardest hit during the Great Recession. Using 2010 census data, the National Women's Law Center, a Washington-based nonprofit organization that focuses on women's economic security and legal rights, finds that the poverty rate has increased faster and risen higher, to 25 percent for Hispanic women and to 25.6 percent for Black women. Therefore, while Delegate Moore did not explicitly mention race and gender in her discussion of how her experiences impact her decision, her sponsorship of a bill that would raise Maryland's minimum wage indicates that both are factors. Her comments reflect an understanding of how the race and gender impact the economic condition of her constituents.

Notably, all of these legislators couch their discussions of identity and representation by stating that not all of their decisions are based on their identities as Black women. They may add this disclaimer because African

American women legislators are aware of the hypervisibility of their race and gender, which often goes in tandem with assumptions that their legislative work is biased or skewed to favor minorities and women. However, the narratives provided above prioritize one identity over another but incorporate the multiplicity of identity in some respect. These women favor an additive approach to politics, even in situations where an intersectional approach may be warranted. Some Black women legislators chose to present their multilayered identities as individual parts in their response to my questions, illustrating that there is variation in how Black women perceive their social identity and the priority that they place on certain identities. Divergent from the tenets of intersectionality theory, the two Black women quoted above hew to an either/or approach to identity-based politics. In this context, the legislators view the totality of their identity as composed of separate and individual parts that combined to make them who they are. Instead of viewing aspects of their identity as mutually constitutive, these Black women easily place themselves in discrete categories that are then mobilized depending on the legislative context. These legislators can then give equal weight to politically salient identities—including race, gender, motherhood, class, or geographic region—in their deliberations of specific legislation.

Rather than articulating an additive approach to identity politics, two other African American women state legislators in this study describe their gender and racial identities as mutually reinforcing. Similar to Gay and Tate (1998), I find that gender and race work in tandem to inform Black women's political identities. The participants in my study identify equally as African American and women, but notably, a new group social identity emerges: that of being a member to a cohort of Black women. This race-gender identity thus melds into one identity that is based on the mutually constitutive distinctiveness of experiencing life as a Black woman. Members of this cohort find that race and gender strongly influence their political attitudes but that intersectional identity does not.

Unlike Delegates Keira Miller and Julissa Moore, other African American women legislators from my sample employ an intersectional approach to identity politics. These women acknowledge that their identity comprises multiple and subordinated subject positions (Crenshaw 1989) that influence their legislative work. For example, Delegate Abigail Watson, who moved to Maryland to pursue a master's degree in education and later accepted a position as a director of Prince George's County public school program for the education of impoverished children, stated, "My identity as a Black woman matters because I see it [legislation] from a different experience. I've experienced some of the prejudices, the not-so-friendly family legislation as it impacts Black women" (Personal interview, March 11, 2009).

In explaining which constituents she feels closest to, Delegate Watson explained that her personal experiences with sexism and racism enable her to empathize with others who experience similar forms of discrimination. She admitted that Black women face additional burdens due to the intersecting nature of race- and gender-based discrimination in legislation that disproportionately affects Black women and their families. Delegate Watson further explained that there are flaws in some state-run services that are intended to protect the needy as well as vulnerable children and adults. She stated that individuals should be personally responsible for their actions and decisions but also said she believes that government policies should give special consideration for race and gender discrimination, particularly when it comes to social service programs. Here, her professional experiences as an educator and program director charged with improving public education in high-poverty areas helps her understanding of the relationship between personal agency and structural inequality. Succinctly, she understands that institutionalized race-gender discrimination and racism and sexism place Black women in precarious positions, but she believes that Black women must also be accountable for their actions. This understanding comes from this delegate's own background. As a survivor of both child abuse and domestic violence, Delegate Watson stated that she understands how race, class, and gender inequalities impact the lives of Black women. Her comments about personal responsibility, however, can be seen as an engagement with right-wing rhetoric.

Delegate Ingrid Jefferson, a union leader who grew up in a lower income, working-class family that often went without basic necessities, contended that her identity offers her perspective that other legislators may not have. Her experiences allow her to view legislation differently and to understand the potential impact of legislation in a particular community: "I can look at a piece of legislation and see it from the perspective of an African American woman who lives in the inner city and have a totally different perspective of a colleague of mine who lives in Montgomery County and has never had to worry about how he would put bread on the table. (Personal interview, March 14, 2009)."

Drawing on her experiences as a low-income African American woman and Baltimore City resident, this delegate acknowledged bringing that perspective to her legislative work. Her observation also evokes awareness of social class issues. According to the U.S. Bureau of the Census, in 2006 only 8.2 percent of Whites were in poverty, compared to the 24.2 percent of African Americans. Poverty rates were highest for families headed by single women, particularly if they were Black or Hispanic. In 2010, according to data from the National Poverty Center, 31.6 percent of households headed by single women were poor, while 15.8 percent of households headed by single men and 6.2 percent of married-couple households lived in poverty. As these examples indicate, Black women in the Maryland state legislature descriptively represent their constituents and are likely to share similar backgrounds with the African American women whom they represent.

In the quote above, Delegate Jefferson articulates identity as mutually constitutive and is unable to parse which part of her identity influences how she interprets legislation. Her quote illustrates the intersectionality of race, gender, and class backgrounds. Yet one can be both intersectionally advantaged and intersectionally disadvantaged (Baca Zinn and Thornton Dill 1996), because no one is ever only privileged or oppressed (Jordan-Zachery 2007; McCall 2005). While Delegate Jefferson indicates that she is familiar with having more month than money, she is now in a privileged position as a state legislator with middle-class economic standing. Yet her experiences afford her a superior perspective on certain legislation—in her opinion—to that of a colleague who does not share her experience.

In sum, African American women articulate different understandings of how identity influences their legislative work. The women use an additive or intersectional approach in detailing how they view their own identities and identity's impact on their motivation as political actors. Some African American women use a mutually reinforcing approach to identity politics, prioritizing one identity over another, while other Black women delegates utilize an intersectional approach to explain how a race-gender identity influences how they view legislation. As the next section will show, the Black women's approaches are highly contingent on the legislative context. I now go on to ask whether this variation then causes Black women legislators to exercise substantive representation of African American women in different ways.

LEGISLATIVE EXAMPLE—POLITICAL INTERSECTIONALITY

Several legislators in this study provided examples to illustrate how their identity influences their representation of their constituents. While I did not include questions about it, the Minority Business Enterprise (MBE) program, which I will discuss shortly, came up frequently during the in-depth, semi-structured interviews and provides an important example of the legislators' policy priorities. The responses that cited this program give an indication of what types of bills are on the legislators' minds. Their examples of legislation spotlight the differences in the ways in which identity is negotiated, with special attention to race, gender, and the intersection of identities that influence the legislators' worldviews. We see instances in which African American women do not believe that their gender and racial identities are in fact mutually reinforcing; we see instead that they use an intersectional approach to discuss the specific policies that they champion. They find that their intersectional race-gender identity as Black women is brought to bear in specific policy issues where race and gender are already functioning as mutually exclusive categories.

While Black women view their identity in ways that differ from one another, their racial and gendered identity leads them to support policies that benefit African American women. This behavior is in line with Mansbridge's theory of the second function of descriptive representation, which elucidates the benefits of providing "innovative thinking in contexts of uncrystallized, not fully activated, interests—descriptive representation enhances the substantive representation of interests by improving the quality of deliberation" (Mansbridge 1999, 628). By using an intersectional approach, the African American women in this study provide a new way of approaching legislation that may have unintended negative consequences for minority women. Because of their lived experiences as Black woman, these legislators believe that they are uniquely positioned to understand how, and keenly aware that, policy can have disastrous effects on African American women.

Minority Business Enterprise

Established in 1978, the MBE program is a "set-aside" program in which a percentage of government contracts are reserved to be awarded to women and minorities. Maryland has one of the oldest MBE programs in the country. It is one of fifteen states with the program, one of four states with a MBE law, and the first state to establish a subgoal for African American-owned firms. It is also the only state to collect uniform data on the progress of its MBE program or to report data on payments to MBEs. The Governor's Office of Minority Affairs (GOMA) has outlined plans to expand the program, primarily into the private sector. During the 2008 fiscal year, the state boasted of receiving $1.1 billion in MBE payments and of making $1.3 billion in awards to minority- and women-owned firms. That translates into $1.8 billion of overall economic benefit in the form of tax revenue, wages, and salaries. The same fiscal year also saw increases in MBE participation. Program "participation rose to 22.5 percent; 27.2 percent for 10 StateStat reporting agencies collectively—the highest in the State's history" (Wilson 2009, 3). According to GOMA, the program has generated 18,639 jobs in Maryland (Wilson 2009). Expanding the MBE program was a major economic development initiative for the O'Malley-Brown administration under the mantra "Minority Business Enterprise—More Business for Everyone" (Wilson 2009).

The 2008 legislative session showed increased attention to the MBE program. The Maryland state legislature unanimously approved SB 606, a bill that required the state treasurer, Maryland Automobile Insurance Fund, Injured Workers' Insurance Fund, and State Retirement and Pension System to attempt to use MBEs for brokerage and investment management services to the greatest feasible extent. Governor O'Malley signed SB 606 into law on May 22, 2008. The goal of this legislation was to diversify the management of Maryland's $40 billion portfolio of pension funds to include more minority- and women-owned firms, because previously only 1 percent of Maryland's pension funds were shared with MBEs (Wilson 2009, 11–13). The bill required that Maryland Automobile Insurance Fund, IWIP, State Retirement and Pension System, and the state treasurer submit annual reports to GOMA and the general assembly on their efforts to increase MBE firms as mangers in brokerage and investment banking services for the state. SB 606 was intended to expand Maryland's pro-minority business climate by advancing public policy and economic practice, according to Luwanda Jenkins, special secretary of GOMA (Wilson 2009, 13). Indeed, Maryland has been recognized by the National Association of Securities Professionals for enacting model legislation for MBE and women business enterprise (WBE) participation in pension funds.

Of SB 606's sixteen cosponsors, ten legislators are African American and five are Black women, including the lead sponsor of the legislation. Cross-filed with HB 1277, the House of Delegates sponsorship also closely resembled the racial makeup of the cosponsoring legislators: of the twenty-nine cosponsors, twenty are African American and seven are Black women. Co-sponsoring legislators represent primarily districts in Prince George's County, Baltimore City, and Baltimore County—areas in the state with the highest African American population. The program shares widespread support among legislators of varying races and ethnicities who represent these three areas of the states. Both Governor O'Malley, former mayor of Baltimore and Lt. Governor Anthony Brown, former member of the House of Delegates representing a district in Prince George's County, also hail from the same areas of the state as the legislators who strongly support MBE legislation.

Maryland's MBE participation goal is 25 percent, with subgoals of 7 percent for women-owned firms and 10 percent for African American-owned firms.

This is the largest MBE goal in the nation. Because this program has separate quotas for MBEs and WBEs, minority women are subsumed within both categories. Minority women can apply for a government contract as either a woman or as a racial minority; there is no category that is reserved for minority women business owners. As a result, Black women business owners are forced to think of themselves as either Black or as women rather than as both racialized and gendered individuals. Whereas the MBE program specifies that women or minority members who are White women of European descent, Blacks, Hispanics, or other minorities are eligible for government contracts, this description ignores the race-gender identities of Black woman (and other racial/ethnic minority women).

A tireless advocate for minority business owners, Senator Raquel Simmons was named the Minority Business Advocate of the Year by the U.S. Small Business Administration in the mid-1990s. Articulating the problem with the program's strictures, Senator Simmons, who grew up in a working-class family in Pennsylvania and later became the president and CEO of a public relations accounting firm, offered an intersectional analysis of Maryland's MBE program that is informed by her race-gender identity. Senator Simmons, as the lead sponsor of this bill, clearly displays a serious commitment to representing minority women:

> Last year I introduced Senate Bill 606 that required the state to diversify its portfolios; it relates to engaging African Americans, more specifically minorities in general, and its investment portfolios, which increased the participation of minorities from about 300 or 400 thousand to about 1.2 billion dollars. This legislation is moving through the general Senate now where African American women, specifically when being certified to do business with the state, have to declare at the time of certification whether they are a female *or* minority. The fact of the matter is they are *both*. And so in changing the legislation to say that an African American woman specifically, or minority woman in general, when being certified by the state to do business can declare themselves as a minority *and* as a female and only at the time of bidding on a specific contract do they have to declare which way they want to go. (Personal interview, March 11, 2009; emphasis in original).

As the lead sponsor of this legislation, Senator Simmons is attempting to rectify the mutually exclusive categorization of Black women as either Black or a woman within the MBE program. She demonstrates the intensity with which an African American woman can represent the interests of other Black women. Scholars have demonstrated that bill sponsorship most clearly establishes the link between constituency interests or preferences and the legislative behavior of representatives (Haynie 2001;

Di Lorenzo 1997; Schattschneider 1960). The fact that this Black woman senator introduced this bill shows the importance that she associates with this piece of legislation and thus serves as a gauge with which to measure the intensity of her interests. Her introduction of this bill shows that there is in fact a connection between the presence of Black women in the legislature and the substantive representation of African American women's interests.

Demonstrating Mansbridge's (1999) assertion that descriptive representation is necessary when there are uncrystallized interests, Black women legislators demonstrate the importance of having a voice in deliberative democracy, which illustrates a larger normative claim of the benefits of descriptive representation. For example, Senator Pamela Price, an entrepreneur who grew up in a middle-class neighborhood in Baltimore City, does not believe that the MBE legislation was intentionally designed to slight Black women business owners. However, she doubts that Black women's perspectives were included when the legislation was first introduced twenty years ago:

> I don't think anybody really thought about it because government thought that they [Black women] would check one group or they would check the other. And I think that people assumed that African American women would choose minority first. And one reason being is that the goals for minorities in the state are larger than the goal for females. So you would think that they would choose that first. By being able to choose both, for example, if in fact someone says to you [referring to me as an example—a Black woman] "female, I would really like you to be on this contract with me" and you say "who's on the contract with you," they have the opportunity to say "well if you have a minority already then I can." Hopefully it works. (Personal interview, March 17, 2009)

Using an intersectional approach, this senator critiques the assumption that Black women place a greater emphasis on their racial identity than their gender identification. The idea that race and gender identities can be prioritized among African American women has long been a contentious debate within Black group consciousness and the women's movement (Giddings, 1984; Hull, Scott, and Smith 1982). Senator Pamela Price articulates that the policy priorities of African American women cannot fit neatly into one group affiliation and shows how this policy limits the effectiveness of the state program by essentially overlooking non-White women. Senator Price adds that she is substantively representing minority women by pointing out the flaws in this bill. The blind spot in the legislation was not considered by the Black men and White women who developed the program over thirty years ago. It is important to note that both Senators Price and Simmons are entrepreneurs and business owners and that their interest in rectifying some of the negative aspects of the MBE legislation most likely stems from their experiences as Black women business owners.

Senator Imani Hayes, an emeritus college professor and dean at a local historically Black university, also noted that the MBE legislation has negative consequences for Black women business owners and that the option to self-select as a MBE or WBE contractor is not suitable.

> Businesses seeking contracts with the state will only pursue Black women if they cannot find a qualified Black man [for the MBE] or a White woman [for the WBE]. Black women are the last resort. I've heard from several Black women that firms just aren't taking their application as serious as they should be. These women feel like businesses would be prefer to contract with anyone who fits the goals of the program beside a Black woman. Really, there are no incentives in the MBE or even the WBE for hiring Black women in particular. There are no incentives for hiring Black women because these goals are not laid out. . . . No incentives or penalties to encourage firms to grow the number of Black women contractors. (Personal interview, July 2, 2009)

Senator Hayes further adds that she is still in the information-gathering stage and has yet to decide what the next step should be to encourage the increase in the number of African American women-owned businesses that contract with the state. She was hesitant to push for a stricter MBE support program but noted that perhaps legislation that requires supplier diversity among the MBE recruitment pool would be advantageous. While I was unable to substantiate Senator Hayes's claim that Black women are the hire of last resort, her comments provide deeper insights about why African American women senators feel strongly about including African American women within the MBE program. Senator Hayes clearly finds that African American women are disadvantaged by the either/or approach to the MBE procurement opportunities for contractors. She states, "Black women need to be equally engaged as a woman and as racial minority" (Personal interview, July 2, 2009).

Senator Bailey Smith, a lawyer from a politically active middle-class family in Baltimore City, explains adroitly how the MBE initiative requires an intersectional perspective:

> I think being a woman affects how I see the impact of legislation. And also being an African American woman, because I have been very involved with minority business enterprise and promoting the state's responsibility for inclusion. I

diligently make sure that minority women are included with the contracts with the state. I bring the perspective of a Black woman to the table, for example, when I make sure that there is equity in re-funding different programs. (Personal interview, March 13, 2009)

While this senator begins her discussion of identity's impact on her legislative work in gendered terms, she concludes with an intersectional perspective of a Black woman. She does not choose between two identities; instead, this senator recognizes that African American women are doubly bound by racism and sexism in the unfair distribution of government contracts that does not account for the multiple facets of minority women's identity. Thus, Senator Smith is substantively representing Black women by working to eradicate government neglect of overlapping memberships within race- and gender-based categories.

To underscore the importance of the role of Black women legislators in the creation of policy that benefits Black women, I include here a quote from an African American male delegate. This Black male delegate expressed that race and gender may matter but that he is not as invested in securing state contracts for African American women business owners. He is a supporter of African American quotas for state contracts and asserts that a gendered analysis is not necessarily needed in his interpretation of the program. "There was a hearing for the MBE bill for the dual legislation for Black women to count as an African American and a woman. I'm sure they are impacted [long pause], the person that is doing that type of work [voice trails off]." (Personal interview, March 15, 2009). This Black male delegate does not seem to have a commitment to Black women's role in the MBE; his statement does not reflect a clear understanding of the legislation's impact on Black women, unlike the previous statements from the Black women legislators.

The male delegate is, however, nicknamed "Mr. MBE" in the Maryland legislature because of his tireless work for the program. During MBE Night at the statehouse, when hopeful minority and women business owners convened in the statehouse to lobby the legislature to increase funding for the program, this Black male delegate was the "go-to person" for the night. He was highly visible, meeting with business owners, the governor, and other key members of the executive branch, as well as other minority legislators and women legislators. "Mr. MBE" proclaimed his commitment to the program by detailing the benefits of the quota system. In my role as participant-observer that evening, I was frequently within earshot of this delegate's conversations. He spoke with various parties about the importance of the governor's office and legislators working in tandem to advocate for the program. However, I did not overhear Mr. MBE mention Senate Bill 606 or the need to reframe the legislation to include minority women. During my personal interview with this delegate, two days after MBE Night, he acknowledged that Black women may be negatively impacted by the current MBE legislation. However, he was not nearly as animated or detailed in his discussion with me about minority women as he was about the program in general. I imagine that my identity as a Black woman researcher may have prompted this delegate to include African American women in his discussion of the MBE program, whereas he may not have been inclined to do so otherwise.

Without the perspective of Black women legislators, it is unlikely that the legislature would revisit MBE legislation to consider including a more comprehensive means of assisting Black women business owners in the receipt of state contracts. The fact that a Black woman senator, Raquel Simmons, introduced the bill, illustrates that Black women may be better able than Black male legislators to understand the importance of gender inclusivity in legislation geared toward assisting a racial minority. It was, after all, the African American women legislators who took this program to task for failing to account for the double minority status of Black women contractors. Without the Black women legislators, it is doubtful that African American women business owners would have the option to negotiate what identity they would like to file under in a bid to receive a state contract. Furthermore, it is noteworthy that the champions of this legislation were business owners themselves or middle-class African American women most likely to take advantage of entrepreneurial opportunities.

That the Black male legislator took no real issue with the mutually exclusive identities for women or minorities in this bill points out that this Black male delegate prioritized one identity—his—over another. This additive approach to public policy is at odds with the intersectional approach to identity utilized by Black women legislators. It is also of note that White women did not mention MBE legislation during my interviews with them. Therefore, this example is a telling illustration of the fact that Black women legislators are needed—and are the best advocates for—for the substantive representation of the interests of African American women.

CONCLUSION

This study provides context for identity politics by investigating how representation and identity are linked for Black women political elites. This chapter echoes the findings of other scholars who contend that descriptive representation enhances substantive representation. Unlike previous studies, however, I uncover nuances in how identity is articulated among legislators sharing the same descriptive background. In so doing, I expose a deeper complexity within identity politics. My work adds to the empirically demonstrated link between descriptive and substantive representation by showing that although Black women represent Black women they arrive at policy positions in diverse ways. African American women legislators in this study describe identity as having a meaningful and significant impact on their work as representatives. Yet the ways in which they articulate how they use identity differ, although the outcome of the substantive policy that they champion is the same.

The African American women legislators in this study demonstrate that identity is relevant in their legislative work. That self-perceptions of legislators' identity are influential in their role as representatives is telling. First, I find that Black women legislators use either an additive or an intersectional approach to articulate how identity informs how they view legislation. Here the African American women legislators prioritize different identities depending on context. Some highlight that one identity may be mobilized in the political process and that they are able to identify when this identity is beneficial, while others find that their race-gender identity is paramount in helping to define their legislative work. As a result, Black women may mobilize different parts of their identity in different ways. Furthermore, the data indicate that Black women legislators recognize numerous aspects of their identity as influential in their legislative work. While race and gender are readily seen as mutually reinforcing, so are other identities, such as class, motherhood, and geographic region. For other Black women state legislators, an identity that is an intersectional framing of race-gender is the driving force behind their view of certain legislation. This nuanced understanding of the complexity inherent in identity is highlighted by Black women Maryland state legislators' first-hand experiences, some of which I have shared here.

Next, the Black women legislators provided examples of when and how they bring identity to bear on their legislative work. Here I contend that they universally employed an intersectional approach in their understanding of a certain piece of legislation whether they would articulate it as such. This intersectional approach indicates that African American women resist being placed into discreet and static categories that fail to account for the overlapping membership in both race- and gender-based groupings. As a result, the Black women legislators were instrumental in bringing inequity to the forefront of debates about the MBE. I argue that, without African American women legislators pointing out the fallacy of gendered versus racialized approach to the MBE quota system, it is highly probable that other legislators would not have advocated for the specific inclusion of minority women. By speaking against the inequity of MBE legislation that asks Black women to choose between their race and gender status, Black women legislators exercise substantive representation.

Lastly, theories of descriptive representation that keep identity constant over time and context fail to account for the value of the substantive work of Black women legislators. Through the use of self-categorization theory we find that social identity varies in highly situation-specific ways. The Black women legislators are attuned to their intersectional situation and attributes but, as individuals, choose to deploy them differently. Here we find that the legislative context matters in the prioritization of social identity in legislative decision making. Scholarship that takes for granted how Black women legislators will behave by relying only on gender-only or race-only perspectives misses the complexity of identity as well as the complicated way in which identity is mobilized.

As the use of representational identity theory indicates, the African American women Maryland state legislators illustrate that there is a strong connection between descriptive and substantive representation. Yet the distinctions in how the women view identity as informing their legislative work vary. By highlighting the complexity and dynamism of social identity, Black women state legislators in this study demonstrate that it is important for scholars to recognize the nuance in identity-based politics rather than viewing subgroups as monolithic. Thus, cross-sectional analysis should play a role in understanding variation and commonality among African Americans, women, and specifically among African American women.

CHAPTER 4

Legislation for the Prevention
of Domestic Violence

Take responsibility for yourself because no one's going to take responsibility for you. I'm
not a victim. I grow from this and I learn.

— Tyra Banks

Recently, I was in Africa monitoring elections when right on the street, this guy started
beating a woman. I got out of my car, pulled her inside and drove her to the hospital. But
after the doctors treated her, she was too afraid to press charges. I've seen this over and
over in America, too.

— Rep. Barbara Lee, (D-CA)

Black women may be the most cohesive demographic group within state
legislatures. Survey research clearly indicates that African American
women state legislators have distinct policy interests (Barrett 1995).
Research by Edith Barrett has shown that African American women state
legislators maintain a high degree of consensus in the types of legislation
they prioritize. Since Barrett's path-breaking study, other scholars have
also found high degrees of uniformity among Black women's legislative
preferences (Bratton, Haynie, and Reingold 2006; Orey and Smooth et al.
2006; Smooth, 2001). However, scholars have yet to investigate which factors, if any, may cause Black women to diverge in their policy preferences.
This research pushes beyond race, class, and gender as the "holy trinity" of
intersectional analysis to critically examine generational affiliation and a
legislator's personal experiences as salient categories for analysis in an intersectional framework. By using select domestic legislation, I investigate
the role of generational identity—legislators born in or prior to 1960 and

those born after 1960—as a contributing factor in Black women's policy-making within the Maryland General Assembly.

Domestic violence, also known as domestic abuse, spousal abuse, or intimate partner violence, is broadly defined as a pattern of abusive behaviors by one or both participants in an intimate relationship such as marriage, dating, family, friends, or cohabitation. The Centers for Disease Control and Prevention estimates that 10 percent of the American population is affected by domestic violence (Tjaden and Thoennes 2006). Domestic violence severely undermines healthy American families and communities as the "most common cause of nonfatal injury to women in the United States with an estimated cost of $50 billion annually" (Bhandari, Dosanjh, Tornetta, and Matthews 2006, 1473). In sum, domestic violence is a major public health concern.

Domestic violence occurs among women and men of all races and classes. Yet, Straus and Gelles (1986) find that African American husbands were more likely to commit severe violence toward their wives than White husbands. As a result, Black women have a unique relationship to domestic violence and to antiviolence programs and politics. Minority victims of abuse often feel pressure from their communities to keep silent about sexual and domestic violence for the purpose of maintaining a united front against racism (Smith 2000). Unfortunately, racial justice organizing has generally focused on racism as it affects men and has often ignored the forms of racism and sexism that minority women face. As a result, minority women have often been marginalized in racial justice initiatives (Crenshaw 1995).

Instead of asking whether race trumps gender (Mansbridge and Tate 1992) in the policy preferences of African American women state legislators, the purpose of this chapter is to examine how Black women's identities are mobilized on issues that disproportionately affect Black women in particular and the Black community as a whole. While not specifically pertaining to domestic violence prevention, research indicates that gender affects the political attitudes of African American women toward sexual harassment, abortion, and the women's movement (Gay and Tate 1998; Mansbridge and Tate 1992; Simien 2005; Simien and Clawson 2004). Research has also shown that race is likely to influence African American women's political attitudes about welfare spending, affirmative action, and busing for integration (Simien 2007). It is clear that African American women's race and gender identities are both influential in their attitudes about politics and public policy. Yet, when policies are both race and gender oriented, do African American women state legislators view this legislation in similar ways? Moving beyond a race-gender analysis, how does a legislator's generational cohort influence her policy choices? By exploring legislation for the prevention of domestic violence proposed in the 2009 legislative session of the Maryland state legislature, I examine how Black women state legislators combine descriptive and substantive representation in their policy preferences. In doing so, they represent not only Black women who are victims of domestic violence victims but the Black community as a whole.

Unlike the White women and Black men I interviewed for this study, Black women legislators shared stories of their personal experiences with domestic violence. This experience enables them to understand how domestic violence legislation uniquely affects African American women. Using Crenshaw's (1991) concept of political intersectionality, which shows how feminist and antiracist politics marginalize Black women's politics that are simultaneously racialized and gendered, I detail how Black women legislators draw from experience, culture, and identity to explain their positions on domestic violence legislation. In so doing they share insights about the legislation's potential impact on their constituents that might otherwise have been left out of the discussion. Similar to Hawkesworth's (2003) finding that minority congresswomen draw upon their own positions and experiences of race and class to critique welfare reform, I contend that Black women state legislators frame domestic violence as a race-gender issue—in the process incorporating other identities, such as their generational cohort—to advocate for African American women who are marginalized and disempowered. Lastly, using representational identity theory, I investigate generational differences in how Black women legislators vote on domestic violence legislation.

In a broader context, the domestic violence bills that I highlight in this chapter are important because they provide an indication of the legislators' policy priorities and underscore the need for the inclusion of historically excluded groups in the policy-making process. They show that Black women are needed at the legislative table precisely because they have different policy preferences than Black male and White legislators. Because I did not include questions about domestic violence legislation in the in-depth, semi-structured interviews, these unsolicited narratives give an indication of what types of bills were foremost in the legislators' minds. It is important to note that during the two-week period in which my fieldwork was conducted, there were several bills championing the prevention of domestic violence before the Maryland House of Delegates.[1] Therefore, delegates may have been primed to provide domestic violence legislation as an example of an issue about which they felt strongly. Not all legislators mentioned domestic violence as an issue during the interview, but it is notable that, unprompted, eleven out of the fifteen Black women delegates mentioned domestic violence legislation. Thus, I conclude that it is an issue that is of special concern to African American women lawmakers. Senators, however, did not mention domestic violence legislation; no domestic violence bills were before that chamber. Hence, the data in this chapter focus solely on the Maryland House of Delegates during the 2009 legislative session. Only one White female delegate spoke in depth about the domestic violence bills.[2] Another casually mentioned domestic violence as a cause to which she, as a woman legislator, feels a special connection. It is telling that of the twenty-two men interviewed for this project, no men of any race or ethnicity mentioned this type of legislation. While I did not originally anticipate that Black women legislators would want to talk about domestic violence legislation in their interviews, I did expect to hear stories about how race-gender identities affect their policy preferences and how they represent of their constituencies. However, because of the high numbers of African American women who are victimized by intimate partners and because African American women delegates have had personal connections to domestic violence, it is unsurprising that this group of legislators prioritized legislation against domestic violence as a distinctly raced-gendered issue, highlighting the overlapping and interdependent nature of gender and race/ethnicity that makes domestic violence a distinctive intersectional issue.

DOMESTIC VIOLENCE AS A DISTINCTIVE INTERSECTIONAL ISSUE

While domestic violence occurs in all racial and ethnic groups and in varying class standings, religions, sexual orientations, and education levels, it is young women, low-income women, and minorities who are at disproportionate risk of suffering domestic violence and rape. "African Americans were victimized by intimate partners at significantly higher rates than persons of any other race between 1993 and 1998. Black females experienced intimate partner violence at a rate 35 percent higher than that of White females, and about 22 times the rate of women of other races" (Rennison and Welchans 2000, 1). African American women in the age group of twenty to twenty-four experience significantly more domestic violence than White women in the same age group. While African American women experience comparable levels of intimate partner violence to White women in all other age categories, they are slightly more likely to experience domestic violence. The effects of domestic violence on women are manifold. Black women who have been victims of domestic violence report more physical ailments, mental health issues, are less likely to practice safe sex, and are more likely to abuse substances during pregnancy than Black women without a history of abuse (Rennison 2001).

Organizations that combat domestic violence find that, when it comes to reporting instances of domestic violence, there may be compounding factors for women from minority communities. These factors include limited access to legal advice, racism, discrimination against women in Black and minority ethnic communities, increased isolation, family or community pressure or collusion to keep the abuse a secret, discriminatory employment practices, and reduced access to services (Wyatt, Axelrod, Chin, Carmona, and Loeb 2000). Research indicates that domestic violence is tied to socioeconomic factors. Indeed, domestic violence within African American communities is often explained by socioeconomic status and poverty rates (Asbury 1999; Barnes 1999; Hampton and Gelles 1994; Hotaling and Sugarman 1986; Lockhart and White 1989; Uzzell and Peebles-Wilkins 1989; West and Rose 2000). Staples (1982) suggests that spousal abuse in lower class Black families is seen as the normative expectation, that there is an expectation that physical violence against the woman is natural or necessary. Dennis et al. (1995) found that domestic violence within the African American community is more prevalent when men have incomes of less than $20,000. Cazenave and Straus (1979) found that when income was controlled, Black respondents were less likely to report instances of spousal slapping at every income range except the $6,000 to $11,000 level. Black respondents at both the lowest and highest income categories were less likely to report violent behaviors than White respondents with comparable incomes. Marsh (1993) contends that abused and economically dependent African American women are imprisoned in abusive relationships that they do not have the personal financial resources to exit.

In addition to poverty rates and socioeconomic status, there are several other barriers to reducing the perpetuation of domestic violence in African American communities. First, Black women have reported that shelters and batterers' intervention programs are not community based and are therefore geographically inaccessible (Asbury 1987; Williams and Becker 1994). The inaccessibility of services is also tied to lack of transportation and the money necessary for accessing certain protective services. Second, African American victims of domestic violence have reported a lack of cultural competence among service providers, making it difficult for case workers to effectively connect with the client (Allard 1991; Asbury 1999; Kupenda 1998). Scholarship has documented that African American women have been denied shelter because they did not sound fearful enough or appeared too strong to require temporary housing (Allard 1991; Kupenda 1998; West

1999). The stereotype of the strong black woman (Wallace 1978) is that the African American woman can sustain anything, has no fear, and can easily protect herself (Collins 1990). As a result of this stereotype, some Black women do not receive much-needed domestic violence services.

Third, racial loyalty serves as a barrier for those seeking domestic violence services. Bent-Goodley argues that racial loyalty is readily seen in "African American women's decisions to withstand abuse and make a conscious self-sacrifice for what she perceives as the greater good of the community but to her own physical, psychological, and spiritual detriment" (2001, 323). It follows that Black women fail to report domestic violence for fear of the discrimination and injustice that African American men often experience in the American criminal justice system (White 1994). Lastly, African American women are often further victimized by social structures (Richie 1996). This gender entrapment—the socially constructed process through which Black women engage in behaviors that are an extension of their race-gender identities, culturally expected gender roles, and violence within their intimate relationships—accounts for abused African American women who are compelled to commit crimes (Richie 1996). Thus, linkages between gender-identity development and crime are part of a larger social structure rather than simply a result of the individual actions of wayward African American women. In fact, Blacks of both genders are more likely to be arrested for domestic violence than White Americans (Beck and Mumola 1999; Fagan 1996). As a result, Black women are more likely to distrust the criminal justice system and are therefore reluctant to use it, and research shows that the criminal justice system can work against Black women who are experiencing or have experienced domestic violence (Plass 1993).

To illustrate how racism and sexism are experienced in tandem by minority women, Crenshaw (1991) uses the example of violence against women as a case study for exploring the various ways in which race and gender intersect to shape the structural, political, and representational aspects that inform minority women's lives. The traditional analysis of identity politics that focuses on a single category of identity fails to understand how violence against women has multiple causes. In her study of battered women's shelters, Crenshaw finds that shelters are not equipped to deal with the multilayered forms of domination that structure the lives of minority women. Many minority women are victims of poverty due to racial discrimination in employment and housing practices. The high rates of unemployment for African Americans make it less likely that minority women can depend on financial support or temporary shelter from friends and relatives. Thus race, class, and gender intersect to further marginalize Black women who are victims of domestic violence.

Black feminists have been on the forefront of addressing domestic violence in African American communities. These activists, practitioners, and scholars recognize that race and class are directly connected to domestic violence. The generalized feminist claim that domestic violence happens and "can happen to anyone" erases the necessity of analyzing how patriarchy and White domination operate in the lives of Black women (Richie 2000, 1135). Thus, to willfully ignore the victimization of those at the margins of power—particularly low-income women of color—often invalidates the anti-violence movements in America. Domestic violence as antiracist politics often silences feminists' attempts to expose patriarchy within the Black community and misses the needs of women of color (Crenshaw 1991). For example, while mainstream feminist communities view increased law enforcement as a solution to domestic violence, many women of color fear increased rates of arrest, incarceration, and detainment of people of color as a response to violence against women (Richie 2000, 1136). Strategies that encourage more aggressive policing of communities of color—which can lead to increased rates of incarceration and amplified police brutality—undermine the work of feminists of color who are concerned about ending domestic violence in communities of color.

Given these concerns, many minority communities find that feminism is a distinctly White endeavor and that White women's issues have little relevance to Black issues (Simien 2006; Simons 1979). Crenshaw's (1991) findings demonstrate that the intersecting patterns of race, gender, and class produce multilayered dimensions of violence against women of color. Not only does domestic violence have disastrous effects on Black women, but it also has an impact on the Black community, and a history of institutionalized racism through law enforcement has left many African American women with nowhere to turn (Plass 1993). These experiences are not represented in feminist or antiracist discourse, and because of their intersectional identities and experiences, the interests of women of color are simultaneously marginalized by both discourses. Black women state legislators are therefore primed to reference their identity as a factor in legislative decision making on this intersectional issue.

DOMESTIC VIOLENCE LEGISLATION

The vast majority of the domestic violence legislation discussed by the Black women legislators during their interviews centered on HB 1181—Denial or Dismissal of Domestic Violence Petitions: Expungement of Records.[3] This bill included a proposal that would have allowed a respondent in a domestic violence protection-order proceeding to request expungement of all court records relating to the proceeding if the petition was denied or dismissed at the interim, temporary, or final protective-order stage. The most contentious aspect of the bill centered on removing a person's name from a public database maintained by the state judiciary's Web site and provided public access from the case record after three years of denial or dismissal of the petition.[4] Opponents, including a majority of the Women's Caucus and the majority of older Black women legislators, noted that victims of domestic violence may not request a final protective order because they may be intimated by their abusers. Eliminating the public record of denied or dismissed requests could erase a record of abuse. Supporters of this legislation, which included younger Black women legislators and several legislators with legal training, expressed their desire to protect individuals who were victims of false and malicious temporary protective orders from having their names appear on a public Web site. They argued that because of the stigma of an unproved abuse accusation, dismissed protective orders available on a public Web site could be used to unfairly deny people jobs or housing. If it had passed, the bill would have removed the domestic violence court records in cases in which a domestic violence petition had been denied or dismissed.

It is relatively easy to file a temporary restraining order (TRO) after accusing someone of domestic violence. Even if the accusation were proven to be completely false, the charge would be in the open record, publically linked to the accused person's name on an Internet database. Some believe that keeping these records as a public record helps defend women from domestic violence and abuse. However, battered women are unlikely to file a permanent restraining order against their abusers. We know that battered women frequently return to their abusers and that abusers routinely threaten women, their children, and the women's extended families if women attempt to flee the abusive situation. Studies have furthermore shown that abusers of immigrant women use the women's immigrant status as tool to keep them from seeking legal protection. As a result, women stay in the abusive relationships or fail to file a permanent order of protection. Women's rights activists feared that HB 1181 would give abusers increased leverage over their victims; that is, the abuser could tell the victim that he or she would hire a lawyer to argue that the petition be denied and his or her record expunged and thus that filing for a court order of protection would have no consequences, effectively deterring the victim from filing the order. The members of the Women's Caucus recognized that victims could be further victimized by the expungement of TROs and asked their colleagues to consider how this bill could have unintended consequences.

Of the more than seventeen thousand temporary protective orders granted in 2008 in Maryland, only about nine thousand were made final. As a result, some legislators and activists have been concerned that laws intended to aid women may have negative consequences for those who are falsely accused. They fear that some parties are using the courts to punish an individual with whom they are angry, filing false domestic violence allegations against him or her. To guard against the institutionalization of false allegations, legislators and activists wanted to provide a process for removing them from public court records.

On February 27, 2009, the House Judiciary Committee, the committee that introduced the legislation, voted eighteen to three to approve the bill but the measure failed in the House of Delegates. Although the legislation generated extensive debate, it was not successful, and HB 1181 died an unusual death on third reading. During this stage of the legislative process, a bill is read with all amendments and is (generally) given the final approval of the legislative body. Bills that have been sufficiently amended and have made their way out of committee are viewed as duly vetted. Once the bill has made it to third reading, it is generally assumed that it will be favorably voted upon and will move to the other chamber for discussion. Committee structure usually guarantees that only passable bills make it to the general assembly floor for third reading. Committees, however, ensure that they have completed proper due diligence before sending a bill to the general assembly because party leadership and committee chairs are humiliated when their bills do not pass in the general assembly.

Newspaper reports on HB 1181 in the *Baltimore Sun*, *The Associated Press*, *State and Local Wire*, and the *Washington Post* during March 10–27, 2009, reflected relatively similar viewpoints (e.g., Bykowicz 2009a, 2009b, 2009c; Helderman 2009; White 2009). The three newspapers highlighted the testimonies of both male and female legislators who themselves had been victims of domestic violence—or had family members who had—making their stories a major focal point. The newspapers all concluded that it was important for victims to understand that their representatives had had similar experiences and that, in light of these revelations, victims should not be ashamed to speak out against abuse. The newspaper articles also reported that there was a split among members of the Women's Caucus; twenty-nine women joined with forty male colleagues to successfully defeat the bill, and fifteen women voted for the measure.

Those who voted for the bill had concluded that this legislation would help those falsely accused of abuse clear their records. In contrast, the chair of the Women's Caucus and domestic violence prevention experts asserted that alleged victims of abuse did not need another reason not to follow

through on protective orders. This camp concluded that the problem of dis-
honestly filed protective orders had been overstated. The bill itself was
clearly controversial and caused extensive debates as a result. However,
legislators' perceptions of HB 1181 provided me with significant insights
about the role of race, gender, and the generational cohort in the legislative
decision-making process.

In the following discussion, I detail African American women legislators'
comments about HB 1181 to illustrate the necessity of employing a methodology of political intersectionality when legislating policies historically
seen as women's issues. I show that neglecting the intersection of other
categories of marginalization—including race and ethnicity—when considering policy legislation for women's issues is highly problematic. I have
included a few lengthy quotations from my interviews with Black women
delegates; these observations are illuminating and assist with our understanding of how identity mediates representation. They also display a generational difference in how legislators view HB 1181, likely attributable in
part to the increased likelihood that the younger Black women legislators
have a legal background, which, when coupled with their race-gender experience, affected their understanding of this particular domestic violence
legislation. Five younger Black women legislators born after 1960 and two
older Black women legislators born prior to 1960 supported HB 1181, and
eight older African American women legislators opposed the bill. This break
suggests that greater and more sustained scholarly attention should be
paid to generational differences within intersectional groups. The differences in the policy preferences of the eight Black women legislators in opposition to the bill in contrast to the seven who supported it highlight that
shared identity alone does not mediate the legislative decision-making process in uniform ways.

GENERATIONAL DIFFERENCES

Intersectionality scholars have yet to pay significant attention to generational differences within groups. This study is among the first to investigate
how group cohort influences Black women legislators' policy preferences.
Building upon the work of political science scholars—most notably Andra
Gillespie (2010, 2012) and Linda Williams (2001), who investigated the
role of generational affiliation in Black politics—I point to the educational
and socialization differences among age cohorts of African American
women legislators to explain differences on policy positions, such as bills
like HB 1181, that disproportionately impact Black women.

A generation is defined as an identifiable group that shares birth years, age, and location and that experiences significant life events at critical developmental stages (Kupperschmidt 2000). As an age cohort, generational groups share historical and social life experiences. The effects of these experiences are relatively stable over the course of their lives (Smola and Sutton, 2002). A cohort develops traits that influence a member's experiences of race and gender. Different scholars conceptualize a Black political identity that prioritizes one's life histories and experiences. For example, the scholarship of Cohen (2010) and Simpson (1998) on the post-civil rights generation's Black youth finds that the youths' experiences with racism and race-based social structures and institutions influenced that generation's connection to Black political identity.[5] This research illustrates a generational divide in public opinion among African Americans, and while my work is situated within these and other studies that point to differences in the post-civil rights generation's politics, I am the first to consider this divide in relation to recent legislative behavior.

Incorporating generation, race, and political behavior, Gillespie's (2010, 2012) work on third-wave[6] Black politicians illustrates that those born after 1960 differ markedly from their predecessors. For starters, they were born or came of age after the civil rights movement. Other similarities include their education; that is, they were educated in Ivy League and other predominately White institutions and often attended law schools as they began to build their political careers. This group is also seen as having more political potential; that is, they have more realistic chances to hold higher executive office than their predecessors (Gillespie 2010, 139). This generation has ostensibly lived the American Dream and represents a generation of Blacks who do not feel cut off from the larger society and are determined to move beyond the moods and methods of their predecessors toward improving Blacks' ability to live the American Dream. Unfortunately, Gillespie's edited volume only includes one chapter on African American women political elites. While her transformative text concluded that there were too few African American women political elites at the national level, the one chapter in this volume dedicated to Black women focused on their political behavior and campaigns, not their post-election legislative behavior (Gamble 2010). In general, the work on generational differences among Black political elites pays little attention to African American women.

More fully incorporating race and gender within a discussion of generational trends, Linda Faye Williams (2001) conducted the first study that disaggregated the political agendas of Black women state legislators according to the civil rights and post-civil rights generation. Using committee assignments and legislative priorities, the women of the New Deal (defined as those aged sixty-five years or older) and the women of the civil rights generations (defined as those forty to sixty-four years old) were studied to "test the thesis that the further we move from the Civil Rights–Black Power Era, the less important the long-term dual agenda of Africans (ending racial discrimination and oppression *and* supporting social and economic justice for all Americans) would be centrally important to Black female elected officials" (Williams 2001, 322–323; emphasis added). In a multivariate analysis, Williams found that Black women state legislators who came to political maturity during the New Deal or civil rights–Black Power eras are more likely to report a strong commitment to civil rights and redistributive programs. She also found that the post-civil rights generation of Black women state legislators does not view redistributive and civil rights issues as a priority, although women of the civil rights–Black Power era did. However, Williams's study does not account for women's interest policy priorities or Black women state legislators' relationships to gender politics.

Building on the Williams's (2001) work, I assert that third-wave Black women state legislators are committed to race-gender issues, as evidenced by their attention to domestic violence legislation. Their understanding of political phenomena is altered by their generation's privileged background of benefiting from the civil rights and feminist movements. Therefore, this vantage point leads younger Black women legislators to view public policy differently than their older civil rights counterparts. The third-wave Black women legislators are more likely to pursue an encompassing political agenda that understands the intersections of race and gender, but their political strategies are not built or sustained around identity alone.

In providing context for third-wave Black feminism, Kimberly Springer (2002) differentiates between generations among Black and White feminists, finding that younger Black women pay homage to their feminist foremothers, after whom they have modeled their politics. In doing so, third-wave Black state legislators show respect for the work of their political foremothers yet part ways with their older counterparts to establish their own political identities that reflect both their race and gender. Hip-hop feminist Joan Morgan (1999) concludes that as daughters of the post-feminist, post-civil rights, post-soul hip-hop generation, younger Black women are reaping the benefits of the struggles that older Black women endured. These third-wave Black women politicians aim to produce a more accepting society of raced and gendered bodies. Morgan theorizes that some Black women of this generation are "college-educated, middle-class black girls, [who] are privileged because we now believe that there is nothing we cannot achieve because we are women, though sexism and racism might fight us every step of the way" (1999, 59). The new generation of Black women legislators is aware of the challenges and obstacles that they face as women of color, yet their individual educational and professional backgrounds prove that they have been more privileged than their predecessors.

This study divides Black women legislators into two cohorts: those born in or prior to 1960 and those born after 1960. This framework overlaps with the terminology used in Williams's (2001) framework of the New Deal and civil rights–Black Power eras and that of the post-civil rights generation and Gillespie's (2010, 2012) categorization of third-wave black politicians.[7] While civil rights–Black Power era terms for generational cohorts and post-civil rights and third-wave Black politicians' terminologies overlap, the waves of feminism are not easily mapped onto the above-described age groups,[8] and the wave analogy often associated with White feminist discourse is not only problematic but also not easily transferred to Black feminists (Springer, 2002). I view younger Black women state legislators as not only having benefited from the civil rights and Black Power movements but also from the second-wave feminist movement during the 1960s through the 1980s that challenged gender inequality within politics, culture, and law.

Delegate Julissa Moore, a young African American woman, supported HB 1181 based on her understanding of political intersectionality coupled with her training as a lawyer, which she notes had enabled her to understand certain terms and legal structures better than her nonlawyer colleagues. Having grown up in a middle-class community in Prince George's County, Delegate Moore notes that her exposure to issues facing victims of domestic violence occurred during her legal training at the University of Maryland. Delegate Moore frames her support for the legislation by explaining her willingness to protect wrongly accused individuals—Black men. She notes that some women were opposed to this bill because particularly, they did not want to be seen as weak on legislation about women's issues. However, she alleged, on the surface the bill appeared as if it were providing protection for domestic violence victims, usually women, yet actually it would have other potential cultural implications. During our interview she described to me the process of obtaining a temporary restraining order (TRO), breaking down legal terms and reasoning before she presented her analysis of the legislation. Delegate Moore stated that the bar is set very low for TROs because the legal system does not want to create barriers for people who need protection. "It's a good thing that the bar is so low because it gives more people access, but, unfortunately on the other side, it gives people who are presumed innocent a huge stigma as an abuser, both men and women." The law, in her opinion, should enable all Maryland residents the ability to petition the court for their personal protection; however, she

acknowledges that individuals who have not been victims can also obtain
TROs by falsifying records and lying.

Because the court records for the state of Maryland are available via
public record, this legislator believes that if a person is found not guilty or
a permanent restraining order is not granted, the TRO should be expunged
from the public record. While Delegate Moore thinks that Maryland residents should be able to easily file for a TRO, she does not believe that that
filing should be viewable by the mass public.

Similarly, Delegate Naomi Young, another young African American
woman delegate and lawyer, agrees that unsubstantiated records should
not be open to the public. As the daughter of a civil rights activist, Delegate
Young is deeply concerned about equality and fairness for Maryland citizens. In the case of victims and perpetrators of domestic violence, she believes that judges should have control over the length of time the file is
open. She stated,

> The issue was whether we should expunge it from public view, not expunge it
> entirely. The judges, prosecutors and police would still have access to these re-
> cords. To me that was what was important. You can be accused of anything and
> then could go to the cops right now and say "keep him or her away from me." And
> the police would give me a stay-away order against you. This will be in your record
> for the rest of your life. The judge may say later "I'm not going to keep this in
> place, but only for that TRO week it's on your record." It could be on your record
> for the rest of your life and you haven't done anything. I feel that if the judge
> doesn't make it a permanent order then, we shouldn't be allowed to do that to
> Black men who have not been found guilty. (Personal interview, March 20, 2009)

Delegate Kenya Barnes, a younger Black woman legislator and a lawyer,
expresses an acute awareness of the negative impact of racialized and gendered biases in legislation that disproportionately affect her district, where
an overwhelming majority of her constituents are African American. "In
Prince George's[9] we have more domestic violence . . . than anywhere else in
the state. Clearly that's a crime that affects more Black women and so you
are conscious of that when you are making a decision about it" (Personal
interview, 20 March 2009). While I was unable to authenticate her claim
about Prince George's County, this delegate's quote presents a rather telling view of the victim in her mind's eye. Because she believes that most
common victim of domestic violence is an African American woman, race-
gender plays an important role in her legislative decision making. Namely,
she is aware of how identity influences the likelihood of abuse, which informs how this delegate views the legislation.

Concerns about the effects that a lasting public record would have on young Black men and the African American community in general are expressed by another young delegate. In explaining the possible negative effects of the bill for Black men, Delegate Barnes explains:

> To have something like this on Black men's record, it makes it harder and you know what happens. I know Black men, just like White men, can abuse their wives or girlfriends. And at the same time, Black men can also be unfairly accused. So in the interest of fairness it was important to vote in favor of the bill, and the Woman's Caucus went the other way. (Personal interview, March 12, 2009)

Engaging in what is fundamentally intersectional analysis, these Black women delegates make connections to race and gender in their positions on this domestic violence bill to conclude that this legislation could have a negative impact on minority communities and in particular on Black women. The legislators' comments, however, address both Black men and women. They want to protect the victims, possibly Black women, but are also concerned about Black men falsely accused of domestic violence, who would be stigmatized due to accusations permanently linked to their names.

In a distinct race-gender analysis of HB 1181, Delegate Yasmin Wood, a young Black woman delegate, elucidates her agreement with the delegates' views detailed above:

> There were a lot of women and men [legislators] who had a problem with this bill because they believed that if we did this [expunge the record] it would be like protecting the abuser. I saw it very different as a Black woman. . . . I supported the legislation because I believe that the public record should not reflect an unsubstantiated claim and not create a stigma for people when the allegations aren't proven to be true. . . . What does it mean then if a Black man can't get a job to support his family? That's not right; especially if the TRO is unsubstantiated, this man should not be denied a job. It adds extra pressure on the Black woman to make ends meet and take care of the family. What does that do for the community? A large number of Black men without jobs is not good for the community as a whole. (Personal interview, March 18, 2009)

A married mother of five young boys, perhaps Delegate Wood can imagine the difficulty of raising a family without the support of her husband. Her vision of a two-parent home, with a man who financially provides for his family or perhaps how a TRO could affect her son's futures may drive Delegate Wood to support HB 1181. The younger African American women delegates agree that legislators should not protect Black men at the expense of Black women. However, the younger legislators' accounts of their legislative decision making around HB 1181 support the narrative of Black male crisis as one to which social policy has responded and in many cases embraced. However, other comments illustrate that these legislators are committed to Black feminism. They critique the social structures that hinder Black advancement, showing a clear understanding of gender dynamics and inequality (Alexander-Floyd 2007; Simien 2006; Smooth 2006). The younger legislators display an understanding that racism plays a large role in society's depiction of Black men and show that they do not want to continue to needlessly disadvantage Black men. They illustrate a willingness to protect Black men and women.

Coming of age in the 1980s, these legislators likely witnessed an open assault on Black manhood (Blake and Darling, 1994). During this period, African American men faced negative socioeconomic and political determinants (Marable 1983). Enduring stereotypes of African American males—that they are immoral, lazy, violent, overly sexual, mentally deficient, rapaciously criminal, or athletic—imposed by White history have made it difficult for society to view Black men as anything other than deviant (Hare and Hare 1984). The lived manifestations of these stereotypes have led to family and social strife for Black men (Karenga 1986), and racist stereotypes and false accusations have caused Black men to be viewed as one of America's biggest problems. However, the crisis of Black manhood is a burden faced by all members of Black communities. African American women struggle with Black men to confront racism, and women indicate their awareness of social and political structures that marginalize Black men. In seeking to support victims of domestic violence but also protecting those who have not been found guilty of crimes, these younger Black women delegates use their race-gender identity to understand how racism, patriarchy, and cultural norms have marginalized some members of the Black community. They bring a different understanding to how this policy affects their constituents.

GENERATIONAL SHIFT AS SEEN THROUGH ROLL CALL DATA

HB 1181 presents an interesting case study for how Black women vote compared to White women and men and Black men. The debates about this bill also illuminate intragroup differences among Black women legislators. On March 10, 2009, the bill failed sixty-four to sixty-nine on third reading.

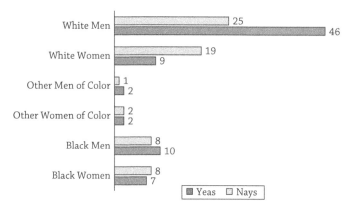

Figure 4.1:
Roll Call Votes on HB 1181 by Race and Gender.

Breaking down the roll call vote by legislators' demographics we find that seven Black women (five of whom were born after 1960—the total number of the young Black women legislators), six Black men, five White women, and forty-five White men voted in favor of the bill. Those voting against the bill were eight Black women, ten Black men, twenty White women, and thirty-four White men. Additionally, one Black man and one White man did not vote. Four delegates were excused from voting, two White women and two White men. Of the nonvoting delegates, all were Democrats except for one of the White women. Figure 4.1 presents a detailed breakdown of roll call votes by race, gender, and ethnicity.

There is no noticeable generational difference among White women delegates. The majority of White women legislators in this study were more likely to oppose HB 1181, and White men were more likely than White women to support HB 1181. This also indicates a gender split among White legislators. However, this split is most likely attributed to partisanship, as the greater part of White women legislators who supporting HB 1181 were Republicans, as were the majority of the White men who supported the bill. There are no partisan differences between the African American legislators since they are all Democrats. Instead, examining the Black women legislators' demographics to investigate their roll call votes revealed that generational cohort influenced intragroup voting. Figure 4.2 depicts the generational differences in how the Black women voted.

As younger legislators enter the governing body, researchers should employ a legislature-specific focus to study generational differences and the policy preferences of these newcomers. It bears noting that despite the generational differences that I have outlined, Black women legislators uniformly

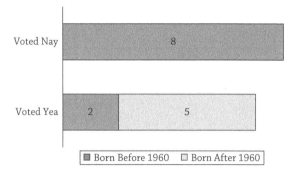

Figure 4.2:
Breakdown of Black Women Legislators' Votes on HB 1181.

acknowledged that domestic violence is an important issue underscoring their representational duties, which leads us back to the idea that Black women's race-gender identities affect what types of issues they champion, whom they represent, and how they represent them.

Therefore, we see the influence of identity in how Black women connect their policy preferences to a new understanding of how race and gender informs the legislation that affects their constituents. As supporters of the bill, the younger Black women legislators operate in conjunction with tenets of Black feminism by asking Black men to take responsibility for their actions if they are accused of domestic violence. These generational perspectives lead to researchers' increased understanding of legislators' policy preferences vis-à-vis social phenomena that disproportionately affect the Black community and Black women in particular.

RIFT IN THE WOMEN'S CAUCUS

It was an unusual occurrence that the Women's Caucus was divided over their support for HB 1181. As mentioned above, the caucus ultimately decided to oppose HB 1181 and rule in favor of not expunging the records. The caucus made the last-minute decision, directly prior to third reading, to rally and defeat this legislation. However, in the process a noticeable rift occurred among the Democratic women, which rarely happens. All of the younger, along with the two older Black women legislators, mobilized in support of HB 1181, but the vast majority of older delegates sided with the Women's Caucus.

Delegate Julissa Moore, a young Black woman, explained the differences that arose on the floor between some members of the Women's Caucus. It is clear that her race-gender identity caused her to view HB 1181 in a different way than some of her female colleagues.

> We had an issue on domestic violence and expunging records from public view when the claims are dismissed or denied. I think that some of the Woman's Caucus felt very strongly about that issue and some felt differently. Well, I don't know if that is a good example. In the minority community we see a lot of barriers to employment, and that may be more of a minority experience than with others. Frequently, arrest records, domestic violence, civil records, and things of this nature—whether they go forward or not—can be a barrier to employment, so we may see more of that in the minority community than others. (Personal interview, March 12, 2009)

While Delegate Moore commented on the explicit connection between barriers to employment and unsubstantiated TROs, she also framed her dissatisfaction with the bill in terms of justice for Black constituents:

> Recently a big issue that came up was our bill that would allow people who are accused—but the complaints are not substantiated for domestic violence—to have their records expunged. The issue for me in the bill was not whether to allow those people to get their record expunged if they weren't determined to have committed the abuse. Women of the Women's Caucus saw that as a woman's issue and domestic violence issue. But, I saw it as a fairness issue for the Black community—my district, my constituents. (Personal interview, March 12, 2009)

Delegate Naomi Young, a younger legislator, is quoted in the *Washington Post* as positing that HB 1181 was a common-sense measure and saying that she could not understand why legislators would oppose the bill. She argued that the courts and police are now better trained to recognize the danger that women endure from abusive partners and noted that temporary restraining orders could be easily obtained. Delegate Young's response shows that she is clearly concerned with those who might suffer from the stigma of an unproven accusation of abuse that might be used to deny them jobs or housing. "Innocent people should be able to clear their records" (Personal interview, March 12, 2009).

Juxtaposed with the Black women delegates' intersectional perspectives on HB 1181 are the comments of one White woman delegate. This delegate was the only White woman legislator in this study to explicitly discuss the domestic violence bills. When asked if she had a particular affinity to any particular group within her constituency, she answered, "because I started coming down to Annapolis advocating for issues on domestic violence and sexual assault, women's issues are my priority. That still remains with me. . . . My soul is women's issues, but most specifically domestic violence, sexual assault, and child abuse" (Personal interview, March 17, 2009). This White woman delegate clearly sees herself as fighting for women's issues. She is known within her district and the Maryland state legislature as a champion of women's issues. Perhaps this is why she spoke explicitly about domestic violence legislation.

As a stalwart feminist and opponent of HB 1181, this White woman delegate expressed a gendered commitment to protecting victims of domestic violence. In keeping with the critiques made of them by women of color and third-world feminists, White feminists often fail to see how race plays an influential role in minority women's lives (Collins 2000; Richie 2000). While White feminists often do take intersectionality into account, this delegate expressed that she was baffled by the younger Black women's view of HB 1181, although two older Black women had also joined the younger women in their support of this legislation. The majority of older Black women held the same view on the domestic violence legislation as this White woman delegate, indicating that there was a gendered commitment to this legislation despite racial differences. Yet only the White women delegate comments on the apparent generational and racial divisions in the caucus. Below, she addresses younger Black women delegates' defection from the Women's Caucus's opposition to HB 1181:

> I assumed that the Women's Caucus might kill this bill and that a natural coalition [of women legislators] would coalesce around this bill to kill it. And much to my shock and education, the young minority women from the urban areas were not against the bill. In fact, they were for the bill. It was really interesting and it's something we are going to have to [have] the Women's Caucus talk about. (Personal interview, March 17, 2009)

When asked to explain why she believes that the young minority women legislators from urban districts supported the bill, this White woman delegate said that she would like to talk with those legislators and learn more about why they favored the bill. While she said that young minority women legislators needed to learn from the women legislators of her generation, this White woman delegate also expressed her desire to learn from the young minority women delegates. She explained that she is looking to expand the dialogue on this subject and to share her experiences as a dedicated women's rights advocate with the women who supported HB 1181:

It was really a very important lesson to me. And I need to share with them what I think and they need to hear from us. I don't think we as pioneers [first sizable cohort of women to enter the Maryland state legislature] can assume that they have the same experiences about domestic violence and child abuse and the whole thing that we fought for. The same as the women that fought for the rights for us to vote, and so many women don't take that or use that right. So it's probably the same thing; we don't realize what everyone had to do to come to this place to give women opportunities. So it's important to me that we talk to both sides and have a dialogue. I'm actually looking forward to it. (Personal interview, March 17, 2009)

This White woman delegate's comments can be interpreted as being parochial and condescending toward the young minority women delegates, yet they show that she understands that Black women's experiences have given them a different perspective from which they view this particular domestic violence legislation. Or perhaps this delegate's comments illustrate her wish to talk about differences in policy preferences on women's legislation.

As a longstanding champion of women's issues legislation, this delegate is committed to the feminist perspective of a universal or essential woman whose gendered identity largely shapes how she experiences and views the world. A singular perspective, as documented in Crenshaw's (1991) and Richie's (2000) findings, does not readily lend itself to antiracist understandings of how legislation can have negative intersectional effects on Black women, Black men, and Black families. This White woman's comments illustrate that a feminist-only approach hindered her understanding of the Black women delegates' favorable views of HB 1181. However, this experience has altered this delegate's views on natural coalition partners and the role race plays in legislating women's issues bills. The controversy surrounding the failure of HB 1181 led her to consider a more complicated and nuanced approach to identity politics and shows that an intersectional approach is not beyond her capacity. Her desire to meet with the younger Black women delegates points toward a willingness to learn from minority women and explore how race-gender identity may have caused them to have a dissimilar viewpoint from her own.

In 2009, almost a third of the members of the Maryland House of Delegates were women, one of the highest percentages among state legislatures in the country. Legislative counsel for the Maryland Network against Domestic Violence, Cynthia Lifson, directly links the increase of women legislators over the past two decades with the increasing visibility of domestic violence and calls for lawmakers to protect victims. Lifson is quoted by the *Washington Post* as saying "It's always helpful to have women in elected positions. Their life experiences are different than men in elected office" (Helderman, 2009, C01). As a result, advocates for domestic violence issues concentrate their lobbying efforts on the fifty-nine women in the Maryland state legislature. Women legislators find it difficult to go against the advice of anti-domestic-violence advocates; however, the increase in numbers of women legislators has also led to greater diversity of opinion in this group. Because abuse issues have long been considered a unifying cause for women lawmakers, the Maryland state women legislators have been expected to support domestic violence legislation regardless of partisanship, race, political ideology, or constituency. However, as the president of the Women's Caucus noted, the split between members may be an important symbol of change. She surmised, "I think it's a sign of social progress. Women do feel free to argue" (Heldman, 2009, C01).

SPEAKING FOR THE VICTIMS

The personal experiences of Black women legislators in this study inform their legislative decision making. Unfortunately, four Black women delegates have had personal experiences with domestic violence, either as victims of abuse or witnesses to it, enabling them to intimately understand who the legislation would affect.

Delegate Ingrid Jefferson was a victim of domestic violence. Her experiences allow her to serve as a victims' advocate in the Maryland legislature. She shared, "I was actually a victim of domestic violence in my first marriage." This delegate said that her husband had abused her for about four years. After a severe beating in 1978, Delegate Jefferson informed her husband that she was leaving him and taking the children to her mother's house in Virginia. Her husband threatened to kill the children if she left. So Delegate Jefferson stayed with him and endured more brutal attacks. During another occasion, her husband had been drinking and later accidentally shot and killed himself with the same sawed-off shotgun that he had threatened to kill her and the children with. She reports on the impact that her story of surviving domestic violence had during a legislative hearing on a 2009 domestic violence bill:

> When we were debating that bill about waiving the waiting period for domestic violence victims to obtain guns, I listened to the attorneys that testified on behalf of the bill. I then realized that I needed to speak as a victim and be the face and the voice of thousands of victims that aren't here in the legislature and don't have a voice. I was able to share my story and put forth my perspective. It was very well

received and very well respected by my colleagues, as opposed to the legalese of the lawyers' testimony on the bill. Most often people look at me and would never think I had ever survived anything so traumatic. My colleagues were very supportive of my perspective. The newspapers carried the story and I was on Fox TV. You know legislators are people too. (Personal interview March 14, 2009)

Similarly, Delegate Angela James also finds that her experiences with domestic violence and other abuses cause her to advocate for victims. Her story of overcoming obstacles from her childhood in rural Georgia and Alabama also allows her to serve as an example for others in bleak situations, and she tells her story to serve as inspiration:

I have been an adult survivor of child abuse. And I come from a home of domestic violence. I've had all of those excuses that people use for not succeeding. Yet, I am a published author, I've written five books. My first book talks about molestation, abuse, drug abuse, and alcoholism—the whole nine yards, which a lot of people can identify with. When people see that, that was not a hindrance of me becoming who I wanted to become, when they see this "successful person" and then realize that this person has not always been here. But it was a process to get here. And when they see that they can say "if she can, then I can too." (Personal interview, March 18, 2009)

Delegate James now draws from her experiences to be a voice for those who are in similar abusive situations or dealing with drug addiction and alcoholism. She finds that her experiences help her to advocate for marginalized groups.

While some delegates do not have personal experiences with domestic violence, others have witnessed the tragic consequences of violence to other Black women. They bring this perspective to the types of legislation that they champion. For example, Delegate Estrella Henderson, one of the oldest members of the legislature during the time of the interview, and who grew up in segregated Baltimore City, commented that she has enormous empathy for domestic violence victims because she has witnessed abuse. As a result, she sympathizes with victims. "A couple of years ago, Delegate Jefferson had this bill about domestic violence. I stood up [in support of the bill]. I have not personally experienced domestic violence. But I've witnessed it in my family. So I understood what she was going through" (Personal interview, March 12, 2009).

Delegate Abigail Watson, a lifelong educator of impoverished children, gave another version of a personal connection to domestic violence. She does not believe that men view domestic violence legislation the same way that women legislators do. "I have personal knowledge of some of the prejudices, some of the not-so-friendly family legislation as it impacts women, like harassment and domestic violence. Even though I have not personally experienced domestic violence, I see what it does for other Black women. So I support that kind of legislation. Yes, you see that type of legislation differently. I don't think men see it from the same perspective" (Personal interview, March 11, 2009). This comment illustrates the need for women to have a seat at the legislative table since they feel they are more likely to represent issues that concern women. Delegate Watson notes specifically that her experiences as a Black woman allow her to recognize how domestic violence impacts African American women.

Similarly, Delegate Olivia Jenkins, a divorced mother of two from a middle-class family in Baltimore county, finds that her identity provides a particular vantage point from which she views legislation: "As a woman, in terms of the gender, I'm going to interpret a lot of legislation differently, for example domestic violence bills. I see it differently from a male colleague" (Personal interview, March 17, 2009). The Black women legislators in this study clearly find that their identity allows them to bring different sensitivities to domestic violence legislation than their other colleagues. Personal experiences either witnessing or having direct encounters with domestic violence also lead these Black women delegates to a different understanding of intimate abuse than legislators without those experiences, providing examples of how experience influences how they substantively represent their constituents.

CONCLUSION

The attention that Black women legislators pay to domestic violence legislation illustrates that they bring different policy preferences to the table than their male and White colleagues do. Illustrating representational identity theory, Black women legislators in this study demonstrate how race-gender identities influence their perspectives on domestic violence legislation. As a result, the public policies that they champion may be both antiracist and feminist. Their multilayered approaches to legislation will hopefully help raise awareness of the intersectional structural barriers that prevent women of color who are domestic violence victims from securing assistance (Crenshaw 1991).

Next, because some Black women legislators have personal connections to domestic violence, they are more understanding and committed to assisting victims of domestic violence. The reality that Black women are more likely than White women to be victims of domestic violence increases the chances that Black women legislators will have personally experienced or witnessed abuse (Lockhart and White 1989). These legislators show that these experiences lead them to an interpretation of legislation that reflects an intersectional approach to the protection of victims. These voices are necessary within a deliberative body because they help convince their legislative colleagues to prioritize the concerns of domestic violence victims. Delegate Ingrid Jefferson's testimony furthermore helped to reach constituents who did not otherwise feel that they had a voice.

Black women's representational styles illustrate the intersectionality of their identity. While the newspaper articles on HB 1181 indicated that both Black and White men delegates also witnessed the abuse of female family members at the hands of their intimate partners, the male legislators I interviewed for this study did not mention domestic violence legislation during their interviews. Black women delegates and one White woman delegate were the only legislators to use the domestic violence legislation as an example of how their identity influenced legislative decision making. While others may have had witnessed domestic violence, they do not cite it as a factor that shapes their identity and consequently their politics. Thus, this chapter demonstrates that both experience and identity matter in the representation of constituents.

Finally, an intersectional analysis of legislative decision making exposes the silences in public policy on discourses of antiracism and feminism. Because of their race-gender identities, the Black women legislators in the Maryland state legislature are attuned to the ways in which the junctures of race and gender impact legislation. Their intersectional vantage point produces different understandings of legislation that may lead Black women legislators to draw conclusions correlated according to their generational cohort.

Anti-domestic violence policy, which silences Black women victims, is ideal legislation for exploring the ways in which Black women legislators contribute to legislative policy making and for highlighting the differences among African American women lawmakers. The younger women respectfully disagreed with some of the older African American women legislators and the members of the Women's Caucus. Expanding Williams's (2001) findings to include women's interest legislation, this study indicates that post-civil rights–Black Power era Black women legislators are committed to Black interest and women's interests although they express their policy preferences differently than their older counterparts.

The younger women's narratives indicate their commitment to continuing the legacy of Black women's struggles to end racism and sexism that disproportionally affect African American women. However, they disagree with the best means to protect victims, and they struggle with their older counterparts to impart that standing up for victims' rights should not come at the expense of those who may have been falsely accused. The younger women display traces of third-wave feminism in their failure to accept "universal" womanhood. Instead, they recognize plurality among women's experiences and challenge the perceived solidarity among women. In doing so, they break the sense of female unity based on oppression common to all women, which serves to align women around their differences with men.

CHAPTER 5

Representation for Whom?

It offends me that the proponents of same-sex marriage are trying to incorporate discrimination language in their argument. As an African American, I know something about discrimination. I was born Black! It was not a decision on my part.
—Bishop Gilbert Thompson, Black Ministerial Alliance of Boston

Black churches have been struggling with both their natural empathy and their reading of Scripture. And this has prompted an extraordinary debate about whether or not the gay rights movement is a civil rights struggle, a human rights struggle; whether it is something that the church can support and embrace.
—Dr. Robert Franklin, Professor of Social Ethics, Emory University   '

I believe all Americans who believe in freedom, tolerance and human rights have a responsibility to oppose bigotry and prejudice based on sexual orientation.
—Coretta Scott King

Maryland became the eighth state to legalize same-sex marriage on March 1, 2012. This legislation narrowly passed the House of Delegates on February 17th, in a seventy-two to sixty-seven vote. It passed in the Senate by a vote of twenty-five to twenty-two on February 23, 2012.[1] Because of a groundswell of opposition after Governor Martin O'Malley signed the legislation making marriage equality legal in Maryland, this issue became a public referendum on the November 2012 ballot. Maryland, Washington, D.C. and Maine approved same-sex marriage, making the three states' voters the first in the country to approve the measures by a popular vote on November 6, 2012. Maryland citizens voted 52 percent to 48 percent to legalize same-sex marriage. On January 1, 2013, gay and lesbian couples were legally able to wed. In an interesting racial breakdown, the six Maryland jurisdictions that voted in favor of the measure were five majority-White counties and majority-Black, Baltimore.

The contentious political debate surrounding same-sex marriage in the state legislature made the religious and racial fissures, which are often masked by partisan ideology, apparent. A significant contingent of socially conservative Black voters made proponents of the ballot measure nervous, and religious organizations and African American religious leaders aggressively lobbied against it, which spurred the process of collecting signatures to repeal this legislation via referendum.

Opinion polls have shown that support for same-sex marriage is growing, which indicates that African American voters may have reevaluated their position on this issue.[2] These statistics indicate a difference of opinion between voters and political elites. Black politics in Maryland may soon see an era in which political elites are challenged to represent a greater spectrum of diversity within the state's Black political agenda. Similar to other African Americans throughout the nation, Black Marylanders in general—and Black Maryland political elites specifically—have been forced into discussions about marriage equality because of the onset of impending legislative action on the matter.

Same-sex marriage has been a political hot-button issue in the media spotlight since the 1990s, and it boiled over into the 2012 presidential election to become an issue of national importance. On May 9, 2012, President Barack Obama formally announced that he supports same-sex marriage. Indeed, many high profile African Americans—from rapper/mogul Jay-Z to Colin Powell, the former Secretary of State under President George W. Bush, to prominent civil rights activists such as Ben Jealous and Reverend Jesse Jackson—have recently decreed their support of marriage equality. On June 26, 2013 the Supreme Court ruled key provisions in the 1996 Defense of Marriage Act unconstitutional. The ruling extended federal benefits to legally married same-sex couples. These declarations have forced Americans, and particularly African Americans, to reevaluate their political and ideological beliefs on marriage equality. The national spotlight on individual states with same-sex marriage legislation, court rulings, and referendums moved conversations about sexual orientation, discrimination, homophobia, citizens' rights, and the rightful scope of government into everyday dialogue for some Americans.[3] These discussions, of course, were not lost on African Americans who were examining marriage equality legislation in light of their own precarious relationship to the state.

In this context, African American Maryland state legislators are similar to other Blacks throughout the nation who are situated between a racially framed opposition to same-sex marriage that relies on a specific interpretation of biblical doctrine and a race-based structural argument that likens discrimination based on sexual orientation to racial discrimination. It is important to explore how one's religious identity and biblical fundamentalism coupled with a homophobic and antigay rhetoric and bigotry has led some Christians, especially some Black Christians, to reject marriage equality (Wadsworth 2010). Because Blacks face sexual stereotypes—which include the emasculation of Black manhood and the devaluation of Black womanhood—that are tied to both gender and race, it is conceivable that African Americans might have mixed attitudes on same-sex marriage. The politics of respectability have been a coping mechanism with which Black Americans have attempted to protect themselves from claims of moral inferiority and sexual deviance. But this strategy has outlived its usefulness, due to its inflexibility and its tendency to view Black moral politics as monolithic.

I investigate cleavages among Black political elites to examine how gender and generation mediate support for marriage equality vis-à-vis Black political identity. Employing representational identity theory to explore how African American women use their political identity, I build a better understanding of when and how Black women's raced-gendered identities impact their legislative decision making. The Maryland state legislature offers a superb case study for considering the implications of Black politicians' positions on same-sex marriage precisely because Maryland recently passed marriage equality legislation despite the protests of some Black constituents, religious leaders, and civic organizations. Many of the older women who I interviewed in 2009 and 2011 for this study were against same-sex marriage, citing a number of factors; however, many younger legislators were supporters of the initiative. By analyzing the voices of the Black women in the Maryland state legislature, I am able to explore how personal identity politics are salient factors in the business of Black politics. Furthermore, by examining the intensity and engagement with which Black women represent the legislative interests of advanced marginalized groups—groups, like themselves, that are stigmatized by society and the dominant culture—my study demonstrates that Black women legislators in fact represent intersectional viewpoints. This analysis is complicated, and I argue that, although there are many consistencies in Black political identities, they are also more fluid and dynamic than widely acknowledged.[4]

Building on an understanding of identity as fluid, this chapter considers the positions of Black political elites and concludes that the representation of advanced marginalized groups is likely stratified along gender and generational lines. I examine how legislators articulate their policy preferences and ask whether the legislator in question is viewing policy through an essentialist or nonessentialist understanding of Black political identity. I then tease out whether Black political elites reinforce or dismantle the boundaries of Blackness and what amounts to an essentialist Black political agenda that is woefully behind the times. I end by concluding that Black women legislators may in fact build bridges between essentialist and nonessentialist forms of Black politics.

Black political elites are expected to pursue consensus issues, "issues that are framed as somehow important to every member of 'the Black community,' either directly or symbolically" (Cohen, 1999, 11). But this pursuit often fails to incorporate the most disadvantaged members within the primary marginalized group. Black politics scholars (Brown-Dean 2007; Cohen, 1999; Warren 2007) argue in favor of marginalized groups mobilizing around cross-cutting issues, which are issues, according to Cohen, that refer "to those concerns which *disproportionately and directly* affect only certain segments of a marginal group" (1999, 13; emphasis in original). She goes on to specify that "cross-cutting issues . . . are also often situated among the subpopulations of marginal communities that are the most vulnerable economically, socially, and politically, and whose vulnerable status is linked to narratives that emphasize the 'questionable' moral standing of the subpopulation" (13–14). In the context of representation and the issues for which legislators advocate, I identify same-sex marriage as crosscutting legislation within the Maryland state legislature to further examine the role that identity plays in representation.

One's religious identity can be read as another political salient identity. While not an ascribed identity, like racial identity, religious identity is a source of identity construction. Religious identities and groups often have distinct ideologies and political views that frame one's social realities. While one may choose his or her religious identity in the United States, people are often born into religious communities. Because a person can experience advanced marginalization because of his or her religious affiliation, or lack there of, religious identity falls into a set of proscribed hierarchies. As Wadsworth illustrates, religious identity is a necessary part of intersectional analyses that seeks to understand how groups assert "their distinctive political experience and fate as analogous to or interwoven with that of another group" (2010; 203). A religious identity co-constitutes another identity, such as race, sexuality, class, or gender. Furthermore, religion has a foundational influence—centered in hegemonic power structures—that both privileges and marginalizes other identities.

Black state legislators, in many cases, utilize a heuristic of Black political identity to understand what populations are deserving of their representation. Classified either as deserving or undeserving, advanced marginalized populations must rely on others to represent their policy interests. When I use the term "advanced marginalized populations," I indicate groups that are partially or wholly located on periphery of the marginalized population. Because Black political identity and the politics of respectability are closely intertwined, African American legislators in general—and Black women legislators in particular—decide to extend representation to marginalized groups that they deem deserving and withhold it from those that they deem undeserving. To examine how a Black political identity manifests itself in decisions that African American women legislators make about representing their constituents, I examine cross-cutting issue legislation designed to benefit an advanced marginalized population, namely, LGBTQ constituents.[5] First, using a multidisciplinary approach, I illuminate the constructions and tropes of Black political identity. Next, I review the political science literature on advanced marginalization, cross-cutting and consensus issues, and how African American state legislators (re)produce hierarchies of marginalization within their political agendas. I go on to illustrate how queerness and Blackness are two sides of the same coin. I use constructions of essentialist and nonessentialist Black political idetity to frame how African American women state legislators articulate which groups are deserving of their representation. In sum, I find that Black politics is not monolithic, as shown by the generational gap in women Maryland state legislators' policy positions on same-sex marriage

POLITICAL MARGINALIZATION: BLACK POLITICS AND THE LGBTQ COMMUNITY

Marginalized groups are often identified by their social, economic, cultural, and political position(s) in relation to the dominant group(s). Blacks in America are a marginalized population; Black same-gender loving individuals are an advanced marginalized group. Building upon the literature that investigates marginalization *within* marginalized groups, I concur that marginalized groups are neither monolithic nor homogeneous. Cohen (1999) finds that advanced marginalization is an indicator of heightened stratification of marginal communities. Advanced marginalized groups are othered within the marginalized population due to their gender, sexual orientation, disability, class, or any other identity that does not advance universal claims about the population as a whole (Strolovitch 2007). Consequently, advanced marginalized populations are situated economically, socially, or politically on the fringes of the broader marginalized population. Furthermore, political inequality is justified when group identities are associated with historical patterns of simultaneous privilege and marginality (Wadsworth 2010). Group identities may create "illegitimate others" when privilege and exclusion converge in both historical and contemporary settings. Meaning that historically constituted power dynamics produce advanced marginalized groups that reinforce privilege on a singular axis of identity.

Hancock (2004) finds that legislators may be unwilling to support cross-cutting issues. Minority legislators, therefore, may be active participants in creating secondary marginalization by failing to advance the cross-cutting issues that affect only advanced marginalized groups.[6] "Lawmakers' status as citizens leads them to similar exposure to the political context and [negative] public identities, shaping the public policy options considered in the legislative process" (Hancock 2004, 17). Specifically, Cohen (1999) finds that Black elites are responsible for replicating the rhetoric of blame and punishment and directing it at the most vulnerable and stigmatized in their communities. She further contends that Black politics has accepted "the dominant discourse that defines what is good, normal, and acceptable stratification among marginal group members is transformed into an indigenous process of marginalization targeting the most vulnerable of the group" (Cohen, 1999, 64). Minority political elites may have an incentive to enhance the public image of the group, only making visible the issues that do not threaten the status of the community. By silencing the political voices of Black LGBTQ activists, Black legislators ensure that the hegemonic structures of sexual morality controlled by dominant groups are maintained. In doing so, Black legislators, as a marginalized racial group, uphold the standards of the dominant group at the expense of Black LGBTQ members. In sum, Black legislators may be unwilling to create policy that is designed to rectify an issue specifically linked to a population with a negative cultural image.

I define essentialist Black political identity as a politics rooted in the cultural norms of African American customs that adheres to monolithic views of Blackness or that reinforces a rigidly fixed uniformity in the performance of Black identity. I contend that African American legislators with an essentialist view of Black political identity are unlikely to advocate on behalf of advanced marginalized groups. Unlike Hancock (2004) and Cohen (1999), who assert that not all facets of the Black community are represented by African American political elites, I argue that Black women state legislators can effectively represent the diverse interests of the broader Black community because they are more likely than African American men to perceive variation within Black political identity. I am able to point to this diversity in Black political representation and, in the process, complicate how scholars empirically study Black political identity. Rather than viewing Black politicians as a monolith, I construct two frameworks for studying Black political identity.

To be more specific, I find that younger African American women are least likely to subscribe to the politics of respectability as a mediating factor of Black political identity. I include gender and generation in my rubric expressly to better understand how younger Black women legislators use their own identity as a mediating factor in the representation of their constituents. As a litmus, I explore the legislators' rhetorical commitment to advocating on behalf of advanced marginalized groups, specifically the lesbian, gay, bisexual, transgendered and queer (LGBTQ) community in the context of the Religious Freedom and Protection of Civil Marriage Act.[7] Marriage equality is a cross-cutting issue bill that helps measure African American women legislators' commitment to advanced marginalized populations mediated through a strong Black political identity.

AFRICAN AMERICANS VIEWS ON SAME-SEX MARRIAGE

Examining representatives' behavior is useful for understanding the attitudes of the general public, and I propose that Black political elites feel the same way about the same-sex marriage as the African American general public. As previously discussed, African Americans, due to racial group consciousness, are particularly likely to use group interests as a proxy for personal interests (Dawson 1994; Gurin, Hatchett, and Jackson 1989; McClerking 2001; Tate 1994). As a result, Black political elites will represent the consensus issues that affect their mostly African American constituents but will not advance the interests of advanced marginalized groups.

The "commonly held belief that homophobia is more prevalent in the Black community than in society at large" (Brandt 1999, 8–9) has largely not been supported by public opinion research. Indeed, studies draw mixed conclusions on the racial variations in public opinion about gay rights. Some have found that Whites hold more negative views than do Blacks, while others have demonstrated the opposite (Hudson and Ricketts 1980; Levitt and Klassen 1974; Lewis 2003; Schneider and Lewis 1984). Studies have indicated that Blacks are more likely than Whites to identify homosexual relationships as always wrong (Tiemeyer 1993) but are more likely to oppose homophobic discrimination than Whites (Boykin 1996). This complicated viewpoint has caused openly gay former Congressman Barney Frank (D-Mass.) to argue that the Congressional Black Caucus's strong support for gay rights indicates that Black voters are not necessarily homophobic (Boykin 1999). Furthermore, African American public opinion on marriage equality is evolving. "In 2008, for example, only 26 percent of African Americans favored gay marriage whereas 63 percent opposed it. In 2012, however, the number supporting gay marriage has increased to 39 percent whereas the number against it has decreased to 49 percent" (Pew Research Center, 2012).

Indeed, President Obama's and the National Association for the Advancement of Colored People's affirmation of marriage equality illustrates that Black America's stance on this issue is much more diverse than has been previously understood. This trend is mirrored in the population at large. In the mid-1990s, 65 percent of Americans opposed same-sex marriage as compared to 30 percent who supported it. During the 2004 election cycle, which was an important election for marriage equality, only 31 percent of Americans supported same-sex marriage as compared to 60 percent who opposed it. Fast forward to 2012, and recent data suggest that that margin is much narrower: 47 percent to 43 percent. This shift in public opinion is largely driven by citizens thirty-five and younger; 63 percent of this younger population favors same-sex marriage.

Despite the mixed public opinion findings and the recent emergence of Black political support for marriage equality, many scholars and activists continue to chastise the Black community for its failure to fully address marriage equality and anti-discrimination legislation for LGBTQ individuals.[8] The issue of same-sex marriage pivots around an array of societal, religious, and cultural norms that spark contentious debates within Black communities. Many Black Christians are politically liberal but socially conservative. They voted against same-sex marriage in Arkansas, Georgia, Kentucky, Michigan, Mississippi, Ohio, and Oklahoma during November 2004, when these states proposed a constitutional ban on same-sex marriage (Ball 2006). However, women are more likely to support same-sex marriage (Pew Research Center 2010). To be sure, same-sex marriage is a conflict-ridden issue within the Black community (Collins 2004), with cultural underpinnings that make it difficult for African Americans to coalesce around a defined position. The relationships between the African American community, the larger LGBTQ community, and the Black LGBTQ community specifically are combative at worst and complicated at best.

The Black Church: Cultural, Symbolic, and Institutional

Indeed, discussions of Black opposition to homosexual behavior most often center on the role of the Black church and Black religiosity as the mediating factor. Black churches are recognized as the most instrumental institution within the Black community (Lincoln and Mamiya 1990). E. Franklin Frazier (1963) referred to the Black church as a "nation within a nation" to point to the multifarious levels of community involvement— ranging from education, worship, social control, to moral nurturance. The cultural womb of the Black community is found within the Black church. Central to the cultural, political, and organizational matrix of Black life, the Black church is a unique undercurrent in Black political identity, which makes it a propagating factor of an essentialist Black political identity. Moving beyond the Black church as an institution, this analysis also incorporates Black religiosity to understand the symbolic, cultural, and expressive space of Black identities. I resist the conflation of the Black church and a specific religious identity and instead highlight the Black church as both a real and symbolic space and place. As a cultural institution, most African Americans are familiar with the teachings and traditions of the Black church, even if they are not active members of or participants in the church. Denominational affiliation deeply influences one's worldview and shapes one's social and cultural realities. However, I draw on Lincoln and Mumiya's conceptualization of the "black sacred cosmos" that illustrates the unique Afro-Christian worldview generated from both African and Euro-American traditions in the eighteenth and nineteenth centuries (1990, 7). The black sacred cosmos permeates Black cultural practices, social institutions and religious practices regardless of ideological bent or denominational affiliation.[9]

As a physical place, the Black church is a Christian-based institution (Billingsley, 1968; Lincoln and Mamiya, 1990). Many African American families report significant church involvement and transmit the importance of their involvement in the Black church to their children (Bell and Bell 1999; McAdoo and Crawford 1990; Haight 2002). Through participation in the Black church, congregants are indoctrinated with social, political, and cultural beliefs rooted within a historical context (Miller 2007). Research also indicates that people who belong to politicized churches vote more frequently and are actively engaged in the political process (Tate 1994; Calhoun-Brown 1996; Harris, F. 1999). One of the added benefits of church involvement is the Black church's legacy as vehicle for social justice, fighting for freedom from race-based discrimination (Lincoln and Mamiya 1990; McDaniel 2008). However, Black LGBTQ congregants may not experience these benefits because of their sexual orientation or behaviors. Because religious beliefs and institutions also (re)produce a hierarchy of privilege and exclusion, groups that are deemed outside of the mainstream are marginalized (Wadsworth 2010).

Traditionally, Black churches have emphasized an interpretation of scripture that opposes homosexuality.[10] However, several scholars have examined the biblical translations from Hebrew, Greek, and Aramaic into English to suggest that neither the Old nor New Testament scriptures provide an indisputable position on homosexuality (Cannon 2008; Farajaje-Jones 1998; Helminiak 2000; McNeil 1993; Scroggs 1983). Notably, these scriptures make reference to homosexual behavior among men, not women, yet the verses are used to repudiate same-sex romantic relationships of both men and women. Regardless, many Black churches demonize homosexuality and refuse to ordain LGBTQ aspirants (Staples 1982; Williams 1999).

However, men who engage in homosexual behavior are involved in key functions in the church. Indeed, some Black queer men—as choir directors, ministers of arts, or worship and creative arts pastors—provide the creative energy for transcendent religious experiences (Fullilove and Fullilove 1999). That queer Black men serve in these roles within the Black church is a widely known but largely unaddressed truth (Miller 2007). This paradoxical relationship points to an "open closet" within the Black church, where queer Black men may sing in the choir but homosexuality is denounced from the pulpit on any given Sunday.

The centrality of the Black church's role in the African American experience has led has led many African Americans to strongly oppose homosexuality on religious grounds (Blaxton 1998; Boykin 1996b; Cohen 1999; Fullilove and Fullilove 1999; Griffin 2000; Harris 1986; Herek and Capitanio 1995; Lemelle and Battle 2004; Lewis 2003; McDaniel 2004; Schulte and Battle 2004). Because the three mainline Black Protestant groups, Baptists, Methodists, and Pentecostals, "originated within the cauldron of American slavery or Jim Crow segregation, these institutions intrinsically have been sympathetic to those who are politically marginalized, especially the poor and racial minorities," although they are opposed to same-sex marriage (Lincoln and Mamiya, 1990). These churches draw similar theological conclusions that interpret the Bible as seeing homosexuality as a sin and an abomination (Boykin 1996: Gomes, 1996). Therefore, many scholars have concluded that religiosity is the strongest predictor of Black heterosexual opposition to homosexuality (Battle Bennett, and Shaw 2004; Blaxton 1998; Boykin 1996b; Constantine-Simms 2000; Herek and Capitanio 1995).

Scholars of Black political participation note the importance of religiosity in African American political activism (Allen, Dawson, and Brown 1989; Calhoun-Brown 1996; Harris 1994; Verba and Nie 1972). While the connection between religiosity and Black legislators' voting behavior has yet to be fully established, I contend that African Americans' racial belief systems are reinforced by an internalized and psychologically oriented religious behavior. This behavior promotes Black political identity, which influences a Black political agenda. My conclusion draws on Harris, who, first, finds that "political actors might feel that with spiritual guidance they can be effective in 'this-worldly' pursuits, including politics. Second, religion might stimulate action through morally perceived political issues" (1994, 48). When faced with legislating moral issues, Black state legislators' religiosity likely serves as a cognitive/psychological resource to help center their legislative positions. Recent politics suggests Black religiosity as the strongest indicator of African American opposition to same-sex marriage. Black Evangelical voters were criticized for their role in passing both California's Proposition 8 in 2008 and North Carolina's Amendment 1 in 2012. I wish, however, to move the conversation toward a more nuanced view of Black religiosity and a Black political agenda to make room for a nonessentialist Black political identity that allows for diversity in Black political life.[11]

When a divisive cultural and political issue such as same-sex marriage enters the legislative agenda, Black women legislators must decide whether they will champion issues of a particular marginalized group or adhere to socially conservative Black political identity. Only one African American in the Maryland legislature is openly gay and can therefore be said to represent the LGBTQ community descriptively. It may be a stretch for Black legislators to represent a constituency with which they do not identify, but, as I will show, young Black women legislators do illustrate their ability to represent advanced marginalized groups. Going forward, I will illustrate that essentializing ideas about Black political identity are forcefully being challenged, and I will show that younger African American women are needed to represent and drive forward the changing viewpoints of a Black political agenda.

Coupling Blackness and Queerness

Since 1995, thirty-seven states and the federal government have mobilized to enact legislative bans on same-sex marriage. At the federal level, the Defense of Marriage Act mirrored state-wide exclusionary and heteronormative efforts based on gender, race, class, and nation (Adam 2003; Appleton 2005) that construct homosexuality as a transgression against gender norms and outside the accepted national identity (Bercovitch 1993)[12].

In addition to being tied to constructions of nation, gender, and race, same-sex marriage is linked to fears about the potential for the uneven distribution of social benefits to an undeserving population. America's rhetoric of rewarding individual responsibility creates large groups who are deemed unworthy of democratic inclusion. These individuals and groups are painted as lazy, as those who cannot "make it" in American society without special assistance (Hancock 2004). Equal rights are spun as special rights for those who are considered unworthy.[13] Americans are unwilling to consider LGBTQ individuals as deserving of the special legal remedies that aid in the prevention of discrimination. Consequently, lesbians and gays are permitted legal status only as individuals. In turn, "the social exclusions enforced against sexual orientation, like race, are denied in favor of juridical monad as the only permissible legitimate status, a doctrine that passively reaffirms White, nativist, and heterosexist hegemony" (Adam 2003, 273).

The institution of marriage is therefore rooted in the politics of exclusion. Nation building has consistently been compared to the family and is often couched in the institution of marriage. Marriage prohibitions based on race that prevented legal recognition of unions between Whites and Asians, Latinos, or African Americans illustrate that national laws have used marriage as a tool to mark exclusion. Viewing marriage through a queer lens disrupts the construction of marriage as a civilizing tool promoting a respectable public image of White, heterosexual, Protestant, and uniquely American vision of public acceptance (Warner 1999). Marriage, then, as such is promoted to defend traditional moral notions that are categorically exclusionary. As Adam notes, marriage in American culture must place itself in opposition to "the single mother on welfare, the promiscuous pervert, or the immature and irresponsible. The hold of religion on civil society has impoverished the alternatives, curbed recognition of common-law relationships and thus the viability of heterosexual alternatives, and shaped the vision of relationship recognition even for gay and lesbian Americans" (2003, 274). As such, marriage is rooted in homophobic discourses that are simultaneously built upon heteronormative Anglo-Protestant, White, and nativist identities.

As I have previously mentioned, same-sex marriage is also a racialized issue for African Americans. Same-sex marriage has been "queered" within the dominant discourse, and Blackness, too, occupies a queered space. Both are constructions of identity that deviate from the expected normalcy of hetero-Whiteness. The social construction of Blackness relates directly to slavery, and, in turn, to measures of morality, intelligence, sexuality, citizenship, beauty standards, and economic independence, which are all tied to racism. This construction has effectively privileged Whiteness and denigrated Blackness. Sexual difference is part and parcel of general regulation of Black culture. The institution of slavery and its aftermath, then, has queered African Americans precisely by constructing them as deviants. As a result, "Blackness" and "queerness" both complement and signify race and sexuality in overlapping and disparate ways (Johnson 2003, 93). African Americans who, via the politics of respectability, maintain socially and culturally accepted behavior are afforded a small sense of economic and racial equality.

As a result, institutions within the Black community—families, schools, churches—have "historically and assiduously avoided addressing the fundamental issue of sexuality. This reticence on the part of Blacks to speak about sexuality in public grows out of a fear that it will confirm the stereotypes that Whites have long held" (Ward 2005, 495). African American stereotypes that developed during slavery—such as the mammy, jezebel, and sapphire, along with the hypersexual Black male buck—have carried over to new stereotypes of the welfare queen and the promiscuous and virile Black man. Overall, Black sexuality is stereotyped as bestial, lustful, lascivious, promiscuous, and wanton (Douglas 1999). To counteract these powerful stereotypes, Blacks developed the race-based survival consciousness, known as the politics of respectability, to resist White domination within the context of colonialism and imperialism (Higginbotham 1994; Crichlow 2004). As such, homosexuality becomes part and parcel of Whiteness. To affirm Blackness in a White supremacist society, some African Americans denigrate homosexuality as a deviant behavior associated with Whiteness. Heterosexuality and heteronormativity within the Black community thus becomes a form of self-affirmation. The politics of respectability still supports an essentialist and heteronormative Black political agenda that neither accepts Blacks' queer membership nor champions LGBTQ policy preferences.

Consequently, Whiteness and homosexuality are linked and viewed as weak and feminine and Black masculinity becomes constructed in hypermasculine terms (Lemelle and Battle 2004). Racism, in turn, has assisted in the development of a Black culture plagued by homophobia. "Because of the conflation of gender and sexuality, to be seen as masculine requires being heterosexual, prompting the hypermasculinization of behavior among males in order to avoid being labeled a 'fag' or 'queer'" (Kimmel and Mahler 2003, 1450). Thus, the legitimation of Black cultural ascendancy requires heteronormativity and homophobia that hypersexualizes, pathologizes, and demonizes Black sexuality (Thomas 1996, 66).

The major arguments against same-sex marriage are analogous to the arguments proffered against interracial marriage, centering on the superiority of Whiteness and heterosexual unions and the wrongness of Blackness and same-sex unions.[14] Indeed, both are hegemonic modes of thinking. Similar to the belief that Whites are superior to African Americans, the argument relies on the idea that heterosexuality is superior to homosexuality. Opponents of same-sex marriage assert that it is "unnatural," encourages homosexuality, and provides a confusing environment in which to raise children (Trosino 1993). White supremacists feared the loss of White preeminence just as heterosexual supremacists fear the loss of heterosexual dominance by allowing what they see as unnatural or immoral unions to enter into the realm of a traditionally exalted social institution to the detriment of society (Coombs 1992). White supremacists argued that interracial marriage would produce inferior children; heterosexual supremacists argue that legalized same-sex marriage will produce deviant men and women who will engage in homosexual behavior (Friedman 1987). The belief that children of queer parents will face psychological harm parallels the assertion that children of interracial marriage were both mentally and physically inferior to pure race children and would also be susceptible to social stigma (Chambers and Polikoff 1999). Although contemporary reasons for prohibiting same-sex couples from marrying resonate as strikingly similar to the arguments used to prohibit interracial marriage, there is pushback from some African Americans about the comparison of interracial marriage and same-sex marriage[15]

Another illustration of the racialization of the same-sex marriage debate is the construction of a one-man–one-woman marriage as the premier institution in which to raise children. Black families have long been labeled deviant in the public eye for failing to live up to heteronormative familial structures. The peculiar history of Blacks in the United States, combined with structural conditions unfavorable to family formation and maintenance, has given rise to a so-called crisis in the Black family.[16] This so-called crisis rests squarely on the backs of African American women who, as mothers, are responsible for (re)creating Black families. The crisis of the Black family would ultimately re-create generations of such families with accompanying moral shortcomings.[17] Made infamous by Moynihan (1965), studies of poor Black families were also conducted by Clark (1965), Drake and Cayton (1945), and Frazier (1939), who concluded "children of single mothers were considered statistically normal and socially acceptable in the poor Black community" (Gans 2011, 318). Painted as sexually lascivious, Black women alone are demonized for failing to control their own sexual reproduction and hence for bringing fatherless children, who must be supported by the state, into the world.

Black men, however, portrayed as insatiably sexual, are subject to another form of sexual policing. Black men are charged with reproducing male hegemony and serving as rightful leaders of the Black family and, by extension, the Black nation. Perhaps most readily seen in constructions of

Black Nationalism, essentialist political ideology requires that Black men assert their maleness as the shepherds of the race in strictly heteronormative terms. While African Americans currently ascribe only moderately to Black Nationalist ideology, it, like an essentialist Black political identity, does not adequately address diversity among Blacks (Price 2009). Black Nationalism implicitly reproduces anti-LGBTQ sentiments among many African Americans by (re)imagining a crisis in the Black family.[18]

The positions that I have outlined here are most readily associated with the politics of respectability, which imagines that the restoration of the nuclear family would serve as a vehicle for a viable, self-sufficient, and autonomous Black nation (Ongiri 1997). Essentialist in nature, constructions of moral and sexual deviance are viewed as antithetical to improving the entire Black race, which is measured against White middle- and upper-class values. Issues that affect a stigmatized population, even when they are traced to historical, cultural, and political constructions, are seen as illegitimate issues and outside the scope of the Black political agenda.

In what follows, I examine how Black women state legislators employ forms of a Black political identity when representing their constituents; specifically in their representation of groups constructed as both deserving and nondeserving. African American state legislators are assumed to have occupied only one particular position during the debates about same-sex marriage legislation. However, the positions expressed by Black women state legislators present a much more nuanced view of Black political identity. Black women legislators, unlike Black men legislators, are afforded the cultural space to disrupt an essentialist Black political identity on this particular issue. This trend, however, is not in evidence among all Black women legislators. The younger and more progressive African American women state legislators push back against the tropes of Black culture that construct same-sex marriage as deviant. They complicate Black political identity by challenging cultural norms to represent this advanced marginalized group. Older African American women legislators' positions on marriage equality indicate that biblical understanding, homophobia, and exclusionary dissemination of civil rights are out of step with a younger generation's view of Black political identity.

CASE SELECTION

On September 18, 2007, a divided Maryland Court of Appeals ruled in a four-to-two decision that it was not a violation of the state constitution to deny marriage licenses to same-sex couples (Harrell 2007). Shortly after this decision, an African American woman representing Prince George's County[19] and a White man representing liberal-leaning Montgomery County, announced they would serve as the lead sponsors of legislation to end marriage discrimination. Following the sudden death of the Black woman senator in early 2008, two White men senators who represented Montgomery County[20] announced they would lead efforts in the Senate to pass the measure. One of the new senate cosponsors was openly gay.

While versions of this bill had been unsuccessfully introduced in the legislature for five consecutive years, other legislation in favor of civil unions had passed.[21] Three domestic partner measures passed and became law in Maryland. One requires health insurance companies to offer domestic partner benefits at the request of an insured individual or their employer. The second requires health-care and post-mortem decision-making rights for domestic partners. The third eliminates the tax paid by an individual when one removes a partner from the deed to the house that they share. On May 18, 2012, Maryland's high court recognized out-of-state same-sex marriages. The court also ruled that Maryland could grant divorces to same-sex couples.

The 2009 identical House of Delegates and Senate bills, HB 1055 and SB 565, the Religious Freedom and Protection of Civil Marriage Bill, established that a marriage between two individuals not otherwise prohibited from marrying, would be valid in the state. This bill prohibited an official of a religious institution or body authorized to sanctify marriages from being required to solemnize any marriage in violation of the constitutional right to free exercise of religion.[22] As previously mentioned, this bill had been introduced five times consecutively in the Maryland legislature. Each time a version of the bill was introduced, more legislators signed on as cosponsors, showing the slow but steady growth in popularity for the bill. A key sponsor of the 2009 legislation credited this growth to extensive lobbying and the support of LGBTQ supporters and constituents. He believes that people in general, and legislators specifically, are starting to view same-sex marriage as a civil and human right that should be afforded to all people (Personal interview, March 17, 2009). However, the 2009 session ended with no action on this bill, although it narrowly passed both houses in February 2012. The data used in this chapter were collected three years prior to the passage of this legislation. Thus, I have a unique point of view about the decision-making process that legislators undertook in the lead-up to the passage of the bill, which highlights questions of Black political identity. The results show how Black state legislators can either reinforce or challenge the marginalization of groups in society via their advocacy for those they see as worthy of representation.

The Religious Freedom and Protection of Civil Marriage Bill met my criteria for a cross-cutting issue during my 2009 fieldwork. I readily acknowledge that same-sex marriage is a polarizing issue and that I might have observed other challenges to Black political identity with an issue that is not as divisive in the Black community. However, I see same-sex marriage legislation as an intriguing vehicle for examining how Black political elites represent advanced marginalized groups lacking the "political, economic, and social resources necessary to participate actively in decision-making that significantly influences and structures their lives" (Cohen 1999, 9).

When asked about the decision-making process or the factors they would include in deciding whether to support or oppose the Religious Freedom and Protection of Civil Marriage Bill, legislators expressed a variety of concerns and considerations. I explore both what the legislators did and did not say. The Religious Freedom and Protection of Civil Marriage Bill caused legislators to articulate their policy preference on an issue that distinctly affects an advanced marginalized population in their constituencies, and I was primarily concerned with the question of how legislators mobilize identity in the legislative decision-making *process* rather than with the results of an outcome or a vote on a particular bill. Here I analyze how legislators prioritize a Black political identity when discussing active legislation that disproportionately impacts specific groups in their constituencies.

REPRESENTATION FOR WHOM?

Four African American women legislators articulated that they think through legislation such as the Religious Freedom and Protection of Civil Marriage Bill using the same decision-making process as they do with uncontroversial bills. Their approach appears to align with Kingdon's (1989) assertion that identity fails to play a large role in the decision-making process. Other legislators indicated that the bill would require them to use traditional decision-making skills. These legislators weigh a combination of their constituents' wishes, tenets of the bill, and their personal beliefs in their decision-making process.

Delegate Keira Miller, the granddaughter of a minister and who grew up in an extremely religious military family, acknowledged that she was unaware of the specifics of the Religious Freedom and Protection of Civil Marriage Bill. When I asked about what factors she would include in the legislative decision-making process on a controversial bill, this legislator shared the detailed process that she uses for evaluating legislation.

> I would certainly review the legislation as it is introduced [since that] is often
> not the product that leads. There are often amendments, and so the first step is
> to look at the actual product that comes out of the committee. The second step
> is to factor whether or not it provides any inequitable benefit. Ultimately I rep-
> resent all of the citizens of the my district and subsequently contribute to repre-
> senting the State of Maryland. . . . I would have to read the fine print and then
> do some research, communicate with some constituents, some opinion leaders
> in my district, some of my colleagues, and some of the sponsors. I try to speak
> with the ones with and against the legislation and look for the balance. I try to
> make sure I have an understanding of both sides of an issue and sometimes
> there are more than two sides of an issue. (Personal interview, March 12, 2009)

For this younger delegate, same-sex marriage legislation was not mediated
through an essentialist Black political identity. She followed her usual pattern of assessing the legislation. Representing the LGBTQ community was
not a controversial issue to her. Her response indicates that identity politics, in terms of both her own identity and that of her queer constituents,
was not a major factor in her decision-making process.

Indicating that she had conflicting feelings about this bill, Delegate
Justine Anderson, an older Black woman raised by a devout grandmother,
surmised that deciding how to approach this legislation would be a difficult
for her. She shared that she believed that her role was to represent a variety
of constituents with diverging interests. She and her constituents did not
share the same the position on same-sex marriage, but she articulated that
she knew she was charged with representing her entire district and not just
those who hold similar viewpoints to her own.

> Being [a member of a] union, I feel that we represent all types of people and I feel
> that everyone should have a right to be and do whatever they want to do. As for my
> own beliefs, I believe that a marriage is supposed to be between a man and a woman;
> but, I don't judge other people based on what my beliefs are. But, I think that every-
> one should just have a right to do how they feel. If they feel that they want to do
> this, then that's their right, but, don't put it on the backs of other people. And I
> don't bring my beliefs to other people. (Personal interview, March 19, 2009)

Acknowledging the controversial nature of this bill, Delegate Anderson
also indicated that her representational style was rooted in her union training. She noted that she had honed her leadership skills in union organizing,
making it possible for her to represent constituents who might not share
her ideological beliefs. She acknowledged that she would not arbitrarily
vote her own opinion would but remain open to opposing views. Unlike the

previous delegate who did not make mention of her own beliefs, Delegate Justine Anderson incorporated her position, although minimally, in the equation. An essentialist Black political identity that opposes same-sex unions may not have played a large role in her legislative decision making on this issue.

Some African American women legislators clearly weighed their own judgment, morals, and background in addition to their constituents' wishes, inserting their personal opinions and belief systems into their decision-making process. For example, Delegate Julissa Moore, another young Black woman delegate who grew up in a middle-class family in Prince George's County stated, "I do look at it from a standpoint of how I feel and how my people feel. My church is totally different. I ask what I can do" (Personal interview, March 19, 2009). This statement indicates that Delegate Moore does not rely on her church to shape her opinion on this issue. Delegate Abigail Watson, an older Black woman delegate and educator articulated that her own views and feedback from her constituency would play a role in the legislative decision-making process:

> I would look at my own personal beliefs. The beliefs of my constituents, and feedback from the members of my church [are factors I would include in the legislative decision making process]. I would put all that into consideration. (Personal interview, March 11, 2009)

Articulating aspects of an essentialist Black political identity, these African American women legislators mention church in the role of cultural indictor and as a factor in deciding on how to vote on same-sex marriage legislation. These legislators' responses may be inspired by their desire (i.e., the electoral calculus) to win reelection. They indicated that they view their positioning on this issue as pursuant to their own beliefs and their constituents' beliefs.

Connecting an essentialist Black political identity to Black religiosity, Delegate Yvonne Scott, an older and deeply religious woman, also noted that her church upbringing influenced her decision-making process about this legislation. This delegate mentioned that her father was a Baptist minister and that she had been raised in the Black church. Consequently, her involvement within the Black church from youth onward had shaped her political position on same-sex marriage. She connected the direct text of the Bible to her opposition to same-sex marriage.

> The marriage piece is troubling. It has to do with my upbringing; my father was a Baptist minister. I have my Bible here that talks about the marriage between a

man and woman; from a moral and religious standpoint that would create some problems for me. (Personal interview, March 12, 2009)

Delegate Angela James, also an older woman who was raised in the Black church, explained that her opposition to same-sex marriage was biblically based. She cited the six verses of the Bible commonly quoted to argue against homosexuality as the basis for her opposition to same-sex marriage. While this delegate personally disagrees with same-sex marriage and noted that she would not support this legislation, she was open to listening to her constituents with diverging viewpoints. Furthermore, she disclosed that she does not see her point of view as discriminatory.

> I don't support same-sex marriage. My Bible is clear: God created man and woman and He created the institution of marriage for one man and one woman. I would not defend discrimination against them. I keep an open door for all my constituents, whether I agree with them or not. (Personal interview, March 18, 2009)

Also making the connection to her personal beliefs on same-sex marriage, Delegate Ingrid Jefferson, an older African American woman delegate who grew up in an impoverished family but did not directly discuss the role of religion in her feminist life history, illustrated how both personal and essentialist Black political identity shape policy. This delegate drew on both her religious upbringing and the opinions of the majority of her constituents in her refusal to advocate for the LGBTQ community.

> I don't support gay marriage because I believe marriage is between a man and a woman. My church upbringing helps me to make that decision. I get a lot of emails going both ways. But I know personally I could not vote for gay marriages; the majority of my citizens don't believe in it. (Personal interview, March 14, 2009)

Senator Pamela Price, an older Black woman senator who recently married her second husband, also struggled with her thoughts on same-sex marriage because of her religious beliefs. She noted:

> Gay marriage is something I have been really struggling with because it's the fairness and equality issue on one hand, and then it's my faith on the other. Biblically I feel as though marriage is between a man and a woman. I have always supported domestic partnerships and other types of arrangements, but I felt as though the action word "marriage" was reserved. And that's pretty much how

I feel. However, I do believe that individuals should have rights, partnership rights. It's just the word "marriage." (Personal interview, March 13, 2009)

While she did not mention the role of religion in her feminist life history interview, this older African American senator added that she supports equality. She clearly did not want the state to deny basic rights to the LGBTQ population. Her opinion was similar to those expressed in other state legislative bodies that voted to grant varying degrees of limited legal protections for same-sex couples. While marriage garners recognition across state and national borders, civil unions and domestic partnerships do not. As a result, states are not required to recognize civil unions performed in other states. The debate about the benefits of marriage as opposed to civil unions indicates that marriage enjoys special status as a social institution in addition to the legal benefits it confers. Civil unions and/or domestic partnerships occupy quasi-marriage status, which links directly to the stigma of homosexuality. As a result, civil unions create a negative effect, disadvantaging those who are not allowed to be married in the eyes of the law (Herek 2002; Link and Phelan 2001). While Senator Price may have viewed the word "marriage" as the only hindrance to her supporting this cross-cutting issue, many in the LGBTQ community argue that having only the options of civil union and domestic partnership in lieu of marriage creates another form of "separate but equal" (Herek 2006).

Similarly, Senator Brenda Perry, a religious older Black woman senator stated that she would not support same-sex marriage but did favor partnership rights:

> I don't support gay marriage. My people know that. Probably one-third of my district are partners, so I told them I do what's right. And I told them I have consistently defended you on every front in terms of housing, employment, healthcare, and all the issues on discrimination. But in this instance this is my religious upbringing that will not allow me to vote for it. . . . It is because of my Christian, my religious upbringing that I cannot vote for it. (Personal interview, March 20, 2009)

This influential Black woman senator's position on same-sex marriage, which is based on an essentialist Black political identity, constructs same-sex marriage as a religious abomination. Going against a sizeable portion of her district's wishes, this delegate unabashedly stated her opposition to same-sex marriage. Senator Perry explicitly informed her constituents that they could vote her out of office on this one issue if they decided that her opposition to same-sex marriage was more important than all the other pro-LGBTQ issues that she supports. Senator Perry went as far as to urge her constituents to find another candidate for her seat if they thought someone else could do a better job of representing their interests. She won reelection in 2010 despite her failure to represent her LGBTQ constituents on marriage equality.

However, this brazen articulation of an essentialist Black political identity weakened Senator Perry's reelection campaign in 2010. For the first time, she faced a competitive election and is now seen as a vulnerable candidate. Delegate Leila Baker, a young Black woman Maryland state delegate open about being lesbian, has expressed interest in Senator Perry's seat (Personal interview, July 1, 2011). Senator Perry may actually have emboldened her constituents who are in favor of same-sex marriage to support a candidate who supports same-sex marriage and at least expresses empathy in respect to their views. In addition to galvanizing those in favor of same-sex marriage, Delegate Baker is now cultivating her political relationships and weighing her options for challenging Senator Perry's seat.

Delegate Cassandra Ross, an older Black woman, also invokes religion to explain why she will not fully support the Religious Freedom and Protection of Civil Marriage Bill. However, unlike the other Black women legislators highlighted above, she also includes her own cultural understanding of this legislation, citing her faith and her identity as a Jamaican immigrant as influencing her positioning on this issue:

> I still can't believe that's how God had intended it to be and so there are some moral issues here that I have to be able to deal with. I have been listening and maybe one day I'll get there. It's my own morality and also keeping in mind the culture to which I was born. My culture doesn't tolerate homosexuality in Jamaica; people have been known to be stoned to death. I think maybe because of that I have not been able to bring myself to totally agree. (Personal interview, March 19, 2009)

Adding complexity and diversity to monolithic constructions of Black political identity, this older Black woman delegate opposes same-sex marriage because of cultural behaviors and beliefs characteristic of Jamaican society. Her comments also illustrate that Black religiosity and an essentialist Black political identity are inextricably linked with homophobic rhetoric. This construction is not merely a phenomenon in the United States but also one that applies to Blacks throughout the African Diaspora (Pieterse 1992).

In comparing the wishes of the constituency groups in her district (Black and Jewish) on same-sex marriage, Senator Bailey Smith, a young Black woman who grew up in a family that was dedicated to advancing Black civil rights, finds that both are opposed to gay marriage. She joked that she does not understand why the Black community pretends that the LGBTQ do not exist within the Black church. "The Black community and the Jewish community are very interesting. The Black community has found stuff to do with their gay folks; they put them as choir directors, they put them in pulpits, and they put them behind the candles. The Jews just haven't found what to do with theirs yet" (Personal interview, March 13, 2009). This light-hearted comment reflects her awareness of the disparities between what the Black church preaches and the lived reality of LGBTQ individuals within Black communities.

Black women legislators born after 1960 were more likely to support the Religious Freedom and Protection of Civil Marriage Bill. This finding is analogous to the finding of Lewis and Gossett (2008), who in their examination of public opinion toward same-sex marriage in California concluded that younger people are more supportive of same-sex marriage than older people. In my study, this younger cohort of legislators framed this crosscutting bill in terms of either human or civil rights. For the younger cohort of legislators, neither same-sex marriage nor LGTBQ sexual relationships are sacrilegious. I therefore contend that these younger women disrupt an essentialist Black political identity and in so doing complicate the African American political agenda. Growing up in an era in which society does not consistently demonize queer individuals and communities has affected younger Black women's views on same-sex marriage. Ultimately, this shows that intragroup differences among Black women legislators have previously been neglected and should have been accounted for in our understandings of Black political identities.

Delegate Yasmin Wood, a younger Black woman delegate and a mother of five, makes the comparison between bans on interracial marriage and same-sex marriage. This legislator is biracial and self-identifies as African American. Her parents' union—between a Black man and a White woman—was illegal when she was born. As a result, she makes a direct connection between what she believes was a nonsensical argument in the 1960s and the similarly situated argument in the present day. This legislator believes that regardless of gender, those who love each other should be allowed to marry. She compares discrimination based on race to that based on sexual orientation:

> To me it's a civil rights issue. Why should anybody tell someone else that they can't marry the person they love? My experience is that my mom is White and my dad is Black; they married in the 1950s. They had to live in Washington, DC,

because it was illegal in Virginia and Maryland. I think it's better for the state as a whole for people to be married and be in committed relationships. (Personal interview, March 18, 2009)

This personal connection to antimiscegenation laws leads this delegate to a marked departure from an essentialist Black political identity. During her 2011 feminist life history interview, this delegate expanded upon how her parents' marriage and the racism that they had faced in the 1950s and 1960s had had a profound impact on the formation of her racial identity. Delegate Wood always self-identified as Black, describing herself as a light-skinned African American woman. When her parents divorced when she was in middle school, she moved in with her Black father and stepmother. She was hyperaware of race-based discrimination and eagerly sought to challenge the social stigma associated with Blackness. This quest for racial equality led her to expand these ideals to include other marginalized groups that experience discrimination. As a result, Delegate Wood sees a direct correlation between her race-based experiences and advocating for same-sex marriage.

Detailing her cosponsorship of this legislation, Senator Bailey Smith, a young Black woman, also makes a direct connection to antimiscegenation laws and the disapproval of same-sex marriage.

I'm a cosponsor of the Religious Freedom and Protection of Civil Marriage Bill. I think what they did in California is wrong. Black churches joined with the Republicans by and large to eliminate gay marriage or same-sex marriages in California and through a referendum or a constitutional amendment. Some civil rights should not be litigated through referendum or public policy because if that was the case I would still be a slave! Sometimes you just have to step up be a leader and do the right thing. In the issue of same-sex marriage, if we line-for-line look at same-sex marriages in the same way you look at *Loving vs. Virginia* case, it would suggest to me that there is no difference. We should be about justice and fairness. (Personal interview, March 13, 2009)

Trained as a lawyer, Senator Smith pulls apart the legal fallacies of prohibiting same-sex marriage. This legislator makes direct connections between same-sex marriage, LGBTQ rights, and Black civil rights. However, her comments reflect an understanding of Black civil rights and gay rights as mutually exclusive. These comments may indicate that she has yet to make the connection that Black LGBTQ individuals do exist. Her legal training, however, leads her to take a proactive stance on securing marriage equality, and Senator Bailey Smith clearly views LGBTQ individuals as an advanced marginalized population that requires legislative advocacy similar to that required by African Americans. Senator Smith adds, "Just as ending slavery was decreed through a constitutional amendment, marriage equality may have to be decided by the Supreme Court" (Personal interview, March 13, 2009). She adamantly opposes a same-sex marriage referendum that would allow citizens to vote on the citizens' rights, believing instead that lawmakers need to step up.

However, a same-sex marriage referendum appeared on the November 2012 ballot as a veto referendum. This measure was a response to the Religious Freedom and Civil Marriage Protection Bill, which countered this legislation by preventing it from being enacted until a statewide vote took place. With or without a referendum, Delegate Fatima Coleman, a young Black woman elected in 2010, opined that same-sex marriage would ultimately have to be decided by the Maryland Court of Appeals as a constitutional issue because it was a contentious legislative issue (Personal interview, July 29, 2011).

While some Black women legislators make a direct connection between racial discrimination and discrimination based on sexual orientation, Delegate Naomi Young, a younger Black woman whose father was a leading civil rights activist in the Maryland, also supports same-sex marriage on the basis of affording citizens civil rights but states clearly that same-sex marriage cannot be equally compared to the struggles that Blacks endured to gain civil rights:

> Believing in civil rights and civil liberties for everyone has swayed me in favor of the gay marriage bill. I do make a distinction that some of the advocates [of same-sex marriage] do not make. I do not think it is in any way the same as the civil rights struggle for non-discrimination when it comes to race. Many of the gay rights advocates say it's a civil rights issue so they assume that because I'm a civil rights advocate that I'm going to be on board. I'm on board because I am one. But the pitch to me is a civil rights issue says that the civil rights movement has failed because of the fact that one, whether or not you choose to be gay, to be married or not is a choice and it is also discrimination. We also know that when it's based on the hue, the pigment and the color of your skin is something that you can never overcome. But you can go through the world and exist without people knowing that you're gay. (Personal interview, March 20, 2009)

Like her late father, she is dedicated to the advancement of human and civil rights, particularly in the state of Maryland. Generally, Delegate Young's point of view is akin to that of many other African Americans who support LGBTQ rights but oppose the direct comparison with the Black civil rights movement. While racism and homophobia are often two sides of the same coin, many Blacks insist that one cannot compare centuries of racial marginalization (slavery, racial violence, disenfranchisement, and an American legal caste system based on race) to the banning of same-sex marriage. However, this viewpoint ignores the historical and contemporary social stigmatization, violence, and state-sponsored discrimination that LGBTQ individuals face in the United States. This mode of thinking about the deep history of discrimination creates a pecking order of oppression, creating in effect an "Oppression Olympics," in which groups attempt to position their discrimination as less than or worse than the prejudice faced by another group (Hancock 2007; Martinez 1993). This tactic allows for Blacks to denigrate advanced marginalized populations because they are deemed less worthy of support in their battle against discrimination and neglects the multiple, cross-cutting, or intersectional identities that we each occupy.

Older African American women provided ambivalent answers when asked what factors they would include in the decision-making process on a controversial bill such as the Religious Freedom and Protection of Civil Marriage Bill. These responses indicate that they were unsure or undecided on their position. Perhaps these legislators were not ready to "go on the record" with a position and may have been uncomfortable with being quoted. Some may have preferred to have kept their position anonymous, but none of the legislators requested to "go off the record" to assure that they would not be quoted. Conceivably, ambivalent comments represent legislators' willingness to speak with me but their reluctance to articulate a definitive viewpoint on same-sex marriage.

Senator Raquel Simmons, an older Black woman senator who was raised in a working-class Black family that instilled the importance of political involvement in her and her siblings and cosponsor of the 2009 bill, did not comment on the legislation because it had not yet come to vote during the time of my fieldwork.

First, the question should be: Will gay marriage come up for vote in this body? At this stage of the game, it won't. Bills that eventually hit that floor are dictated by leadership. . . . No, it never hit the floor. Civil marriage may eventually one day get to the floor. I don't care who marries who, I really don't. Is it the argument of what does the Bible says? I always say the Bible is interpreted by men, so what the Bible says is what man says or whoever did all of this anyway. I really had no opinion one way of the other, if you [referring to me, a woman researcher] want to marry Lisa and John wants to marry Joe, I don't care one way or the other; as long as they are happy and are paying their bills and taxes, I don't care. (Personal interview, March 11, 2009)

It is interesting to note that this Senator Simmons is part of the state senate leadership and a cosponsor on this bill but is not truly committed to the legislation; if she had been committed to the bill, it would have been easier for her to bring the bill to a vote rather than leaving it for a junior cosponsor without a leadership position to do. For her, this bill may have been a way to take a stance on an issue to please her constituents without having to directly advocate for it.

A few African American women legislators refused to directly address the issue of same-sex marriage. For example, Delegate Tanisha Harold, an older African American women delegate who did not explicitly mention the role of religion in her daily life, shifted the conversation to civil unions:

> When it comes to civil unions, I believe that the religious community should not be mandated to do anything. Civil unions in my opinion are talking about personal benefits. They are not talking about religious benefits. These are personal civil benefits. It's whether or not you get to ride in the ambulance if your partner has a stroke, heart attack or accident. Do you have to ride behind in another car? You usually have your significant other with you to calm you down; it's a partnership. I know that if I'm in an ambulance I'm terrified. I may not be thinking clearly, I need someone to be there, it may be my partner or it may be my spouse. But, it should be someone that I choose to have there. The government shouldn't intervene in that. (Personal interview, March 17, 2009)

As previously noted, civil unions create separate but equal legal status for same-sex couples who wish to be married. Delegate Harold seeks to side-step the question of marriage by highlighting her approval of civil unions, but her response nevertheless indicates that she favors placing LGBTQ partnership within a framework of second-class citizenship. She is classifying marriage as only permissible within religious institutions. Delegate Harold may be trying to empower civil unions so that they offer the same civil benefits as marriage. However, while seemingly well-intentioned, her position on same-sex marriage actually reinforces heteronormativity by refusing same-sex couples the right to marry. I posit that these ambivalent answers reveal that the majority of Black political elites remain unaware of the advanced marginalization within their communities. Legislators with this view are participants in the advanced marginalized of their LGBTQ constituents.

In examining African American women state legislators' views on the Religious Freedom and Protection of Civil Marriage Bill we see a number of the factors included in their legislative decision making, not least of all the intensity and variety of their approaches to this particular kind of cross-cutting legislation. African American women state legislators are not a monolithic group; they employ notions of Black political identity differently and have varying relationships with Black cultural and political tropes. Black women's gender identities provide them with an (arguably limited) opportunity not afforded to Black men—that of challenging aspects of essentialist Black political identity. Because they are not bound by the constraints of hypermasculinity and the widely interpreted direct condemnation of male homosexuality found in biblical scripture, Black women can express more progressive views of same-sex marriage than African American men generally can because the heteronormativity that informs Black manhood is central to essentialist Black political identity. The Black men in this study do not have the same flexibility of opinion on same-sex marriage because the issue is mediated by an essentialist Black political identity to which they are beholden.

Black Men Maryland State Legislators and Same-Sex Marriage

To further illustrate the inflexibility of Black political identity, African American men legislators' views of the Religious Freedom and Protection of Civil Marriage Bill were similar to those of the older women delegates. Because there was no generational divide in how Black men legislators articulated their views on marriage equality, I incorporate African American men legislators of all ages as a comparison group to further explore how gender mediates Black political identity. The thirteen male legislators who gave their opinion on this cross-cutting issue were more likely to oppose the legislation than support it. Like the older African American women legislators, Black men who opposed the legislation also cited religious reasons for their adversarial positions.

Out of the thirteen African American men interviewed for this study, the majority opposed same-sex marriage due to theologically driven homophobia. Five specific examples of this type of response are presented below. Because the male group serves only as a comparison, I chose not to include the entirety of the African American men's responses. Instead, these responses represent the types of answers the men provided when I asked them about same-sex marriage and the factors that influenced their decisions about legislation related to the issue.

Drawing a more direct connection to his religious beliefs, one African American male legislator connects his spiritual and moral convictions to his opposition of same-sex marriage. This legislator views homosexuality as wrong. While he acknowledges that equal protection under law should apply to everyone, he does indicate that some groups should not be entitled to this protection.

> I'll be honest with you, and I have had a long time to think about that. That's an act that they will answer to God for. So I'm not going to play God because I'm not. We can't have our cake and eat it too when we talk about equal protection under the law. Spiritually and morally I know it's wrong but they also know it's wrong. But I'm not going to be the one that has to stand in judgment and say "I condemn her and her and him and him." (Personal interview, March 17, 2009)

The African American male legislators in this study cited direct interpretation of the Bible as their rationale for opposing same-sex marriage specifically and homosexuality in general. Several reiterated that homosexuality is wrong and that they do not support same-sex marriage because of their religious beliefs. Take, for example, another African American legislator who states that he is not a "gay basher" but believes that homosexuality is an "abomination." He noted that because he does not understand homosexuality or identify as queer, he does not support marriage equality. He explained:

> If you are a believer in a Higher Being, which I am, and you are a person who studies and believes the King James Version of the Bible, it says there that it is an abomination. So I have to factor my personal beliefs, my spiritual beliefs, when I look at that particular situation. Now with that said, I'm not a gay basher but at the same time it's something that I don't understand the origins of. And I can't believe something that I don't understand. It would be hard for me to support something that I don't understand. (Personal interview, March 20, 2009)

One African American legislator is a Baptist minister. Unlike other Black men who detailed religious reasons for opposing same-sex marriage, this delegate did not. Providing one of the shortest responses to this question, this legislator simply noted that he is in opposition to the legislation because of his religious beliefs, along with a host of other reasons. "I'm against it. Not only for religious reasons but it is bad economic policy, social policy, educational policy, it's just bad policy period" (March 12, 2009). He did not provide specific examples or expand on his rationale for considering same-sex marriage bad public policy. The 2009 bill and the 2012 bill both included strong language to guarantee and ensure that each religious entity "has exclusive control over its own theological doctrine, policy teachings, and beliefs regarding who may marry within that faith" (SB 241, 2012).

However, this Baptist minister and legislator is nevertheless among the most prominent opponents of the bill. He is often quoted in both local and national media outlets strongly opposing the bill on religious grounds. This legislator was an active member of the religious coalition that put marriage equality before the public as a referendum in November 2012. However, his 2009 interview with me was much more nuanced and less direct than his 2011 comments on this legislation. Perhaps he became more passionate about this issue over the five consecutive years in which this bill was introduced.

Similar to the Black women legislators, Black men base their policy considerations on a mixture of their constituencies' wishes and personal beliefs. Black men and older Black women legislators use different explanations for why they are opposed to same-sex marriage, yet the majority of Black men legislators begin with the premise that same-sex marriage is wrong, as this delegate indicates:

> On a bill like this I think, the first thing is I would try to ask myself is it right or is it wrong? And that's what I have to ask myself. Then the process becomes "Okay, what do my constituents want? What is the pulse of my community? What are their feelings on this bill? Am I doing the right things to represent my district?" On the civil marriage bill I share the same beliefs as my constituents. We have a pretty conservative group down there [in my district]. (Personal interview, March 20, 2009)

This delegate indicates that his legislative decision-making process starts with him assessing his individual feelings about the bill. Once he knows how he feels about an issue, he then looks to his constituents' positions on the legislation. Here, both the delegate and his constituents oppose same-sex marriage, implying and interpreting homosexual relationships as unacceptable and morally wrong.

Another African American delegate notes that he has a sizeable LGBTQ community in his district and that he therefore has to endorse certain bills that his progressive Baltimore City constituents support. However, he self-identifies as a socially conservative, middle-class Black man with traditional values who does not readily champion same-sex marriage legislation. Overall, his comments were tied to conceptions of the crisis within the Black family. He indicated to me that his belief was that same-gender-loving couples undermine strong African American families.

> The first thing I would look at is my constituency as far as I have a sizeable gay community. Not enough to put you in office but enough to maybe put you out

office if you are just completely anti-gay or lesbian and transgendered. I look at it as, do I want to pass a bill that puts them out of the process where it can only be seen as a marriage to a man or woman? [Do I want to] make [that] part to the constitution. I don't want to do that. However I'm reluctant to cosponsor any gay marriage legislation. I understand where they are coming from. But as a Black man with family and raised by [a Black family]—I was very close to my father when he was alive—there are certain things that my community has taught me about relationships that don't always coincide with the gay community. Being from an African American socially conservative community that also goes into factoring how I would vote or support that issue. (Personal interview, March 18, 2009)

This quote highlights a trope of Black homophobia aided by a Black Nationalist ideology that is informed by heteropatriarchal gender norms. Thus, this legislator's concern is rooted in an essentialist Black political identity that constructs African American homosexuality as a transgressive and therefore as engendering manifold assaults on the Black family.

Only one Black male legislator interviewed for this study supported the Religious Freedom and Protection of Civil Marriage bill. Like the African American women who supported the bill, this delegate likened same-sex marriage to civil rights.

Gay marriage is not controversial to me. I think every single person on the face of the earth should have the same right as every other single person on the face of the earth. That is the way Martin Luther King Jr. felt about it when he was doing the Civil Rights Movement, that you had to look at each and every one personally as if they were you, as your brother or as your sister. If you look at person like that then how can you not want to support that person's rights? It doesn't really matter even if I were an extremely religious person, which I am. I believe in God I believe in church, I believe that Jesus gave his life to die for our sins. I also believe that there is a separation between the church and the state that exists not only in the state but also in the church itself. God wants there to be a difference. We can do the work of the state without it being center of the spirituality because you are basically giving a person the right to be free. (Personal interview, March 14, 2009)

Connecting human rights to the struggle for same-sex marriage, this legislator links the separation of church and state as reasons why he supports the legalization of same-sex marriage. He shows that viewing this legislation as an opportunity to secure rights for an advanced marginalized group is not automatically positioned as a deviation from one's Christian beliefs.

This delegate challenges an essentialist Black political identity; he does not see same-sex marriage as controversial.

Both women and men legislators, noting cultural context, presented similar arguments in support of or against this cross-cutting bill. In this regard, I observed a few gender differences between older Black women and the majority of the men legislators who reinforce an essentialist Black political identity among African American elites. This finding further supports scholars' claims that African Americans have a strong group consciousness activated by racial identification (Dawson 1994; Mansbridge and Tate 1992; Tate 1994).

CONCLUSION

The interviews presented in this chapter show that the older and more traditional Black women legislators were as likely to oppose same-sex marriage as Black men, who, with one exception, opposed it regardless of their generational affiliation. Younger Black women legislators, more likely to support gay marriage, were also more likely to frame the Religious Freedom and Protection of Civil Marriage bill as a civil- or human-rights issue. My data support Cohen's (1999) argument that some Black political elites, regardless of gender, create or ignore submarginalized populations by failing to advocate on their behalf. However, the younger Black women legislators as a group are more likely than Black legislators in general to support same-sex marriage, which points to divergent generational and gendered attitudes toward same-sex marriage for African American legislators. In this instance, younger Black women prove to be the optimal representatives for a nonessentialist Black political agenda. Similarly to younger voters, women in general, and Black progressives, the Maryland state legislators who are young Black women represent the evolving position of Americans in general and African Americans in particular on same-sex marriage. Perhaps they can build bridges between legislators operating within essentialist and nonessentialist Black political frameworks and within Maryland's Black communities. This would help ensure that politics does not lag behind public opinion.

While the debate on the Religious Freedom and Protection of Civil Marriage Bill was framed around providing government benefits to same-sex partners, many of the older Black legislators cited religious reasons for opposing the bill. The bill explicitly stated that religious institutions do not have to solemnize a marriage that they oppose; however, certain Black women legislators nevertheless said that religion and their faith were major concerns. Along with adhering to an essentialist Black political identity, these older and more traditional Black women legislators and Black men cited faith as a guiding influence in the decision-making process. Consequently, we see the influence of the Black church in social policy.

Generational affiliation is a factor. Black women born in the 1950s were more likely than Black women legislators born the 1960s and 1970s to oppose same-sex marriage. The younger and more progressive Black women disrupt entrenched forms of Black political identity by challenging African American cultural norms that link Black homosexuality to deviant anti-Black behavior. Furthermore, a representational identity illustrates that Black women legislators do not act a unified group on same sex marriage legislation. We see a variation in both in what African American women think about marriage equality and LGBTQ rights. We also find that these women draw from differing parts of their identities and experiences to articulate their views on the Religious Freedom and Protection of Civil Marriage Bill.

Couched within legislators' conversations about this cross-cutting legislation, however, are discussions of and decisions about their roles as legislators and which interests or constituents to represent. For instance, legislators' comments illustrate competing and contradictory viewpoints. Political representation scholars contend that the goal of political actors is to make their constituents' voices heard by advocating on their behalves (Pennock and Chapman 1968; Pitkin 1967; Schwartz 1988.) Legislators may therefore take on one of two roles, or perhaps a hybrid of the two. As a delegate, a legislator follows her constituents' preferences. As a trustee, the legislator follows her own judgment for the best course of action (Pitkin 1967). As mediated through an often hegemonic and prevalent essentialist Black political identity, African American Maryland state legislators acted as trustees in their articulation of same-sex marriage. The legislators used their racial identity as a proxy for their constituents' wishes on same-sex marriage; essentialist Black political identity binds legislators and constituents together in their conception of Blackness. Because the vast majority of the African American legislators represent majority–minority districts, their positioning on marriage equality was similar to those of their constituents. When legislators represented a sizeable LGBTQ constituency, however, they still, in many cases, opposed same-sex marriage. Drawing almost exclusively from their own identities, experiences, and personal beliefs, these legislators did not include their constituents' wishes as factors in their legislative decision-making process, which indicates that African American state legislators are likely to act as trustees as opposed to delegates.

This analysis indicates that a form of Black political identity is only primed when issues are racialized. Advocates and proponents of same-sex marriage both used the African American experience as a proxy for understanding marriage equality. Thus the issue of same-sex marriage and the LGBTQ community were incorporated within the racialized tropes that legislators used to articulate their support or opposition for the Religious Freedom and Protection of Civil Marriage Bill.

The legislators in this study did not evoke the "nature vs. nurture" debate about sexual orientation. A few African American legislators, however, did not feel that this community required special advocacy because of their advanced marginalization. When I asked about the marginal communities that the legislators feel need their voices in Annapolis, a great majority of the legislators responded that senior citizens and children did. Not a single legislator mentioned the LGBTQ community as needing or as deserving of their advocacy.

Legislators overwhelmingly saw the members of the LGBTQ community as outsiders. Only one African American legislator, a lesbian, identified with this population. Interestingly, only one of the legislators connected the LGBTQ as a population with any particular racial identity. The African American legislators, with the exception of one, were not descriptive representatives of this group,[23] showing how this group has been constructed as mutually exclusive to Black communities. While the younger, more progressive African American women legislators were supportive of same-sex marriage legislation, the majority of them could not personally identify with this population. All the openly queer-identified legislators supported marriage equality legislation, however, giving us the intersectional perspective to conclude that descriptive representation matters.

African Americans do not have to have a race-based political identity to advocate for others who have experienced discrimination. Blacks may have a joint commitment to fighting injustice in all forms because they understand and empathize with others who bear society's inequalities. Yet, as we find in this case study, legislators are most likely to use an essentialist Black political identity to advocate for groups with whom they share a social identity. When an issue is decidedly racialized but does not immediately conjure images of a Black constituency, legislators fail to empathize with groups that also bear discrimination and inequality. This may be the case in part because African Americans have previously extended their political capital to groups who later exploited the economic and political disadvantages of Blacks.[24] Perhaps marriage equality is such an instance. While the NAACP has publically supported same-sex marriages, GLAAD has yet to reciprocate by extending itself on the political on issues that dispropor-tionately affect African Americans, such as by calling for federal attention to Black unemployment rates.

It may be wise for African Americans to use an essentialist Black politi-cal identity in their articulation of whom they will advocate for if other groups use similar essentializing ideological measures. Legislators often build coalitions with other groups or make policy concessions to ensure that their legislation is passed, and perhaps some legislators did not feel as if the LGBTQ advocacy groups were adequately willing to arrange mutually beneficial cooperation. This nuanced consideration of quid pro quo neces-sitates that groups are prepared to reciprocate certain legislative favors in return. Perhaps some legislators who opposed same-sex marriage did so because they found same-sex marriage advocates had not adequately ad-dressed Black issues and concerns in return.

In sum, the data reveal that the vast majority of Black political elites reinforce the boundaries of Blackness. In light of the 2012 referendum that institutionalized marriage equality, recent public opinion polling and na-tional African American leaders' support of same-sex marriage, state legis-lators' refusal to advocate for marriage equality demonstrates that they lag behind on this issue. Indeed, some Black politicians—both men and women who adhere to an essentialist Black political identity—seem most comfort-able representing constituents who prioritize policy preferences around consensus issues. However, younger African American women elected to the Maryland state legislature demonstrate the evolving nature of Black politics. Rather than steadfastly holding on to an essentialist form of Black politics, this group of legislators expressed their openness to viewing mar-riage equality as an opportunity to extend representation to an advanced marginalized population, rejecting the idea that this population is unde-serving of representation. In this manner, younger Black women's voices are necessary precisely because they articulate another conceptualization of—and new possibilities for—Black politics.

In the near future, as more young legislators take office, perhaps Black women legislators will prove wrong Cohen's (1999) finding that Black po-litical elites are active participants in further marginalizing disadvantaged subgroups, particularly since Black women currently outpace Black men in gaining elected office (Smooth 2006). Or, perhaps as Hancock (2011) sug-gests, we may see both young Black men and women state legislators sup-porting same-sex marriage in the future because Black Millennials have more progressive views on issues involving sexual orientation. The conclu-sions in this chapter certainly show the benefits of utilizing a generational analysis when comparing intragroup policy preferences.

While perhaps the most interesting aspect of same-sex marriage in Maryland centered on voters' decisions on November 6, 2012, the importance of the state legislature's role in championing equality cannot be understated. Maryland became the first state below the Mason-Dixon Line to affirm gays' and lesbians' rights to marry. By providing civil protections for gay and lesbian couples and protecting religious institutions that choose not to perform same-sex marriage, legislators crafted a model bill that other states can use as a template.

Next, students of Black political participation and electoral politics are reminded of the impact of Black voters and political elites in calling on America to live up to the tenets of liberalism and ensuring equality and justice for all of her citizens. It is clear that African Americans are involved and actively engaged with the democratic process, particularly on issues of equality. A national exit poll found that African American voters favored legalizing same-sex marriage at 51 percent, compared with 47 percent of White voters (Kumar 2012). While many in the Black community remain opposed to marriage equality, Maryland's recent ballot initiative indicates that African American voters are making a difference in both American politics and culture. As a result, perhaps older Black political elites should read the writing on the wall and pursue a political agenda that is inclusive of advanced marginalized groups.

CHAPTER 6

Caregiving as a Race-Gendered Issue

It's not the load that breaks you down, it's the way you carry it.
—Lena Horne

It's so clear that you have to cherish everyone. I think that's what I get from these older Black women that every soul is to be cherished, that every flower is to bloom.
—Alice Walker

Taking care of the elderly is primarily a women's issue. Indeed, the National Organization of Women has declared caregiving a feminist concern (www.now.org) and details that women make up 90 percent of the professional caregivers and 75 percent of the informal caregivers in the United States. Caregiving is a feminist issue not only because women are more likely than men to be caregivers of a spouse and parent but also because women are the majority of the elderly who will eventually need care (Ingersoll-Dayton, Starrels, and Dowler 1996). The interdependent and overlapping nature of race and gender makes caregiving a distinctly race-gender issue. Furthermore, research shows that women caregivers are most likely to be Black (Navaie-Waliser, Spriggs, and Feldman 2002). Because caregiving is an issue that disproportionately affects Black women, this chapter examines, comparatively, legislators' support of the Financial Exploitation of the Elderly Bill, which takes up issues related to the gendered nature of caretaking. It provides an important comparison to the previous chapter on marriage equality and shows that Black women elected to public office are unified, regardless of age or generational affiliation, in their support for the bill.

I have previously argued that whether an African American legislator hews to an essentialist or nonessentialist Black political identity impacts his or her willingness to represent an advanced marginalized population. The departure of younger Black women from the strictures of essentialist Black political identity allows them to advocate for marriage equality. By placing Black women within a racialized narrative, I find that a racial identity is relevant to forging an understanding of how Black women politically represent advanced marginalized groups—populations that are further stigmatized within a larger marginalized population. This finding is significant because it illustrates how much race-gender identification influences legislative advocacy. This chapter explores African American women's willingness and eagerness to represent the elderly, and so I present here an analysis of Black women state legislators' views on protecting the elderly. Unlike White women, White men, and Black men, African American women couch their support for the Financial Exploitation of the Elderly Bill, which would make it a crime to take advantage of a senior citizen for financial gain, within their own experiences of caregiving for elderly relatives. While all legislators agree that the elderly are a group that deserves their advocacy, the legislators use different thematic constructions to frame their support of this bill. By comparing the Financial Exploitation of the Elderly Bill to the Religious Freedom and Protection of Civil Marriage Bill, I further investigate how legislators determine which populations are worthy of their representation. Comparing these bills allows me to understand whether there is something unique about how intersectional identities determine legislators' support for groups they, along with dominant society, construct as deserving or undeserving of political representation. Representational identity theory, the concept that Black women legislators use their race-gender identities and experiences as Black women to shape their legislative behavior, helps me to illustrate that Black women, as a group, use their perceptions of the interests of Black women to guide their policy positions on this bill.

The themes in the narratives of Black women are central in this chapter, although I also include the voices of Black men, White men, and White women to highlight the unique nature of African American women's relationship to representing the needs of the elderly. I also examine to what extent, if any, African American women view representation for the elderly as a women's issue and whether they see themselves as representing women's interests. Here, as in other instances throughout the study, intersectional analysis helps me to account for the distinctive experiences and worldviews that Black women have forged based on their encounters with both racism and sexism.

In using this issue to compare Black women to three other demographic groups of legislators, I highlight how race-gender identities make Black women legislators distinctive in their legislative behavior. Perhaps the obvious choice would have been to compare Black women and White women's legislative decision making on a gender-issue bill, just as the previous chapter compared African American women and men's positions on a racialized bill. However, the data revealed that both Black and White men, surprisingly, use similar cognitive frameworks to women when they explain their support of this legislation. The main distinction is that the Black women legislators in this study comprise the only group that actively serves as caregivers for elderly parents, an experience that uniquely influences their legislative decision-making process on this bill.

Legislators advocate for groups in different ways depending on the group's social status and on whether the legislation is a consensus issue, that is, an issue that impacts the Black community at large, or a cross-cutting issue, that is, an issue that affects groups across identity categories and thus requires cross-group mobilization. By exploring how Black women respond to specifically gendered legislation, I show that a race-gender identity plays a role in determining legislative support for legislation. I have furthermore selected the Financial Exploitation of the Elderly Bill as a comparison case to the Religious Freedom and Protection of Civil Marriage Bill precisely because it did not center on a stigmatized and marginalized population. Comparing these bills allows deeper exploration of Black women's political advocacy, their decisions about how to best represent their constituencies, and the role their race-gender experiences play in their legislative work.

The unique perspective that the Black women in this study share is grounded in their personal experiences with caregiving for the elderly. My central argument posits that Black women perform caregiving in ways that are different from Black men, White women, and White men. Reading the Financial Exploitation of the Elderly bill through the lens of race-gender identities and experiences complicates identity politics. Here, I illustrate that a race-only or gender-only approach to understanding legislator's motivation to support this legislation does not take into account the lived experiences of Black women legislators.

CAREGIVING AS A WOMEN'S ISSUE

Women legislators are expected by activists, voters, and researchers to champion women's issues—issues that are broadly related to women's traditional roles as caretakers—and to substantively represent women

(Reingold 2008, 130). Women's policy leadership is visible in all areas of the policy-making process surrounding this issue, from bill introduction to committee hearings and floor speeches (Dodson and Carroll 1998; Norton 2002; Swers 2002). Feminist theorists have argued that women's role as caregivers was developed out of gender socialization (Kessler 2001). As a result, women's caregiving is a socially determined and gendered activity. Yet, caregiving for the elderly—unlike other types of family caregiving provided by women—is unrelated to reproductive sex differences, meaning that there is no bond of motherhood presumed. Caregiving also places undue burdens—both economic and health—on women. Research has shown that caregiving reduces women's participation in the labor force (Wakabayashi and Donato 2005), because women have difficulty in maintaining employment if elder care includes providing assistance with the activities of daily living (i.e., bathing, dressing, eating, and using the toilet) and managing the finances of the elderly. The vast majority of disabled elders live in the community and depend on informal (unpaid) help of women close to them (Boaz and Muller 1992).

Many women in heterosexual relationships live longer than their male counterparts. These women take care of their children, husbands, and community while paying little attention to their own well-being (Boneham and Sixsmith 2006). Younger women have been characterized as "women in the middle," who take on the role of caregiving daughter while still fulfilling obligations to children and their husbands and perhaps also while working for income (Brody 1991, 471–80).

Cultural differences and race-related life experiences may explain why Black caregivers, Black women in particular, express different views on caregiving than their White counterparts (Haley et al. 1996). First, older Black women are valued in their families. This esteem for older Black women is independent of their ability to perform instrumental roles within the family (Dilworth-Anderson and Anderson 1994). Second, Black families may not view the decline of an older relative as important. The cultural value of older individuals does not diminish when his or her cognitive and behavioral functions start to falter (Haley et al. 1996). Yet while African American families readily take on the role of caregiving for elderly family members, research indicates that African American caregivers use less formal support and suffer from higher levels of caregiver burden, depression, and worse physical health than Whites (Pinquart and Sorensen 2005). Data from the Census Bureau indicate that elderly African Americans have more severe functional limitations than do their White counterparts (U.S. Bureau of the Census 1995). However, older Blacks are half as likely to be institutionalized as Whites (Belgrave, Wykle, and Choi 1993). The above-reviewed literature details that caregiving for an elderly relative is substantively different within Black and White families.

Examining the caregiving roles of daughters, Mui's (1992) study of 117 Black daughters and 464 White daughters revealed that Black daughters reported less overall role strain than White daughters. Black women described that while they had fewer demands on them as caregivers, they experienced poorer health and less access to respite support. White daughters, however, faced more work conflict and strained mother–daughter relationships. In their research on the dynamics of caring for an elderly family member with dementia, Lawton Rajagopal, Brody, and Kleban (1992) found that after controlling for socioeconomic status, Blacks were more likely than Whites to believe that caregiving was not a burden. Indeed, Black families reported a unique satisfaction in caregiving and did not find this work to be intrusive, although their White counterparts did. Allen and Chin-Sang's (1990) qualitative study of thirty African American women found that older women volunteered in caregiving activities in their churches and in senior centers after their retirement. After retiring from mostly domestic and service work, these Black women continued their service to others and themselves, even in their old age. Indeed, Black women report that caregiving for the elderly is expected and continuous because "we have no choice"—expressed as statement but not as a complaint (Haley et al. 1996, 127).

This literature on caregiving and its race-gender elements aligns with the narratives of Black women, which are distinct from those of Black men, White women, and White men in the discourse surrounding the Financial Exploitation of the Elderly Bill. The narratives of Black women in this study resonate clearly with the above-reviewed literature, setting them apart from their racial and gendered counterparts in the Maryland state legislature. I have thematically organized legislators' articulations of what factors they included in the legislative decision-making process surrounding the Financial Exploitation of the Elderly Bill, and the narratives in each theme represent all the different frameworks that legislators used to explain their support for this women's interest bill.

FINANCIAL EXPLOITATION OF THE ELDERLY BILL

Financial exploitation of the elderly takes a variety of forms. A 2009 MetLife study found that the elderly victims of financial exploitation lose as much as $1 million a year, amounting to $2.6 billion in annual losses. The majority of the victims were women in their seventies and eighties.

Women who need help with health care or home maintenance were twice as likely to be victims of elder financial abuse. More specifically, this study identified the "typical" victim as a White woman between the ages of seventy and eighty-nine, who might be described as trusting, lonely, frail, and cognitively impaired.

The MetLife study found that fraud was committed by strangers, family members, friends, neighbors, the business sector, and by Medicare and Medicaid (MetLife 2009). Perpetrators tended to be men between the ages of thirty and fifty-nine. Lastly, the study found that the dollar losses were highest during the holiday season due to fraud perpetrated by family, friends, and neighbors. While fraud committed by family members and caregivers is more common, the financial losses caused by investments scams are higher. Victims of elder financial abuse suffer the long-term effects of fraud in addition to their immediate financial loss. They report having credit problems, health issues, depression, and a loss of independence. The elderly are also a prime target for financial abuse because they are neither aware of nor fluent in technological advances.

In contrast to the cross-cutting same-sex bill explored earlier in this book, legislators frame the Financial Exploitation of the Elderly Bill as a consensus issue—one that is framed as somehow important to all group members (Cohen 1999, 11). The Financial Exploitation of the Elderly Bill prohibits a person from knowingly and willfully obtaining—with intent to deprive the individual of the individual's property by deception, intimidation, or undue influence—the property of an individual that the person knows (or reasonably should know) is at least sixty-eight years old. While this bill does not consider financial exploitation of the elderly as a hate crime, many of the legislators liken this bill to hate crime legislation. This bill was unanimously passed in the House of Delegates (134–0) on March 19, 2009, and the Senate (47–0) on April 7, 2009, and signed into law by Governor O'Malley on May 7, 2009.

Unlike the Religious Freedom and Protection of Civil Marriage Bill, the Financial Exploitation of the Elderly Bill was unanimously supported, becoming law in Maryland after passing both chambers unanimously and being signed by Governor O'Malley. When I asked about the factors that contributed to the legislative decision-making process for the Financial Exploitation of the Elderly Bill, many of the legislators who I interviewed drew first from their personal identities, citing his or her personal station in life as a reason why they would support this bill. Others explained that they came to Annapolis to protect the most marginalized, who, in their opinions, are children and the elderly. As we have seen in the previous chapter, the legislators did not view the LGBTQ community as in need of special advocacy. I therefore seek to understand which groups legislators believe are worthy of representation and how they make those decisions. All legislators, regardless of gender and race/ethnicity, supported the Exploitation of the Elderly Bill, so I asked legislators to discuss how, if at all, identity mediated their decisions about the representational process. In particular, within the context of our discussions about this bill, I asked representatives whether and how their identities influence what groups they advocate on behalf of.

Rather than highlighting the race and gender of the legislators, I divided their responses into four guiding thematic rubrics: legislators who questioned whether this bill was good public policy, legislators who supported this bill because they themselves are senior citizens, legislators who expressed a personal responsibility to advocate for and protect the elderly, and legislators who currently take care of or have taken care of elderly parents. Again, the goal is to understand how identity mediates representation and how legislators draw from their personal histories when representing their constituents. I present how legislators use their experiences, personal identity, and/or attempt to create good public policy. I examine how legislators articulate their policy positions on a consensus bill—in this case, considered women's issue legislation—that is designed to benefit a particular segment of the population.

Good Public Policy

Richard Fenno posited that members of Congress have three goals. "All House members, we would argue, try to achieve, in varying combinations, three basic personal goals: reelection, power inside Congress, and good public policy" (1978, 137). Although the Exploitation of the Elderly Bill unanimously passed both chambers, a small number of lawmakers expressed reservations about supporting this legislation. Specifically, they asked whether this bill duplicated existing policy and whether this legislation was a necessity. Driven by their desire to create good policy, some legislators wondered whether the legislation was problematic. It is interesting to note that the legislators who were unsure about the bill did not make reference to their identity or personal experiences. Nor did this group of lawmakers suggest that it was their responsibility to protect seniors as a marginalized group.

A lawyer by training and a former legislative aid to two members of Congress, Delegate Kenya Barnes stated that the Financial Exploitation of the Elderly Bill was "symbol over substance. I like remedies to have substance not symbolism. Political symbolism is a big deal here [in the Maryland state legislature]." (Personal interview, March 20, 2009). In her view, this bill added an unnecessary penalty to an already punishable crime. Although she eventually voted in favor of the bill, she reported that she was "against it in concept. I don't think it's a hate crime. I actually don't agree with the concept of a hate crime so much. I believe that a crime is a crime. . . . There is a penalty under law regardless of the motive behind it. If you prosecuted someone for committing a crime and if you are successful, there would be an adequate penalty there" (Personal interview March 16, 2009).

Similarly, a young White male legislator, also a lawyer, reported that he found this bill unnecessary. He echoed Delegate Barnes's sentiment, saying that the Maryland legislature has been known to pass legislation that criminalizes something that is already criminal based on popular happenings or current events. This legislator noted that "last year a woman appeared on Oprah who survived a vicious attack. After being doused with gasoline from a Sprite can she was lit on fire and left for dead. So last year, a bill was introduced entitled assault by arson, but, arson and assault are already both crimes" (Personal interview, March 13, 2009). He equated the previous year's bill with the current Financial Exploitation of the Elderly Bill, which he referred to as a "spotlight bill"—legislation proposed to make the point that it is particularly egregious to take advantage of senior citizens who might be vulnerable. However, he quickly added that he is "not averse to passing spotlight bills, particularly ones that Maryland thinks is an egregious crime" (Personal interview, March 13, 2009).

Another young White male delegate, also a lawyer, also indicated that he thought that the bill was unnecessary. This legislator sought to frame his response in terms of his opposition to excessive crime and punishment laws. He added that the legislature heavily criminalizes and penalizes citizens for minor crimes. As a member of the judiciary committee, this legislator felt that there were too many laws that severely punish citizens, making it harder for individuals who have been convicted of crimes to find employment, banning them from federal educational aid, and hindering their becoming active community members. This delegate opined that the Financial Exploitation of the Elderly Bill was unnecessary. "What are we doing here, what are the penalties that already exist? Is this something so that we can pass the bill and feel good about it or is it something we really need?" (Personal interview, March 18, 2009).

Neither race nor gender served as a factor in the legislative decision-making process on this particular bill for these three legislators. Perhaps the fact that the legislators who objected are all lawyers is the more relevant aspect framing their outlooks on the Financial Exploitation of the

Elderly Bill. Their legal training may sensitize them to the factors that contribute to the legislature's desire to pass a bill that merely places a spotlight on an issue that has already been criminalized. As practicing attorneys, these legislators may be better versed in current statute and law than other legislators. While these legislators did not couch their remarks in terms of professional identity and training, it is not unimaginable that their legal background provided the impetus for their questioning of the necessity of the Financial Exploitation of the Elderly Bill. Interestingly, only three lawyers—a Black woman and two White men—challenged the necessity for this bill, although there are several other lawyers in the legislature. Regardless, their professional identity played a salient role in their legislative decision making.

While the other legislators I spoke with did not make explicit reference to their professions, this finding points to a difference. The vast majority of Black women and men legislators do not mention profession as a factor in their legislative decision making (Witko and Friedman 2008). While profession or career identity leads to experiences that may influence legislative behavior (Burden 2007), in the case of this bill, I found that the Black legislators in were the least likely to highlight its role in their legislative decision making.

Elderly Legislators

A select number of Black women legislators attributed their support of the Financial Exploitation of the Elderly Bill to their own advanced age. Delegate Cassandra Ross, a Jamaican immigrant and nurse, finds that no one should be exploited and that it is a particularly flagrant offense to manipulate the elderly:

> Since I am over the age of 68, I believe that they need to be arrested and fined. They need to be locked up. I don't think there should be exploitation of any individual. And never mind someone who has worked all their lives and have contributed and paid taxes in the state and in this country, that anyone should come and exploit them of their life earning at the time when they are getting ready for retirement when they most need their funds. (Personal interview, March 19, 2009)

Delegate Bella Campbell, one of the oldest members of the Maryland state legislature, also supports this legislation. "I don't want anybody to take advantage of the elderly. I am at that point myself. I know how I feel about the whole thing. I'm 81 years old. Don't try to take advantage of me" (Personal interview March 20, 2009). Similarly, Delegate Estrella Henderson, the second oldest African American women in this study, noted that she was in favor of the legislation. "It's good; I support that [Financial Exploitation of the Elderly Bill] because I'm going to get old. Really, I'm already old" (Personal interview, March 12, 2009). Similarly, an older African American male legislator noted that he supports this bill because "it's not controversial and because I'm over the age of 65. This bill could help me" (Personal interview, March 13, 2009). Due to their own advanced ages, the legislators had an explicit understanding of who would benefit from this legislation. Their own identities played a role in their legislative decision making in respect to this bill, an active illustration of how descriptive representation informs substantive representation.

Responsibility

A recurring theme that framed legislators' responses was their sense of responsibility for taking care of seniors as the most vulnerable members of society. When I asked about the factors in the decision-making process determining their support for the Financial Exploitation of the Elderly Bill, the vast majority of legislators made the normative response: that the elderly are a group deserving of political representation. Legislators linked their responses to their personal experiences and identities to explain their positions. Regardless of their race or gender, legislators expressed that they had a responsibility to protect the elderly. This feeling can be attributed to personal connections or moral compass.

Delegate Julissa Moore, a young delegate who grew up in a middle-class Prince George's County family, said that she supports protective legislation for the elderly because "seniors are our most vulnerable population. We are judged by how we treat vulnerable populations" (Personal interview, March 12, 2009). Similarly, Delegate Keira Miller, who grew up in a close-knit military family, posited, "We will be judged by how we take care of those who can least take care of themselves" (Personal interview March 12, 2009). Senator Imani Hayes, an emeritus professor, commented that she would likely support the bill because

> I think we should be doing everything we can to protect seniors; they have protected and provided for most of us all of our lives so whatever we can do, we should. There are a lot of scams out there, especially about this whole mortgage buy-back thing. I think what they are doing is exploiting senior citizens. So, whatever we can do to protect our seniors I think we have the right and responsibility to do it. I'll be out there doing that. (Personal interview, March 17, 2009)

Lastly, Delegate Justine Anderson, who was raised by her religious grandmother, also spoke about feeling responsible for protecting the elderly and pointed to her legislative record, saying "I've worked to protect our seniors. I've done that since I moved into Prince George's County—even before I became a legislator. I have worked to protect the elders and those who cannot protect themselves" (Personal interview, March 19, 2009). Delegate Anderson expanded on her advocacy efforts on the behalf of seniors both in her work as a union leader and as a community activist and concluded by noting, "One day I will be a senior and I want to be treated like I treat them. I will definitely vote for that bill" (Personal interview, March 19, 2009). All of these legislators seem to make this both a personal and political issue.

Similarly, White women legislators noted their support for senior citizens. Directly echoing the sentiments of the Black women, one senior White delegate said, "Lawmakers have a serious duty to protect the elderly. We are judged by how we take care of those who cannot take care of themselves. Seniors are a vulnerable population. My devotion to human and civil rights has actually increased because of my desire to protect the most vulnerable populations" (Personal interview, March 11, 2009). Similarly, another White delegate repeated her colleagues' sentiments that the bill was uncontroversial. A member of the Commission on Aging, she declared that she cared deeply enough for the elderly that she had specifically sought out membership on that committee. One long-term member of the Maryland House of Delegates also referenced her personal work with the elderly. She stated, "The elderly are being exploited so this bill is a no-brainer for me. It's something that we need to do. And I'm glad that I can be resource for the elderly" (Personal interview, March 19, 2009). In sum, legislators of all backgrounds were united in support of the bill.

As a sponsor of the bill, one White woman senator addressed criticisms of the bill, in the process reinforcing her support for this legislation. She said,

> We need to be careful that we are not force-feeding the bill and that we balance our end goal with the appropriate ramifications. However, this is not a controversial bill. It's a good bill. It boils down to this: Human beings are human beings and all deserve to be treated equally as long as they have earned that [based on their] treatment of others. It's my responsibility to see that the law protects those that cannot protect themselves, those that are vulnerable, and those that may not be treated equally. (Personal interview, March 17, 2009)

This senator was the only legislator in this sample not to explicitly reference seniors as a group that directly needs special advocacy. Her comments on equality and the necessity of the law to protect everyone, regardless of their social position, echoed throughout her interview. She concluded that this bill just made good moral sense.

African American male legislators also shared that they believed it was their legislative and moral responsibility to take care of senior citizens. For example, one middle-aged Black man said, "My whole theory in life is that there are two groups of people that I'm very concerned about. That would be the youth and the elderly. The old folks taught us and now we need to protect them. As a political mover and shaker, it's my responsibility; I have to make sure that I give back something to somebody" (Personal interview, March 19, 2009). Another younger Black male delegate boasted about his strong record for protecting senior citizens and shared that seniors in his district were among the largest demographic of people who had voted to reelect him: "Anything exploiting the seniors—I am going to be front and center making sure it doesn't happen. Seniors are the ones that helped me get to where I am today. I am heavily mentored by seniors in my community or in my fraternity, my neighborhood, and my church. Seniors know that they have a real voice with me" (Personal interview, March 18, 2009).

These legislators' protection of the elderly is based on a sense of responsibility to those who had once looked after them. The majority of legislators who I interviewed for this study felt that this bill was not controversial, and I noted no difference in opinion owing to gender, race, age, legislative tenure, or constituency. The legislators all represented the elderly as a group deserving of special advocacy. Black political identity was not deployed in their decision-making processes because this issue was neither implicitly nor explicitly racialized. However, as the next section indicates, this bill is gendered, since women are disproportionately tasked with the role of caregiver, although both men and women legislators expressed their support of this legislation because of their caregiving experiences with elderly relatives.

Personal Reflections

Some legislators drew personal connections to specific senior citizens—either because they themselves are seniors or were caretakers of elderly parents—making a direct association with the people this bill could help. Several mentioned their family commitments as the reason why they would support this bill. Specifically, legislators who had cared for elderly parents or managed their parents' finances championed this bill.

For example, one White male legislator spoke about feeling a personal commitment to this bill because he had witnessed his elderly mother's concerns over finances and the tormenting she had endured from her stepson. He shared the story of how his eighty-nine-year-old mother was asked by her stepson to sell her house to him after her husband died. He harassed the legislator's mother and had tried to pressure her into signing over the house to him. Because of his stepbrother's harrasment and realizing that his mother was in a vulnerable position after the death of her husband, this delegate decided to put his mother in an assisted living home and protect her savings:

> What I did was convert all her assets into tax-free bonds. She had no concept of handling money at all. She thought that she would run out of money before she died. I told her that was not going to happen—that I made sure she was in good shape. From this process I learned that the elderly need attorneys and accountants who will advise them. I told elders that I am there to help them. I've seen that within families—in families with stepchildren, that the elderly especially need financial advising. (Personal interview, March 16, 2009)

This delegate was the only male legislator of any race in my sample who said that he took care of an elderly parent, and it is interesting to note that he is the only legislator who reported taking financial responsibility for his mother's affairs. However, different from the African American women legislators I discuss later in this chapter and all of whom physically took care of their parents, this delegate moved his mother into an assisted living facility.

Delegate Ingrid Jefferson, a product of low-income family in Baltimore, for example, referenced her mother as the reason that she supports this bill. She stated, "I want you to know I take care of my eighty-six-year-old mother. I think the penalties should be as stiff as they can possibly be, in reference to our seniors" (Personal interview March 14, 2009). On her part, Delegate Yasmin Wood's observation of her father's deteriorating health led her to support this legislation. She explained, "I am very aware that the elderly change. I have a ninety-year-old father who lives with us. He is not the man he used to be. He needs more help" (Personal interview, March 18, 2009). As a part of the sandwich generation—people who support their children and care for their aging parents—Delegate Wood takes care of her five young sons in addition to her elderly father. Another African American woman senator spoke of how her parents suffered from dementia, leading her to support this bill. Senator Pamela Price, an entrepreneur from a middle-class Baltimore City family, is a former board member for Alzheimer's Association of Greater Maryland. She opined:

I believe victimizing the youth and the elderly is absolutely horrible and the exploitation either one of those extremes because it's almost the same population
except that one has a number of years. The older you get the more child-like you
become because you lose your faculties. Both of my parents had dementia and I
took care of both of them. I have also seen how people are victimized by [finan-
cial] scams on television. (Personal interview March 17, 2009)

These Black women legislators were or are currently are caretakers of elderly parents. None of the Black men or White women legislators detailed
that they were physical caregivers to their parents, nor did any of them
make direct connections between this bill and their parents' advanced age.
This finding is consistent with studies that indicate that, because of traditional gender roles, male caregivers are fewer in number than women caregivers (Applegate and Kaye 1993; Harris 1998) and the studies that I referenced earlier that point to cultural differences in how Black and White
families take care of elderly family members.

Delegate Tanisha Harold, a divorced mother of two adult children, has
direct experience helping a family member who had been financially exploited years before the bill was proposed. While lengthy, her story is important to read in its entirety; it explains particularly well the personal
connection that she feels to the legislation and how this experience aided
in her legislative decision-making process.

That bill is kind of personal. My mom died several years ago. I moved out when I
was really young. My mom had a stroke; she was about 72–73 years old. I was one
of the only children who would never move back home; but, when she had her
stroke my sister and brother had moved in with her and had been living there for
years and it didn't matter to me. The house was paid for and I figured they would
figure out how they were going to buy the food and pay utilities and all of that. I
knew that they weren't making a contribution. Once my mom had her stroke she
had to come and live with me because my house was all on one floor, she could get
her physical therapy. I knew I had physical therapist in my community. Everyone
called and wanted to volunteer their help, so, I had the best possible set-up for her.
However, as a citizen legislator, I had to go to work. And my sister was not working
so she was to come to my house every morning and watch my mom in the morning
and I would come home for lunch she would stay until I got home from work, and
then my sister would leave. But, she convinced my mother that I was so busy and
it was such a huge inconvenience that it was time to go home. I was very busy, but
I never let that show or neglected her. She said to me "you never sit down." That's
because when I get home I have a lot of stuff to do; she decided that she wanted to
go home. And my sister took her to an attorney without the rest of us knowing,
switched her checking account into my sister's name, who was unemployed and

was making no contributions to the household. Once all of this happened, I didn't know it and my mom was getting progressively worse. My mom decided she wanted to go to a nursing home; she told me but she didn't tell me why. I told my sister okay, we had a family meeting where all of us could decide, and that is when my sister told me she had power of attorney. I had social services come in to prove my mom was extorted. It was horrible; I still don't speak to my sister. I just cannot bring myself to forgive her; for years my mother took care of her. So, I know there are people out there that are doing that. I tried and go through the legal system, but, not everyone is authorized—you need power of attorney. I understand that bill. I lived that bill. (Personal interview March 17, 2009)

Delegate Harold's unfortunate story underscores the importance of legislation such as the Financial Exploitation of the Elderly Bill, which many other legislators articulated but did not have the sort of direct personal experience to render so clearly. Women's roles as caregivers are often portrayed as conflict free, as moments in which women join together in committed, shared devotion to taking care of the old and sick. Rarely understood is the social, emotional, physical, and economic costs associated with being the primary caretaker or the toll that caretaking takes on families. Delegate Harold's story illustrates the exhausting "women's work" of caretaking and how families can be torn apart by the stress of taking care of loved ones.

A feminist analysis of caregiving exposes how the character of extended families and broader communities has been created and maintained by both women's "first shift" (i.e., paid work) and "second shift" (i.e., housework and caregiving; Hochschild and Machung 1989; Wharton 1994). This labor- and gender-oriented approach illustrates that the work that women do as caregivers is undervalued both by society and in contemporary social policy (Gerstel and Gallagher 2001). While her story may be an extreme one, this delegate believed that government intervention might have halted some of the financial abuse that her mother experienced and alleviated some of the pain that her family experienced. Delegate Tanisha Harold strongly believes that if such a bill had been in place during the time of her mother's decline, her family might not have been saddled with the additional economic burdens caused by her sister's exploitation of her mother's resources.

CONCLUSION

While caregiving and issues surrounding the elderly are generally considered women's issues, none of the legislators in this study made an explicit connection to the Financial Exploitation of the Elderly bill as a feminist or gendered issue. Nor do any of the legislators bring up race or use a racialized framework as a factor in the legislative decision-making process surrounding this bill. As I have shown, caregiving can be constructed as both gendered and racialized, and it was surprising that neither gender nor race was incorporated into the legislators' analysis of the bill. Instead, legislators' ages, roles as caregivers, and—perhaps in some cases—their professional identities were primed in the discussion of this legislation. While some legislators were able to make specifically personal connections to senior citizens, either because they themselves were seniors, were caretakers of elderly parents, or were mentored by senior citizens, most of the legislators were able to identify whom this bill would help.

African American women legislators appeared in each of the thematic rubrics that articulated which factors influenced the legislative decision-making process in regard to the Financial Exploitation of the Elderly bill. Interestingly, none of the White male legislators expressed that the responsibility to advocate for and protect the elderly was a factor in their decision-making process. Perhaps because caregiving is a race-gender issue, White men do not view it as part of their legislative purview. Furthermore, only African American men and women stated that their own advanced ages made them more likely to support this legislation. While I interviewed several older White legislators—indeed, all of the White women I interviewed were over the age of fifty-five—the age of the legislator herself was not a salient factor for White legislators in discussions about this legislation. Only three legislators—one African American woman and two White men—expressed concerns about the necessity of the legislation and its usefulness. Black men and White women legislators did not articulate the same concerns. Because Black women are the only demographic group that appears in each of the four thematic categories of analysis, I conclude that Black women may have the most diverse cognitive framework for articulating their support for the Financial Exploitation of the Elderly bill.

Perhaps the most interesting factor here is the connection between African American women legislators and caregiving. Many of the Black women legislators have elderly parents who live with them or who have lived with them. Indeed, only this group shared that they are or have been their parents' primary physical caregivers.[1] While the legislators did not provide intimate details about their caregiving (e.g., the extent to which they cared for their parents by bathing them, taking them to doctors' appointments, feeding them, etc.), they did portray themselves as taking active roles in caring for their elderly parents. They did not institutionalize or place their family members in assisted living communities; instead, the parent or parents remain in the homes of the legislators and their families. Black women state legislators also do not explicitly disclose whether they control their elderly parents' finances. It cannot be assumed that they do not manage their parents' money, but based on the data I cannot conclude that the legislators do have a hand in their elderly relatives' finances or that the Black women legislators and their families decided that it was more fiscally advantageous to keep the elderly relative at home. For one, the elderly family member may not have medical problems that necessitate that he or she be cared for in a nursing home. For reasons to which I am not privy, these African American women legislators and their families decided to keep their elderly relatives in their homes and to assume a caregiving role.

Unlike the Religious Freedom and Protection of Civil Marriage bill, the Financial Exploitation of the Elderly bill enjoyed unanimous support in both chambers. While some legislators had reservations—such as a Senator Bailey Smith, who took issue with characterizing *all* elderly as vulnerable, stating "the part of the bill that is bothersome to me is the designated age of sixty-eight years old as warranting special protection. Some sixty-eight-year-olds are pretty swift—Bernie Madoff being one of them!" (Personal interview, March 13, 2009)—overall, the legislators felt a responsibility to protect what they regard as a vulnerable population. This is a marked difference from the legislators' views of the LGBTQ community as neither needing special advocacy nor as vulnerable. Seniors, however, are classified as a deserving group because of their status as a vulnerable population. Through no fault of their own and because of declining mental and physical abilities caused by the normal aging process, the elderly are susceptible to abuse. This population is often held in high regard for their past work in the community and for their ability to share tidbits of wisdom with younger generations (Mutran 1985).

In sum, while legislators did not use either a gendered or race-gender framework to articulate the factors guiding their decision-making process on the Financial Exploitation of the Elderly bill, they did incorporate other politically salient identities. I wish to go farther by arguing that elderly caregiving may, in fact, not be viewed as a women's issue bill among these legislators. Indeed, both men and women of all races and ethnicities unanimously supported this bill, and none articulated that race, gender, or race-gender were salient factors in their decision-making process. However, because the Black women legislators are most likely to serve as caregivers for their elderly parents, they have a more intimate and hands-on awareness about the beneficiaries of this bill and the consequences of failing to protect the elderly.

This supports the intersectional findings that caregiving is women's work and the idea that it is disproportionately Black women's work. While not explicitly referencing their identity, Black women demonstrate that their race-gender identities and experiences, illustrative of representational identity theory, influence their legislative decision making on the Financial Exploitation of the Elderly bill. Thus, representational identity theory assists us in the finding that African American women rely on their race-gender identities and experiences to choose which bills to sponsor and to understand the potential impact of legislation on both Black families and women.

CHAPTER 7
Conclusion

Only the BLACK WOMAN can say "when and where I enter, in the quiet, undisputed dignity of my womanhood, without violence and without suing or special patronage, then and there the whole *Negro race enters with me*."

    —Anna Julia Cooper, *in* A Voice from the South, *1892; emphasis in the original*

The colored woman feels that woman's cause is one and universal . . . not till race, color, sex and condition are seen as the accidents and not the substance of life . . . not till then is woman's lesson taught and woman's cause won—not the white woman's, nor the red woman's, but the cause of every man and every woman who has writhed silently under a mighty wrong.

    —Anna Julia Cooper, *in a speech at the World Colombian Exposition in Chicago, 1893*

African American women have a long history of advocating for equality, not only on behalf of African Americans and women but also as African American women who occupy a precarious position at the intersection of race and gender. For example, Dr. Anna Julia Cooper, teacher and principal of the M Street High School and a leader within the Black women's club movement, tirelessly spoke about the social and economic difficulties that African American women faced. Cooper pushed for Black men's equality and that of women of all races. She tied Black women's status in America to advocacy for the betterment of all Blacks and women. She urged society to make room for the contributions of Black women, to recognize the unique barriers and opportunities that African American faced, and to acknowledge the humanity of Black women. In many ways, the women of this study are carrying out Dr. Cooper's legacy by continuing to work with and struggle against White women and Black men to assert and acquire African American women's rights. Furthermore, both Anna Julia Cooper and the

African American women state legislators in this study illustrate how Black women draw from their personal experiences to make political claims.

I have sought to reveal how Black women legislators' interests shape policy debates on issues that disproportionately affect African American women, in the process giving voice to an underrepresented group. Elected Black women best represent the interests of all Black women. Black men and White women typically do not advocate for issues that are pertinent to African American women as strongly or at all. Nevertheless, although Black women legislators adopt largely uniform policy priorities, they propose vastly different identity-based policy solutions and deploy a specialized range of legislative tactics to achieve desired outcomes. African American women challenge an essentialist Black political identity, and my theorization of Black women legislators' political behavior uses representational identity theory to account for both the similarity and diversity within Black women's legislative decision-making processes.

Listening closely to the voices of Black women strongly supports my findings. In four different policy areas—the Minority Business Enterprise legislation, the Religious Freedom and Protection of Civil Marriage Bill, and the Financial Exploitation of the Elderly Bill, I found that the multiple identities Black women occupy were important explanatory variables. Moving beyond simply concluding that race and gender matters for African American women state legislators, I show that race and gender identity influences their legislative decision making and find that Black women Maryland state legislators use an intersectional approach to identity when they are proposing, developing, negotiating, or advocating for legislation that affects marginalized groups. Adding complexity to difference allows me to move beyond race, class, and gender to illustrate how generation, sexual orientation, motherhood status, nationality, and religious beliefs influence African American women legislators' political behavior. Rather than viewing political representation from an institutional vantage point, I have shown that accounting for identity as a factor in African American women state legislators' legislative decision-making processes lends credence to the idea that the women occupy an intersectional perspective. This finding adds nuance to and deepens scholarly understandings of how identity constructs or informs legislative behavior.

REVIEW OF FINDINGS

By combining humanistic and social science techniques, such as feminist life histories, elite interviews, and participant observation in conjunction with legislative case studies and bill sponsorship data, I have presented a fuller description of how identity informs Black women state legislators' descriptive and substantive representation. Linking personal narratives to political behavior, I have illustrated how Black women's lived experiences have influenced their legislative decision-making and policy preferences. Through a systematic exploration of the relationship between personal identity, community, society, and, by extension, political representation, *Sisters in the Statehouse* has demonstrated the inevitable influence of social forces on individuals and the influence of individuals upon the problems and solutions of the society they hope to make better. I connected *who* a legislator is with *what* she does, thereby demonstrating that a nuanced understanding of politically salient identities adds to a richer scholarly awareness of representation.

Data show that Black women pay the most attention to issues that disproportionately affect African American women. To examine how identity mediates the decision-making process I sought to identify legislation representing a range of issues that would provide several decision-making contexts within which to examine the role of identity. For example, I compared a controversial bill with a noncontroversial bill. I also focused on one cross-cutting issue and one consensus issue. As a cross-cutting bill, 2009 Religious Freedom and Protection of Civil Marriage Act, addressed a divisive issue among most constituencies, with African American legislators in particular and legislators in general divided on same-sex marriage. The 2009 Financial Exploitation of the Elderly Act was selected as the consensus issue; it was unanimously approved by both chambers and is currently law. I also investigated legislation to revamp and renew Maryland's Minority Business Enterprise program, a set-aside policy under which a percentage of government contracts are reserved for women and minorities. This legislation would have renewed the state set-aside program for minority business owners and allowed Black women to choose whether to be counted as women or as Blacks in a contract. Next, I investigated legislation that was introduced under the title of Denial or Dismissal of Domestic Violence Petitions: Expungement of Records. This bill included a proposal that would have allowed a respondent in a domestic violence protection order proceeding to request expungement of all court records relating to the proceeding if the petition requesting the protection order was denied or dismissed in the interim, temporary, or final protective order stage of the proceeding. Although this legislation generated extensive debate, it was not successful. Studying these bills allowed me to unearth how the intersection of race, class, and gender affect the decision-making process on the part of Black women legislators.

I found that identity plays an important role in shaping how legislators view both controversial and noncontroversial legislation. Black women legislators explained how their identities influenced their perceptions of these bills. I found that legislators are more comfortable in representing groups that are legitimately seen both socially and politically as needing special advocacy. Additionally, I discovered generational differences among Black women legislators that affect their policy preferences. Taken as a whole, these chapters present evidence that race-gender and other politically salient identities play an important role in debates within legislatures and in the decision-making process undertaken by Black women state legislators.

IMPLICATIONS

At the beginning of this book, I indicate that Black women's politics have normative implications for both representative democracy and Black politics. I detail that Black women legislators prove the necessity of moving past a binary approach to identity politics. My findings highlight an area that social scientists have traditionally overlooked in studies of Black women's political representation.

Theories of descriptive representation that keep identity constant over time and context fail to account for the substantive work undertaken by African American women legislators. While political science literature tends to treat identity as stable, feminist scholars have recognized that it is not fixed. Yet, feminist scholars such as Yuval-Davis (2012) push back against identity politics and the usefulness of intersectionality. As a remedy, I have sought to provide an example of how to theorize political representation when identities are not fixed in place but instead work together to advance group-based policy preferences. In dialogue with political theorists such as Mansbridge (1999), I show that diversity within deliberative institutions is healthy for democracy. This link hinges on how legislators perceive the effects of their identities on their legislative work. I connect Black women's life histories to their understandings of the importance of race-gender identities in their political decision-making and provide a nuanced explanation of how descriptive representation enhances substantive representation, in the process examining how an intersectional approach to legislative populations can improve scholars' understandings of political representation.

Lastly, this project adds to the scholarly understanding of the dynamics of race and gender within legislatures. Rather than utilizing primarily White women's or Black men's experiences as the sole basis for examining the benefits of descriptive representation, this project focuses on African

American women state legislators' experiences to examine how combined race-gender identities influence representation. Ultimately, this project helps build a fuller scholarly understanding of the importance of diversity among elected representatives. My contribution to a growing body of scholarship on Black women and representation acknowledges and evinces the complexity of identity while revealing a range of personal, social, and political factors as contingencies.

LIMITATIONS TO THIS STUDY

It is unlikely that I have convinced all readers of the legitimacy of focusing this study entirely on African American women who are Maryland state legislators. As in other studies of state legislative politics, it is difficult to generalize across states, since each state legislature has a different political culture (Haynie 2001; Weissert 2000). Yet I believe that much is to be learned from the African American women in the Maryland state legislature, given this legislature's unique and consistent history of large delegations of Black women legislators (Bratton, Haynie, and Reingold 2006; King-Meadows and Schaller 2006; Smooth 2001). Because I analyze only one state's legislature, I am able to make central my analysis of Black women legislators' voices, therewith providing detailed and in-depth analyses of the role of race-gender identities for Black women state legislators.

This book is not intended to be the final word on how race-gender identities influence Black women state legislators' decision-making processes. Instead, I hope to draw attention to the shortcomings of using an additive approach by showing that the variations in Black women's identities are missed when race, class, and gender are the only categories of analysis. My theory points scholars in a direction that helps accounts for the dynamism and nuance within groups to illustrate how difference affects legislative decision making. I find, in the process, that Black women's race-gender identities do indeed inform their political behavior—Black women bring their personal experiences into the statehouse. Yet I also find that race and gender are experienced differently by individuals and that scholars cannot therefore assume that Black women will behave as homogenous political bloc. Legislators' race-gender identities in fact become influential when a particular aspect of identity is primed in respect to specific bills. More research will be needed to see whether and when race-gender identity is deployed in other settings. We cannot assume that Black women will view all legislation through a race-gender lens, but it would be useful to fully examine the context around the theory that identity is neither constantly in flux nor static. My case studies demonstrate the plausibility of my theory, but my findings cannot be construed as proof that the theory will work in every legislative setting.

It is also possible that critics may take issue with the policy issues that I have chosen to form the core of this book. Like all researchers, I had to take advantage of the policies discussed in the state legislature during the period in which I conducted my fieldwork. The policies under discussion happened to be relevant to African American women and the Black political agenda. The selected issues were a mixture of "easy," meaning that they could be understood by voters regardless of their level of political sophistication, and "hard," requiring a sophisticated decision-making calculus leading to a reasoned attempt to use policy preferences to guide electoral decisions (Carmines and Stimson 1980). The legislation surrounding the Minority Business Enterprise program and the preventative domestic violence legislation was composed of hard issues. Same-sex marriage legislation and the financial exploitation of the elderly legislation were easy issues. Only marriage equality legislation was considered a "moral issue" in which "at least one advocacy coalition involved has portrayed the issues as one of morality or sin and used moral arguments in its policy advocacy" (Haider-Markel and Meier 1996, 333). Lastly, the legislation discussed in this book represents what might be referred to as "crystallized issues"—issues that have been on the political agenda for a long time (Mansbridge 1999). None of these issues could be called "uncrystallized," because "candidates have not taken public positions on them and political parties are not organized around them" (Mansbridge 1999, 643). The issues covered here show Black women legislators taking an active role in shaping debate.

FUTURE DIRECTIONS IN INTERSECTIONALITY RESEARCH

Scholars have begun to locate the intersection of race and gender—analyzing the importance of intersectionality—in descriptive and substantive representation (Garcia Bedolla, Tate and Wong 2005; Hardy-Fanta, Sierra, Lien, Pinderhughes and Davis 2005; Paxton, Kunovich, and Hughes 2007). This scholarship breaks from the additive and multiplicative approaches to studying Black women political elites, approaches that combine theories of race and gender but do not explore the ways in which race and gender interact to produce a new category for understanding identity, instead focusing on intergroup representation. While an intersectional approach to understanding the effects of both race and gender in representation is necessary, more research is needed to forge a stronger understanding of intragroup representation (Orey and Smooth et al. 2006).

My research advances the idea that scholars should explore the intragroup differences among Black women legislators. It points to the need to create models for empirically studying the ways in which difference is recognized within groups and not just between groups. While scholars have long advanced the notion that African American women as a group have aspects of identity that are informed by the intersection of both race and gender in their lived experiences that provide them with a unique worldview, it is necessary to go further and explore differences *among* Black women. For example, this research points to generational intragroup differences between Black women legislators. Other social markers such as experiences with discrimination, sexual orientation, and parental status are social identities that produce cleavages between Black women legislators in this study. These differences point to the need to create a variety of specific models. To fully utilize an intersectional approach to studying difference, scholars should investigate differences within groups while paying special attention to subgroup membership.

Finally, there are enormous benefits to incorporating an intersectional analysis into the study of political representation. Such an approach should delineate complexities in identity to further showcase how White males are the unmarked norm in American society in general and among political actors in particular. An intersectional approach would allow scholars of representation, not just scholars of women and Black politics, to investigate how Whiteness and maleness are privileged and examine the ways in which constituents' identities, and the identities of political elites, inform representation. Utilizing an intersectional approach to identity would ultimately problematize the idea of a static and monolithic American citizen. I agree with Ange-Marie Hancock, who asserts that "the goals of American democracy require us to integrate groups that are marginalized" (2004, 154). Similarly to other theorists (Williams, 1998) espousing that diverse voices are beneficial for deliberative democracy,[1] I find that the perspectives of marginalized groups contribute to the legitimization of political decisions reached through democratic deliberation. It is clear that many different forms of social diversity enhance the deliberative process and "that marginalized group perspectives constitute a dimension of pluralism which will contribute at least as much to the comprehensiveness of political decisions as any other" (Williams, 1998, 131). Marginalized groups may see things and understand social forces differently than the majority. This marginalized perspective on social forces may be extremely valuable for the formulation of good public policy (Cohen and Rogers, 1995, 42–43; Young

1997). An intersectional analysis can illuminate how the perspectives of marginalized group members demonstrate how social policy might be improved and how the social structures of inequality could be dismantled.

ADVANCING A NEW METHODOLOGICAL FRAMEWORK IN THE FIELD OF LEGISLATIVE STUDIES

Black feminist scholars have challenged both objectivity and truth claims while highlighting that projects that do not recognize differences such as race, class, gender, and sexual orientation—all of which exist on the margins—perpetuate a White middle-class bias (Hallam and Marshall 1993). As a feminist and an Afrocentric political scientist, I encountered challenges in using Richard Fenno's (1978, 2003) qualitative method to research state legislators when I first arrived in the field. Once I had begun my fieldwork in the Maryland state legislature, the project proved to be filled with racial and gender biases that would impact the outcome of my project. I found that my insider status as an African American woman and my outsider status as a social scientist led to a critical examination of both my research goals and methods. As result, I become highly self-reflexive in both processing and recording my observations and in understanding the narratives that legislators shared and how they shared their stories with me. As I have argued elsewhere (Brown 2012), Black feminist epistemology is a useful tool for making new knowledge claims within the existing body of knowledge within the race and representation literature.

My experience as an African American woman researcher situated within Black feminist epistemology, whose work centers on Black women Maryland state legislators, shaped my access to subjects and data interpretation. The points of information that legislators shared with me, my access to the legislators, the assumptions that they made about me, the gaps in conversation, and the contexts in which they shared about their policy positions were all mediated by my own identity. The prevailing paradigms and epistemologies in legislative studies are insufficient for fully assessing the multiplicities of identity-based politics. Because few legislative studies scholars employ feminist ethnography or other interpretivist methodologies for exploring legislative behavior, these studies lack both epistemological and methodological frameworks necessary for analyzing the existing power/knowledge relationships between the researcher, legislator, legislative staff, and constituents.

Feminist ethnographers have employed Donna Haraway's (1988) concept of "situated knowledges" to highlight the partiality and shifting nature of standpoint theory, which argues that knowledge is socially situated. They assert that marginalized groups are positioned to ask questions, are aware of and have a clearer view of what is going around them than non-marginalized groups, and that research on power relations should originate with the lives of the marginalized (Collins 1990; Haraway 1991; Harding 1991; Hartsock 2004; Smith 1974). Informed by standpoint theories, feminist ethnographers construct self-reflexive strategies for field research to make the often implicit processes of research explicit. The process of reflexivity, characterized by introspection and the willingness to learn about oneself, one's research purpose, and one's relationships with the social world, exposes the varied strategies confronted at the beginning of the research process (Naples and Sachs 2000). A Black feminist epistemology, which is grounded in Black women's experiences and cognitive styles, contends that those who are multi-marginalized draw from personal experience as insiders who are oppressed within their social order. Black women's distance from power enables them to critique the system. Turning to my own experiences in the Maryland statehouse and the benefits of using a Black feminist epistemology that prioritizes self-reflexivity, I can offer a different vantage point to power relations that illustrates how the field of legislative studies can profit from interpretivist methodologies.

During my fieldwork, I remained culturally conscious of the social structures that mediate knowledge production and of the fact that social identities are ever present in the research process. In sum, I was cognizant of the myriad ways in which identity can become salient in the research process. Research is an intersectional process, and I acknowledged that social structures created crossing lines and traversed inner workings of identity that allowed me to engage as an insider/outsider with legislators and within the Maryland state legislature to better understand how the "researcher's multiple and varied positions, roles, and identities are intricately and inextricably embedded in the process and outcomes of research" (Milner 2007, 389).

In the course of conducting the interviews, I found that the African American legislators were candid about the role that race plays in the legislative process. Indeed, all of the women of color with whom I spoke went into detail about the intersection of race and gender and its effects on representation.[2] Undoubtedly, my identity as an African American woman greatly contributed to their willingness to speak with me. Next, my identity also factored into the comfort and candor with which the legislators spoke about issues regarding race and gender. In sum, my identity added to what legislators told me and how they phrased certain culturally relevant ideas.

Interprevist methodologies were vital for this study because they allowed me to contextualize the experiences of the legislators and to better understand how my own identity became part of the data collection process. I paid special attention to the claim that one's racial and gendered identity influences what research subjects share with the researcher. My insider status granted me access to African American legislators to whom I am sure that I would not have gained if I were not a Black woman with connections to their culturally imbedded identities. My research experience was furthermore entangled with multiple systems of power based on gender, race, and age (Dowling 2000; Vanderbeck 2005). While my identity was privileged with legislators of color and women, it also had negative effects with White male legislators. In two instances, White male legislators on the Judiciary Committee actually turned their backs to me as they saw me approaching to ask for an interview.

My youthful appearance helped me garner more interviews. As a member of Generation Y or the Millennials (those born between 1981 and 2004), my age became a focal point for some staffers and legislators. For example, the 2009 chair of the Legislative Black Caucus of Maryland, a Black woman, instructed caucus members to "help the baby and give her an interview" because I was one of their own looking to further research on "us." The Legislative Black Caucus of Maryland chair served as my liaison to Black legislators. As a result of her urging, a few members of the Black Caucus personally introduced themselves and said that they would be more than happy to interview with me. Next, the narrative of being a "poor college student" and my appearance as a petite woman opened up additional spaces where legislators and their staff could connect with me. Numerous comments were made about my small stature: "What are you, a size 1?"; or, "I know you don't eat—your pants are falling off you"; and my favorite, "Baby, you look like you need a meal—you're an itty bitty thing." By providing lunch and other meals during my fieldwork, my "other-mothers" in the state legislature went beyond simply providing nourishment; they helped to provide access to their fellow legislators and explained specific details of the Maryland state legislature to which I otherwise would not have access. Because of my status as a PhD student—and later as an assistant professor—my size, and my age, both staffers and legislators granted me rare personal access in which we engaged in informal conversations about themselves, their families, and their experience in the legislature. During these conversations I naturally also shared personal information about myself. We began to build a rapport that led to my increased access to the legislators. My identity and self-presentation influenced how legislators interacted with me in addition to what they told me.

A reflexive understanding of identity is necessary for producing new insights into political phenomena. The effect of the race and gender of the researcher produces different outcomes in the process of data collection. Scholars must be cognizant of their own identity in preparing for, conducting, and analyzing research. This reflexivity exposes bias and advantages in how researchers understand the experiences, meanings, and politics of those whom they research. In this way, identity is doubly used as a lens to simultaneously explore power and social relations in a more complex manner than solely presenting findings on the identity of the researched. Studies that consider seriously the complexity of identity must also include how context affects the questions asked and answered, the ways in which subjects view the researcher, and how privilege and access are built-in markers of identity. This study illustrates the need for additional and more systematic research to investigate the ways in which the scholars' identities may impact what we know about legislative representation.

Next, this study raises questions about Black feminist ethics and the production of knowledge. A Black feminist ethic seeks to give voice to the concern of Black and minority women through a holistic feminist approach centered on caring and justice. As a Black feminist researcher, I seek to clarify obligations between me and the women in this study precisely because we are not paradigmatically equal. By removing the names and concealing some of the more personal narratives of the legislators in this study, the findings offer limited accessibility. I sought to carefully select the silences and chose how to present the legislator's stories. Although all their interactions with me were on the record—indeed, I had a tape recorder and took copious notes—in the vast majority of my interactions with the legislators and their staff, much of what was shared with me may not have been meant for public consumption. While the legislators knew that I was working on a research project that would one day be published, their interactions with me were often relaxed, familiar, and personal.[3]

The hypervisibility of Black women—meaning the prominence of Black women on the national, cultural, and political landscape—pushes Black feminists to reimagine how we present Black female subjects and voices. The hypervisibility of recent African American women political actors, such as Jennifer Carroll, Mia Love, Cynthia McKinney, Condolezza Rice, and Maxine Waters, marks a new period Black women's politics. Black women do not have agency over the ways that images of their bodies, politics, and representations are proliferated within American political discourse. Indeed, the hypervisibility of Black women politician's images resembles the stereotypical and controlling images of Black womanhood. Take, for example, Mia Love, the mayor of Saratoga Spring, Utah, congressional candidate, Republican, Mormon, daughter of Haitian immigrants, and stay-at-home mom. While heralded as a breath of fresh air for the Republican Party, Mia Love faces sharp criticism from opponents who see her as inexperienced and lacking a clear political agenda. Her identity is more complex than she is given credit for as a Black woman, and her image and politics are consistently diminished by challengers who say she is simply a Tea Party radical with little more than an anti-Obama platform. Local voters and national commenters alike find that she lacks a clear political message. In this way, she is stereotyped as an angry Black woman with little substance to back her anti-Obama rhetoric.

I made the decision to combat the hypervisibility of Black women politicians by providing my subjects some anonymity in this study. Because these women are also running for public office I sought to remove parts of their narratives that would jeopardize their relationship with constituents, colleagues, and their family members. I have sought to preserve a modicum of privacy in their very public lives. My adherence to a Black feminist ethic and the desire to provide a semblance of anonymity necessitates that I keep some very personal aspects of the legislators' narratives private. Thus, the findings that are presented in *Sisters in the Statehouse* are mildly sanitized.

The explication of my Black feminist ethic is to remind readers of the political component of knowledge production. The contextuality of knowledge production, the moral consequences of researchers' decisions, and the nature of the unequal relationship between the researcher and her subjects plays a significant role in Black feminist ethics. I have chosen to publically acknowledge my methodological constraints and choices to highlight the fact that some things will always remain absent in academic scholarship. The decisions of what to include and exclude naturally affects the final outcome of the research project. Therefore, I recommend that scholars honestly and openly disclose their own research ethics.

This discussion alerts scholars to a few necessary considerations in the reading and evaluating research interviews, particularly important for scholars who might be interested in using interpretivist methods to study the politics of identity. As a scholar, as with the individuals and populations that we study, there is only so much control that we have even over, our own identity. As such, interpretations based on our own researcher identity can affect us all, from the seemingly unmarked White man to the too-often othered Black woman. Future studies should consider methodologies that discuss the multiple facets of the researcher's identity, even if these may not provide the in-depth information that ethno-personal interviews yield.

Alternative Approaches

Expanding the focus to other policy areas would be helpful for more fully examining the effects of Black women's multiple identities on their legislative behavior. Given the present study's focus on domestic violence, marriage equality, minority business enterprise programs, and financial protection of the elderly, other policies that have a distinctly feminist or Black politics emphasis would be useful lenses through which to assess my representational identity theory. This inclusion of alternate lenses would more fully interrupt Mansbridge and Tate's (1992) finding that race sometimes trumps gender for Black women. Furthermore, the multiple identities of Black women and their own political objectives will illustrate the complexity of their policy positions.

Take for example legislation on reproductive justice or, more specifically, abortion policies. In 2010, the Georgia legislature saw the introduction of the OB/GYN Criminalization and Racial Discrimination Act (SB 529/HB 1155), which sought to criminalize providers who supposedly performed race- and sex-selective abortions. Chief among the statutes of this proposed bill was the probation of the abortion of a fetus based on race, color, or sex. This bill focused explicitly on women of color (and perhaps White women who were impregnated by racial/ethnic minority men) but most distinctly signaled out Black women and women of Asian descent. Several advocacy groups for women of color, reproductive justice advocates, feminist organizations, and pro-life groups organized to defeat this legislation. Undoubtedly, women legislators of color in the Georgia statehouse also used their race-gender identities as an experiential basis for their opposition to this legislation. Like marriage equality legislation in the Maryland statehouse, the bill before the Georgia state legislature produced strange bedfellows within African American politics. Here we saw coalitions of religious leaders, Black conservatives, and pro-life activists who mobilized around ending what they called "Black genocide."

Gesturing toward issues like this 2010 legislation in Georgia illustrates the complexity of Black women's positions on abortion. As state legislators continue to place abortion policies on their agendas, an intersectional approach will become even more necessary for understanding Black women legislators' policy positions. Furthermore, issues like abortion reveal the complicatedness of Black politics—namely, they expose the difficulties of an essentialist Black political identity. Similar to the findings on same-sex marriage in Chapter 5, African American women legislators have demonstrated diverse opinions abortion legislation. By potentially viewing abortion as a policy issue, I expect to find Black women legislators drawing from their identities and experiences as part of their decision-making processes. A simplistic view of Black women legislators as either pro-life or pro-choice distorts the complex legislative decision-making process and reduces the intricate ways in which Black women draw from their identities and personal experiences to arrive at difficult policy decisions.

Lastly, while conducting feminist life histories with the Black women Maryland state legislators, I heard many voluntary comments about their hair and how their decisions to wear their hair impacted how their colleagues and constituents viewed them (Brown, forthcoming). These remarks on hair were frequently coupled with comments about skin tone. The legislators' articulation of the politics of hair and skin tone points to a unique aspect of Black women's legislative experience. This culturally relevant expression of self is in fact a political matter for Black women state legislators in their efforts to interact with their colleagues in the statehouse and represent their diverse constituents, both of whom use hair as a political heuristic. Examining the multiplicity of Black women's identities and experiences will lead scholars to other topics, such as hair and skin color, that warrant a more complicated view of identity politics and Black women's political behavior than is currently common in scholarship.

SIGNIFICANCE OF FINDINGS

Theories of descriptive representation that keep identity constant over time and context fail to account for the substantive work of African American women state legislators. The connection between descriptive and substantive representation, in the case of Black women legislators, hinges on how such legislators perceive the effects of their own race-gender identity on their legislative work. I have extended the argument that descriptive representation influences substantive representation of race and gender groups by investigating differences within these demographic groups. Although I have shown that Black women legislators descriptively and substantively represent the interests of African American women, I revealed several distinctions within the legislative work of these legislators to provide a broader perspective that exemplifies how an intersectional approach can enhance our understanding of political representation.

Standing on the shoulders of Black women's studies scholars who investigate Black women's politics, such as Jewel Prestage and the foremothers of Black political activism such as Anna Julia Cooper, I have sought to draw continued attention to Black women's politics. *Sisters in the Statehouse* has made central the voices, experiences, concerns, and policy priorities of

African American women Maryland state legislators who, by sharing a similar race-gender lineage with Prestage and Cooper, make known the "messiness" of Black women's politics. Rather than neatly fitting within a discrete and tidy category of identity politics, the women in this study explode conceptualizations of a monolithic political identity. As a group, they share policy preferences but draw from their experiences and identities in different ways.

By making room for Black women's politics within the discipline of political science, along with other Black feminist scholars, I call for a deeper critical engagement with the intersections of identity politics and representation literature. Here we see the limitations of existing studies, which maintain race, gender, and class as a constant and fixed identity. The examination of the simultaneous effects of multiple identities on one's political behavior renders visible the complexities of group-based politics and the individual political objectives of African American women Maryland state legislators. My main assertion, that scholars need a more robust understanding of the role that identity plays in descriptive representation, must allow for the investigation of the complex role of intragroup identity politics in policymaking.

Identity is not static or one dimensional for Black women state legislators. Indeed, the ways that these women bring their personal experiences to the statehouse illustrates that race and gender identities do affect their political behavior but in a nuanced manner. Indeed, the powerfulness, complexity, and dynamism of Black women's representation pose bold challenges to a race-only or gender-only approach to political representation. These challenges to a collective Black identity and uniformity of Black women's legislative behavior invites scholars to ask new questions about our current understanding of race, gender, and the intersection of these identities as they affect the outcomes of legislators' political behaviors.

APPENDIX A

DATA COLLECTION

The data for this study come from fifty-one in-depth, semi-structured open-ended interviews that I conducted with Democratic Maryland state legislators in the spring of 2009 and from eighteen feminist life history interviews with Black women state legislators during the summer of 2011. During the 2009 legislative session I spent ten days in the Maryland state house. Later I spent two months in Maryland during the summer of 2011, collecting detailed life histories with the Black women state legislators. Because all the African American women legislators were Democrats, I interviewed only members of this party. Controlling for party identification also allowed me to highlight intragroup differences.

In 2009, I faxed and emailed all the Democratic legislators with a letter—written on university letterhead—requesting an interview. The letter broadly outlined my project and asked legislators to talk with me about their legislative decision-making process during a fifteen-minute interview. I conducted forty-nine of the interviews between March 11, 2009 and March 20, 2009. Over this time period I engaged in focused ethnography, which is characterized by short-term field visits steeped in data. There was, however, sufficient time to explore the questions posed in this project, and data saturation—the point at which I no longer heard or saw new information[1]–occurred at the end of my second week in the field. I conducted the majority of the interviews in person in the Maryland state legislature and two additional phone interviews on June 30 and July 2, 2009. All interviews were on the record and lasted from eleven minutes to one hour. The majority of the interviews lasted twenty minutes. I made detailed notes during every interview, which took place in various settings according to the legislator's schedule and accessibility. Most interviews took place in the legislator's office; however, I conducted several in committee meeting rooms and a few with legislators as they walked to or from meetings.

While I informed the legislators that their interviews were "on the record," I have replaced legislators' names with pseudonyms due to the candid nature with which some legislators engaged me in conversation. While it was impossible to remove all identifying information, I believe that the pseudonyms provide a healthy amount of anonymity for the women in this study. The pseudonyms allow readers to remember the subject from chapter to chapter as she appears in the different issue areas and via elements of common personal histories throughout the text. This method allows me to connect the threads between chapters and the larger theoretical implications and to present a cogent picture of the Black women in this study while maintaining analytical rigor.

I conducted interviews with all twenty of the African American women serving in the Maryland legislature. In addition, I interviewed a number of their Democratic colleagues. I chose these legislators based on gender and race, a selection that included five White women, thirteen Black men, nine White men, one Latina, one Latino, and two Asian American women. Qualitative methods are well suited for studying American state legislators. Unlike members of Congress, state legislators are available and willing to engage in in-depth interviews.

All fifty-one interviews were transcribed from audio to text by a professional transcriber, providing for greater accuracy of the interview data. I coded all the interviews based on themes that emerged from the transcripts and then looked for patterns from which to draw comparisons. I organized the interviews thematically by context and legislator identity once I had discerned distinct patterns. Because I was using the transcripts to thematically organize the interviews and to look for connections and disconnections, part of the process of coding simultaneously involved data analysis. This book is therefore based on my interpretation of the data and is shaped by my considerations about what stories to tell. I selected quotes from the recorded interviews, participant observation, biographies, and case studies that illustrate how Black women's identities aid them in the legislative decision-making process. The process of selecting quotes is a subjective element of the analytical process.

NARRATIVE AS METHODOLOGY

Identity narratives are instrumental for studying the key scenes, turning points, and pivotal episodes in an individual's life. The disciplines of sociology and psychology use relational models of identity processes to examine the social, cultural, and historical factors that influence a person's identity (Fivush and Haden 2003). The complex process in which an individual combines cognitive, emotional, and interpersonal factors that join together to facilitate change are often at the center of how she expresses, displays, and make claims about who she is. As a result, the self is never a unified or coherent; rather it is "multifaceted, composed of parts sometimes highly interdependent and sometimes not, some conflicting and some reinforcing" (Stryker 2000, 79). One's multiple aspects of identity may compete for representation in ways that may foreground certain elements of identity or push others into the background. An aspect of an individual's identity may reflect another, making both visible as mutually reinforcing identities (Stryker 2000). Every narrative identity illustrates how an individual makes sense of his or her life and the multiple factors that often lead to change. As such, people are likely to include events in their life narratives that led to an important change in their life (White 2009). My study was therefore designed to solicit representational narratives that made meaning from people's lives. Representational narratives are socially oriented and allow the individual to reflect on themselves and how their identity is defined or (re)created. Ochs and Capps state that "most narratives of personal experience function as a sense-making process rather than as a finished product in which loose ends are knit together into a single storyline" (2001, 15). It follows that personal narratives provide important information about the social construction of self.

I view the life history narratives as partial and subjective evaluations of events in the women legislators' lives. Their stories reflect the processes by which they have constructed events and their personal histories to fit into their own self-concepts (Mishler 1999). As a result, these narratives indicate what each woman believes to be an important point in her life, and I use these points to illustrate how these events, beliefs, and perceptions affect her legislative behavior. While feminist life histories cannot depict accurate facts and are in fact a portrayal of reconstructions and potential biases, they are instructive for viewing how a person makes sense of her life (White 2009). In analyzing the women's narratives, I pay special attention to the peak experiences, interpersonal dynamics, social, historical and economic factors that shape each women's identity.

I conducted the feminist life histories with eighteen out of the twenty African American women Maryland state legislators over the summer and fall of 2011. I call them feminist life histories because feminist theorists across several academic disciplines have argued for the importance of locating and historicizing the lives of women (Bell and Nkomo 2003; Collins 1990). The life histories provided me with valuable insight about how identity has influenced legislators' decisions and challenged me, as a researcher, to understand my subjects' current attitudes and behaviors and account for how they might have been influenced by previous decisions made in other times and places. In the course of these feminist life histories, the Black women state legislators whom I interviewed crafted their narratives by drawing on native imagery and representing cultural mores that are indigenous or organic to their own biographical, generational, cultural, historical/material, and geographical situations. I use these life histories to explore how identity matters in the legislative context and how legislators use identity to support, oppose, or champion legislation. In order to more fully explain the richness and complexity of the legislators' behavior, I used life histories and participant observation techniques to further investigate their narratives. Studying the legislators from more than one standpoint has increased the creditability and validity of my findings.

Feminist life history interviews rely on what the woman elects to disclose (Bell and Nkomo 2003; Berger 2004). Any narrative is a set of choices leading to a particular self-presentation, and subjects may decide to revise history by changing the ways in which they frame stories and seeking to alter how they may be perceived. To soften any potential bias, I place the women's narratives within a broader historical and cultural framework. The reliability of generalizations is thus unusually tentative.

Identity narratives are instrumental is studying the key scenes, turning points, and pivotal episodes in an individual's life. The disciplines of sociology and psychology use relational models of identity processes to examine the social, cultural, and historical factors that influence one's identity (Fivush and Haden 2003). The complex process of which an individual combines cognitive, emotional, and interpersonal factors that join together to facilitate change are often at the center of how an individual expresses, displays, and make claims about who they are. As a result, the self is never a unified or coherent, rather it is "multifaceted, composed of parts sometimes highly interdependent and sometimes not, some conflicting and some reinforcing" (Stryker 2000, 72). One's multiple identities may compete for representation in ways that push other identities into a significant or reserved position. Furthermore, an aspect of an individual's identity may reflect another aspect of her identity and make itself visible as mutually reinforcing identity (Stryker 2000). Every narrative identity illustrates how an individual makes sense of their lives and the multiple factors that often lead to changes in one's life. As such, people are likely to include events in their life narratives that led to an important change in their life (White 2009).

My study was designed to solicit representational narratives that made meaning from people's lives. Representational narratives are socially oriented and allow the individual to reflect on themselves and how their identity is defined or (re)created. Ochs and Capps state that "most narratives of personal experience function as a sense-making process rather than as a finished product in which loose ends are knit together into a single storyline" (2001, 15). It follows that personal narratives provide important information about the social construction of self.

I highlight themes in the legislators' narratives to illustrate the commonalities and differences in the women's experiences. Using closed codes, I searched the transcripts of the interviews for narratives of personal experiences, and then I examined the types of narratives and content. I found that the Black women state legislators in this study experience race, gender, and class differently but still use these social constructions as organizing principles for how they view both the world and legislation. To examine the role of context, I identified the settings in which certain aspects of a legislator's identities were primed. Legislators' narratives revealed that neighborhood, college, and family relationships were locations where their identities were constructed and where they often experienced situations that reinforced aspects of their identities. By allowing individual experience to illustrate how identity mediates legislative preferences, the Black women state legislators demonstrate that race, class, and gender are predominant—but not always equal—factors in their experiences.

As a result, the life histories have enabled me to situate legislators' verbal articulations of the legislative decision-making process in the broader context of identity politics and legislation. As a result, I am able to reveal how the legislators view and interpret their own life courses, which allows me to investigate the socially defined roles and events that a woman enacts over time. By capturing the subjective meaning of experience over the course of a person's life, I am better able to examine development within specific contexts and explain how outside factors have influenced the women's legislative decision making. Therefore, legislators' narratives, built on personal memory, are the starting points for my study. By focusing on Black women's narratives, this study yields valuable insights into the tropes of gender, race, and class that have defined the world in which these women became legislators.

BENEFITS OF QUALITATIVE METHODS

The benefit of case study analysis, as opposed to survey methodology, is the personal connection that is forged between the researcher and research subject. I was able to connect with the Maryland state legislators and their staff members on a one-on-one basis. These relationships led to legislators and staffers sharing their candid opinions and views on controversial legislation, politics, and interpersonal relationships among colleagues. Interpretivist methodology allows me to discern gaps between what legislators said and did, which opens up what I think of as hidden transcripts—critiques of power that play out offstage—that the power holders themselves neither see nor hear (Scott 1990), which skirt political correctness or social desirability. I also attended and, in a limited capacity, participated in committee meetings and hearings, caucus meetings, and delegation nights.

For example, I assisted the Baltimore City delegation with preparation for their delegation night. I worked along staff and interns to plan and organize the program. I also spoke with constituents and other Maryland government officials about the efforts of the Baltimore City delegation to improve community outreach among teens and young adults in the city. Additionally, when staff or interns were unable to assist legislators during community meetings, hearings, and caucus meetings I would often step in to help the legislators. Infrequently, I would relay information to their legislator's staff or colleagues about a particular bill. But more often, I would make sure that legislator was prepared and comfortable during these meetings. This meant that I would ensure that the legislator had a bottle of water or coffee and that she had her notes and other relevant information regarding a particular bill present during a meeting. While I participated more fully within Senator Raquel Simmons's office, I also spent a good deal of time with Delegate Justine Anderson and her staff. I assisted her staff in a limited capacity during a meeting with the Legislative Black Caucus of Maryland when Delegate Anderson was the chair of the caucus in 2009. Furthermore, I spent the last week of my fieldwork in the Judiciary Committee of the House of Delegates. I became friendly with the committee staffers and assisted them in their administrative day-to-day activities between conducting interviews with the members of the committee.[2] Such ethnographic data help to substantiate information provided through the interviews, roll call data, bill sponsorship and confirm or challenge the legislators' words and actions.

Indeed, interpretivist methods place meaning making at the center of analysis. Significant emphasis is placed on the humanity of the researcher and the research subject (Yanow and Schwartz-Shea 2006). The centrality of local knowledge is prioritized in interpretive research, similar to Donna Haraway's assertion that feminist scholars must undo the god trick by offering better accounts of the world that account for transcendence and the splitting of the subject and the object (1988, 190). I do not claim that this is an objective study; rather it is based on my partial view. As an African American woman interviewing African American women state legislators, I was able to avoid the position of research-as-stranger (Clifford 1986) because I am familiar with the cultural norms and meanings that are common to Black women. Black feminists assert that African American women have a shared historical reality based on the dual subordination of both race and gender. This subordination enables a clearer understanding of the relationships among systems of oppression (Collins 1990). Therefore, the marginalization of Black women, as members of a specific group characterized by their gender and race, creates a shared experience. Black feminists argue that there is a complex dual relationship in both Black culture and the dominant culture that Black women have to negotiate in their daily interactions (hooks 1984). Thus, as a Black woman researching Black women, I was considered a racial and gendered insider.[3]

During interviews, Black women were comfortable making culturally based statements. As a result, we engaged in what Few, Stephens, and Rouse-Arnett refer to as "sister-to-sister talk," defined as "Afrocentric slang to describe congenial conversation or positive relating in which life lessons might be shared between Black women" (2003, 205). Engaging in sister-to-sister talk requires a form of cultural competence that mandated that I adopt an approach that "both reflect[s] and respect[s] the values, expectation[s], and preferences" of the Black women Maryland state legislators (Pinderhughes 1989, 163). The legislators' candid conversations about identity and political representation were peppered with cultural references and sister-to-sister talk, and I attribute the legislators' openness to our shared racial and gender background.

Even with the use of sister-to-sister talk, my experiences within the Maryland state legislature indicate the complexity of insider/outsider status. As a "native researcher" I was cautious not to exaggerate this familiarity, as one cannot assume a homogenous culture (Moffat 1992). In the United States, where race-based group membership is a salient part of one's sociopolitical identity, insider status is still constituted by other factors that may make race a secondary consequence. "Thus, the meaning and impact of racial difference are complicated by age, class, accent, education, national origins, region, as well as sexuality" (Winddance Twine and Warren 2000, 9). As intersectionality scholars argue, Black women's identities are more complicated than the realization that race, gender, and other categories coincide (Hancock 2003; Jordan-Zachery 2007; Simien 2006; Smooth 2001). Identity is fluid and, at times, also fixed because it is primed by context and situation. As a result, simply sharing the same race and gender as the Black women state legislators did not guarantee that I would be able to gather more data from them than another researcher (Few et al. 2003). Indeed, I had access to different data because of my shared/overlapping identities with the legislators (Brown 2012).

I was aware of the differences—or nuances of identity—based on generational, parochial, economical, and motherhood status between the Black women legislators and myself, and, as a nonpolitical elite, I was cognizant of my outsider status as an ordinary citizen. Lastly, as a New Jersey resident, I was not seen as an insider in the way a Maryland denizen—and therefore familiar with the intricacies of Maryland politics—would be. These differences illustrate that one can be an outsider even when conducting fieldwork in one's own racial/gender in-group. As a result, Moffatt's claim that identifying with "them" does not necessarily mean "you are like them, or that they are like one another, or that they all trust or identify with you, or that they want to be studied by you" (1992, 207). My insider status as an African American woman could only take me so far.

The women whom I interviewed are, after all, politicians and therefore given to crafting carefully measured responses that shift subtly from one audience to another. There can be a gap between what a legislator will say on the record and what she believes. Indeed, as Smooth (2001) asserts, self-reports may never tell the entire story of legislative influence. There is also often a gap between how legislators see themselves and how their colleagues view them, regardless of the measured outcomes of their legislative success. The tactics of self-representation that these Black women legislators employ do not necessarily represent prevalent norms for all the Black women legislators who fall within the purview of this study. Self-reports also do not illustrate clearly how self-representation affects various Black women's legislative initiatives. Despite these limitations, however, exploring Black women legislators' views of how their identity mediates their legislative decision making is a useful model for scholars who are working to understand how the race-gender identities of legislators intersect to influence representation.

Little has been written on local political women, although the study of local political leadership is vital to political science. Trounstine (2009), for example, finds that examining politics at the local level should be integral to political science since many of the decisions made at the local level influence national politics. Thus, I argue that it is prudent to study local politics as a starting point; this allows scholars to understand both the political and sociodemographic contexts that influence and structure political behavior. By examining the Maryland state legislature, I am able to empirically examine the relationship between Black women's identities and their legislative behavior.

Structure of the Maryland State Legislature

The Maryland legislature is highly professionalized (high salary, large staff, longer session) and comprises part-time representatives who dedicate an annual ninety-day period to law making. Maryland's political culture is regarded as akin to that of a business because individual legislators broker deals and orchestrate political favors (Elazar 1972). While the party structure is highly organized, legislators have the ability to act as individuals, especially in policy areas in which they have specialized knowledge (Smooth 2001). Maryland's short legislative session requires a structure that facilitates lawmaking at a relatively quick pace. Delegates have only ninety days to act on over 2,300 pieces of legislation, including the state budget. As a result, Maryland has a highly organized committee structure, and leaders in both chambers are responsible for assigning other members to serve on committees. The members must elect the president of the Senate and the speaker pro tempore in the House of Delegates. The speaker pro tempore is an African American woman, Delegate Olivia Jenkins. The deputy speaker pro tempore is Delegate Abigail Watson, also a Black woman. Maryland is currently the only state in the nation to have Black women serving in this capacity.

The Democratic Party controls both legislative chambers and the executive office. The party head easily confers influence within the Democratic majority in the state legislature. The party whips, deputy whips, floor leaders, and deputy floor leaders reward and punish legislators according to their willingness (or lack thereof) to follow the party line. Alongside and in addition to party leadership, the Maryland legislative structure is comprised of county delegations made up of caucuses representing the state's twenty-four counties. The county delegations also have an elaborate leadership structure. They work to secure powerful committee assignments and leadership roles within the legislature for their members. These delegations wield legislative power because they essentially serve as brokers for individual counties, bringing back goods and services to the legislators' individual districts. There are seven standing committees within the House of Delegates. Delegate Bella Campbell, a Black woman, was the chair of the

Rules and Executive Nomination Committee until her death in 2013. There are six standing committees in the Maryland State Senate. An African American woman, Senator Brenda Perry, is chair of the Education, Health, and Environmental Affairs Committee. In this position since 2007, Senator Perry is responsible for many "firsts." She is the first African American, the first woman, and the first Black woman to chair a standing committee in the Maryland state legislature.

Maryland enjoys a highly organized caucus system. The Women Legislators of Maryland was founded in 1969 and holds the distinction of being the first women's legislative caucus in the United States. Currently, women comprise 28 percent of the lower chamber and 23 percent of the Senate. African American women consistently serve in leadership positions within the women's caucus—indeed, all of the 2012 committee chairs are Black women and the president is an Asian American woman. The caucus has an executive director, several committees, and is bipartisan. Next, with forty-three current members, the Legislative Black Caucus of Maryland is one of the largest groups of Black legislators in the United States. Founded in 1970, the caucus was established to act as a legislative body for the Black community. The current president of the Legislative Black Caucus is Delegate Julissa Moore, an African American woman. Like the women's caucus, African American women also enjoy several leadership positions within the Black caucus. The key positions held by African American women within the Maryland state legislature indicate that they are incorporated into the leadership structures of the institution (King-Meadows and Schaller 2006).

Maryland state legislators serve a term of four years in the lower chamber. Members of the Maryland Senate are elected every four years, in off-year elections in the middle of four-year terms for presidents of the United States. All 188 lawmakers faced election in the fall of 2010, including Governor O'Malley, a Democrat. The elections are not staggered but rather, all 47 Senate and 141 House of Delegates seats are up for election on a cycle of every four years.

Demographics of the Maryland State Legislators

Among Maryland state legislators serving in the 2011 session, none of the Black legislators were without a high school degree, and White males were the only group that did not have any members with a doctorate. Overall, both Black men and Black women have higher educational levels than White legislators in the Maryland State Legislature. Lastly, only one-half of the Black women attended a historically Black university or college (HBCU) for some aspect of their schooling, compared to Black men, who received their degrees from HBCUs in larger percentages; Maryland is home to four HBCUs: Bowie State University, Coppin State College, Morgan State University, and University of Maryland, Eastern Shore. Both Morgan and Coppin are in Baltimore. The majority of legislators who attended a HBCU attended Morgan State University or Howard University, which is located in Washington, DC.

NOTES

1. The terms African American and Black are used interchangeably throughout this book. As such, the term Black is used as a proper noun in recognition of a specific cultural group. To that end, I have chosen to capitalize the "B" in the word Black. Currently, both terms are used to refer to people of African descent living in America. However, there is one legislator in this study who is an Afro-Jamaican immigrant. It is not my goal to reduce the complexity of diasporic identities; thus this legislator is only referred to as Black in this study.
2. By marginalized, I mean the relegation of a group to an unimportant or less powerful position within a society.
3. By identity, I mean the social categories in which an individual claims membership and the personal meaning with which a person imbues these categories (Ashmore, Deaux, and McLaughlin-Volpe 2004).
4. The Combahee River Collective has been credited with coining the term "identity politics," which they defined as "a politics that grew out of our objective material experiences as Black women" (Harris 2001, 300).
5. See Harris (2009), Johnson (2003), and Thompson (2010) for challenges to essentialist notions of Blackness.
6. I do not include an Afro-Latina in my list of Black women Maryland state legislators. This delegate was born in the Dominican Republic. Although she is a member of the Legislative Black Caucus of Maryland, she self-identifies as Latina. She is, however, included on the National Organization of Black Elected Legislative Women's roster and is listed as Hispanic (only) on the Center for American Women and Politics roster. This example points to the difficulties of studying race and ethnicity as mutually exclusive categories in Black politics.
7. Previous research has shown that women are more likely to run and win in multi-member districts than in single member districts (Carroll 1994; Diamond 1977; Sanbonmatsu 2002), which helps to explain the prevalence of women lawmakers in the Maryland state legislature.
8. The majority of Black members represent Baltimore County, Baltimore City, and Prince George's County. While there are a very few Black legislators who represent districts in Montgomery County and Princess Ann County and liberal White legislators who represent Baltimore County, Baltimore City, and Prince George's County, the majority of Black legislators represent majority–minority multimember districts. According to the 2010 Census, Baltimore County is 64 percent White, 26 percent Black, 5 percent Asian, and 4 percent Hispanic. Its population is 805,029. While Baltimore County is considered suburban, the towns and

municipalities closest to Baltimore City, located in Baltimore County, resemble inner cities. The 2010 Census counted 620,961 Baltimore City residents. Demographically, Baltimore is a majority-minority city with 63 percent Blacks, 29 percent White, 2 percent Asian, and 4 percent Hispanic. Baltimore City is commonly spoken of as having two sections: east and west. East Baltimore is a largely Black community with low-income neighborhoods. West Baltimore is more diverse, its population ranging from middle- to upper-class African American neighborhoods, low-income White neighborhoods, Jewish neighborhoods, and pockets of Black poverty. Baltimore City has also enjoyed two African American women mayors: Sheila Dixon (2007–2010) and Stephanie Rawlings-Blake (2010–present). As of 2010, Prince George's County, Maryland, has a population of 863,420 and is the wealthiest county with an African American majority in the United States (Howell 2006; Chappell 2006). The county is currently 19 percent White, 64 percent Black, 4 percent Asian, and 15 percent Hispanic. Fifty-four percent of the county's firms are owned by African Americans and the median income is $70,647. The county is divided into five sections: North County, Central County, the Rural Tier, the Inner Beltway, and South County. The Inner Beltway is majority African American; Central and North County also have a large population of Blacks. Bowie, the county seat located in Central County, is 48 percent White.

9. As of 2013, the Baltimore City delegation in the House of Delegates has eighteen members, eleven of whom are African American. The Baltimore City delegation in the Senate has six members, five of whom are Black. Moving to the twenty-one-member Baltimore County delegation in the House of Delegates, there are three African Americans. The Baltimore County delegation in the Senate comprises eight members, of which only one is African American. The Black legislators in Baltimore County all represent District 10. The largest contingency of African American legislators is found in Prince George's County. Of the eight-member Prince George's County delegation in the Senate, three are Black. The Prince George's County delegation in the House of Delegates has twelve African Americans.

10. Asian American and Latina legislators were removed from this analysis because of their small numbers in the Maryland state legislature.

11. Completely reliable statistics on Asian Americans serving in state legislatures are difficult to obtain, since few were serving outside Hawaii; most states did not list Asian American as a separate category, instead lumping them with other minorities under "Other." This estimate is based on data from California, Colorado, and Hawaii state legislatures.

12. Estimate is based on Prestage (1977); no Hispanic or Native American women state legislators at that time.

CHAPTER 2

1. Only one woman practiced Catholicism.
2. The other serves in the Georgia state legislature.
3. Delegate Baker has been estranged from her wife for a number of years. She is currently in a long-term committed relationship with another woman.
4. While she has been separated from her wife for many years, Delegate Baker was unable to divorce her because neither currently lives in Vermont, which is a state requirement. However, Maryland courts recently decreed that same-sex couples could be divorced in the state even if they were not married in the state, which opens the possibility for a divorce.

CHAPTER 3

1. Self-categorization theory can also be problematic. Visible identities or external labeling is, most of the time, unavoidable. The color of one's skin, texture of hair, thickness of lips, nose, and hips are marked cues of overt physical otherness in the American context. So are language and cultural practices. However, these attributes are easier to change than physical traits. Gender and visible manifestations of biologically sexed bodies are often also hard to disguise. The somatic "othering" of bodies by external factors creates group boundaries either imposed, self-selected, or both. The main issue, however, is that choice in identity acquisition is not as readily available among members of low-income-status groups (see McKenna and Bargh, 1998). These less permeable groups are theorized as having an internalized group identity. This category of individuals are "united by some common characteristic" apparent to outsiders and a group in which members "are aware of their similarities" and define themselves on that basis (Jenkins 1996, 23). Identity choice is as significant as identity formation because "membership in a group shapes and influences an individuals' identity" (Huddy 2001, 141). To illustrate, McKenna and Bargh (1998) have found that "individuals with a strong identity as a member of a marginalized group (e.g., sexual and political) are more likely than those with a weak identity to accept their identity, share it with friends and family, and feel less estranged from society when they participate in a group-related electronic news group" (Huddy 2001, 146). However, other scholars have found that identity can be and is performed by low income or low status groups. For example, Ballroom culture, a Black and Latino/a queer community in North America, use performance to create performance to engage in HIV/AIDS prevention (Bailey 2009).

CHAPTER 4

1. HB 1181 was one of the many pieces of domestic violence legislation considered during the 2009 legislative session. This bill was heard during the same time period in which Governor O'Malley's introduced two proposals, one of which would allow the authorities to confiscate guns from the subjects of protective orders and the second that would enable those seeking protective orders to carry handguns. Both state legislators and women's rights activists viewed the domestic violence legislation introduced as contradictory.
2. Out of five White women who were interviewed.
3. Court records—including those relating to a domestic violence proceeding—that are maintained by a court are presumed to be open to the public for inspection. Generally, a custodian of a court record must permit someone who appears in person in the custodian's office to inspect the record. The Maryland State Judiciary's Web site also includes a link to a database that provides public internet access to information from case records maintained by the judiciary. Maryland District Court traffic, criminal, and civil case records and Maryland circuit court criminal and civil case records are available. Records can remain in the database indefinitely and are not removed except by court-ordered expungement. Subject to certain exceptions, a court record that is kept in electronic form is open to inspection to the same extent that the record is open to inspection in paper form. In September 2008, there were 1,667 final protective orders that were denied or dismissed for various reasons (e.g., denied because the petitioner could not meet

the burden of proof or the petitioner was not a person eligible for relief under the statute or dismissed because of a lack of personal jurisdiction, lack of service, the petitioner failed to appear, or the petitioner requested dismissal). In October 2009, there were 1,288 final protection orders denied or dismissed, and in December 2008 there were 1334 final protective orders denied. Senate Bill 467/ House Bill 1181 (both failed) would have provided for the expungement of court records relating to domestic violence protective order proceedings if a domestic violence petition was denied or dismissed.

4. A court order (a temporary restraining order) can be denied or dismissed, and, consequently, a final protection order (a permanent restraining order) will not be issued. However, this case will remain on the Judiciary's Web site. A person's name would be publically accessible and linked to a case regardless of its final outcome. If passed, the bill would have removed the domestic violence court records if a domestic violence petition was denied or dismissed. Although this legislation generated extensive debate, it was not successful. Indeed, HB 1181 was defeated on its third reading. The temporary protective orders, which judges grant after hearing only from the accuser, do not often materialize as final protective orders. If a final order is not granted, proponents of the bill would like the record to be expunged from the public record of court hearings.

5. While Cohen's (2010) and Simpson's (1998) scholarship on the political preferences of post-civil-rights generation of African Americans are instructive for framing the theoretical expansion of Black political identities, these studies focus on the political opinions of Black youth (either college students as in Simpson's work or Black youth ages eighteen to twenty-five in Cohen's work). Gillespie's (2010, 2012) and Williams's (2001) work is more closely related to this study because it deals directly with elected officials who were born in the decades directly after the civil rights movement.

6. The first wave of Black politicians achieved electoral success directly after the Voting Rights Act of 1965 during the time period 1965–1988. The second wave of Black politics is characterized by the prevalent use of a deracialized campaign strategy during the late 1980s and early 1990s, such as the mayoral races of David Dinkins (New York City), Norm Rice (Seattle), John Daniels (New Haven, Connecticut), Chester Jenkins (Durham, North Carolina), and Douglas Wilder for governor of Virginia (Gillespie, 2010, 142).

7. The two generations prevalent in this study are also often called the baby boomers (boomers) and generation X or gen X-ers (www.census.gov). For the purposes of this research, I classify boomers' birth years as beginning in 1940 and ending in 1960. Generation X birth years begin in 1960 and end in 1980. Boomers were profoundly affected by the Vietnam War, the civil rights movement, the Kennedy and King assassinations, Watergate, and the sexual revolution (Bradford 1993). This cohort witnessed political, social, and religious upheaval that resulted in a lack of respect for and loyalty to authority and social institutions (Kupperschmidt 2000). This cohort also feels the pressures of taking care of their aging parents and their own children (Kupperschmidt 2000). Gen X-ers grew up with "financial, family, and societal insecurity; rapid change; great diversity; and a lack of solid traditions," which caused them to have an increased sense of individualism over collectivism (Smola and Sutton 2002, 365). This cohort grew up in homes in which both parents worked (Karp, Sirias, and Arnold 1999) or with only one parent due to increased divorce rates (Kupperschmidt 2000). This has forced gen X-ers to turn to small enclaves of friends for support although they

value a stable family (O'Bannon 2001). This group is untrusting and cynical, as they are influenced by MTV, AIDS, and worldwide competition. This group is comfortable with technology. Because this group is the most diverse generation in American history, gen X-ers believe in emphasizing similarities rather than differences (O'Bannon 2001).
8. Third-wave feminism, which began in the 1990s, does not overlap with the above-mentioned terms. This particular wave of feminism is informed by post-colonial and postmodern thinking. Third-wave feminists have challenged the stabilization of cultural constructions of gender, sexuality, heteronormativity, the body, as well as the notion of universal womanhood. However, I am hesitant to apply the label of third-wave feminists to the younger Black women legislators.
9. According to the 2010 census, Prince George's County is 64 percent Black and 11 percent Hispanic. Prince George's County is the seventieth most affluent county in the United States by median income for families and the most affluent county in the United States with an African American majority.

CHAPTER 5

1. As of December 23, 2013, same sex marriage has been legalized in 17 states (CA, CT, DE, HI, IA, IL, MA, MD, ME, NJ, NM, NY, RI, UT, VT, and WA) and the District of Columbia.
2. July 2012 polling by Public Policy Polling has found that 57 percent of likely Maryland voters said that they would vote to support same-sex marriage and that only 37 percent said that they would oppose the law. African Americans are almost 30 percent of the state's population and a larger percentage of the electorate than anywhere outside the Deep South. A late October 2012 poll conducted by the *Washington Post* found that 42 percent of African American voters support marriage equality and 53 percent oppose it. There is a noticeable racial divide among Democrats. While 76 percent of White Democrats favor same-sex marriage, support is at 40 percent among Black Democrats (Wagner and Craighil 2012).
3. To be sure, the Black community is not monolithic, meaning that it does not hew to a single viewpoint or ideology, and it is not necessarily against marriage equality. Unlike other American citizens, however, many Blacks view the fight for marriage equality through the lens of race. Indeed, African Americans have a recent institutional memory of *Loving v. Virginia* in 1967, which centered on race and marriage. By uniquely tying same-sex marriage legislation to the memory of the de jure prohibition of interracial marriage and to conversations about civil rights on one hand and Black religiosity on the other, many African Americans view struggles for marriage equality as akin to their own struggle for full inclusion in the American polity, whether they are for or against same-sex marriage. This racialized view of marriage equality was perhaps most readily seen in the ad campaigns prior to North Carolina's 2012 Amendment 1 debates, in which both sides compared controversy about same-sex marriage to Blacks' struggle for civil rights. Black political elites, religious leaders, and average citizens were united in a race-based framing of this issue although they were divided in their opinion of same-sex marriage.

4. In turn, I must extend the same complexity to LGBTQ identities by not presuming that same-sex marriage is priority for the totality of this group.

5. There is no presumed overlap among the groups by the legislators. Of course, this is a fallacy, as one can identify as both Black and queer.

6. Policy "sends a message about what government is supposed to do, which citizens are deserving (and which not), and what kinds of attitudes . . . are appropriate in a democratic society" (Schneider and Ingram, 1993, 334). As legislators are single-minded reelection seekers and strive to produce good policy (Fenno 1973; Mayhew 1974), they anticipate the political implications of supporting policy that impacts a specific target population. Legislators' understandings of social constructions of target populations, in turn, determine how they assess policy.

7. It is not assumed that the majority of the LGBTQ community favor same-sex marriage. Indeed, this group is also heterogeneous, with group members of varying opinions on this legislation (Polikoff 1993; Soule 2004).

8. However, Andrew Kohut of the Pew Research Center contends that opponents of same-sex marriage are much more politically active than its supporters. There is a great deal of mobilization and political engagement among the opposition. In contrast, its supporters are less likely to be single-issue voters. For example, North Carolina's Amendment 1 passed with just 34 percent of the state's eligible voters weighing in on the amendment to the state constitution making marriage between a man and woman the only legal union recognized by the state. Exit poll data revealed that Black North Carolinians supported the constitutional ban by a two-to-one margin. While opposition to same-sex marriage has decreased in the Black community in recent years, the outcome of North Carolina's May 8, 2012 vote underscores the conservatism of many African Americans on this issue.

9. The values of freedom and allegiance to God are an integral part of the Black sacred cosmos undergirding the Black church.

10. Specifically, Black clergy have used six verses of the Bible to oppose homosexuality and reinforce heterosexism. "Genesis 1–2, 19:1–9; Leviticus 18:22, 20:13; 1 Corinthians 6:9; Romans 1:26–27; and 1 Timothy 1:10 have been interpreted as evidence that homophobia and heterosexism are scripturally normative" (Miller 2007, 52).

11. It is important to make note of the diverse beliefs of African American religious leaders on same-sex marriage—some high-profile Black pastors have recently made public pronouncements in support of marriage equality. On May 16, 2012, Reverend Jesse Jackson urged President Obama to push for federal equal rights for same sex LGBTQ marriage. Reverend Delman Coates of Prince George's County, Maryland, also supported same-sex marriage and creating equal protection under the law for all citizens. By contrast, Reverend Emmett Burns, a Baltimore minister and member of the state legislature, is an active opponent of marriage equality. In an interview with CNN, Burns, who had campaigned for President Obama in 2008, expressed his outrage over Obama's decision to support marriage equality and forecasted that the president would be defeated over this issue in his November 2012 bid for reelection. Reverend Burns announced that he "love[s] the president, but . . . cannot support what he has done" (Gilgoff 2012). Similarly, Reverend Derek McCoy, executive director of the Maryland Marriage Alliance and an African American minister, chided lawmakers for failing to follow the will of the people, noting that his organization has collected over two-thirds of the

required signatures to put the referendum on November's ballot (Siegel 2012). While many other Black religious leaders are now publically agreeing with Obama in their assessment of LGBTQ rights as a matter of equality, others maintain that same-sex marriage goes against their religious beliefs. Delegate Emmett Burns, an African American Maryland state senator who represents a district in Baltimore County, ignited a wave of controversy on August 29, 2012, when he sent a letter to Steve Bisciotti, owner of the National Football League team the Baltimore Ravens, protesting a player's open stance in support of same-sex marriage, urging him to "inhibit such expressions from your employee and that he be ordered to cease and desist such injurious actions" (Rosenwald 2012). Burns's letter was written in response to a 2011 YouTube video posted by Baltimore Ravens linebacker Brendon Ayanbadejo, in which the football player spoke in favor of marriage equality and urged Maryland voters to support the initiative on the November 2012 ballot. Burns's letter to Bisciotti elicited an aggressive, witty, and profane written response in support of Ayanbadejo and same-sex marriage from Minnesota Vikings punter Chris Kluwe, which was posted on Deadspin.com and later picked up by both the *New York Times* and the *Washington Post.* The national fall-out from Burns's comments illustrates the timeliness of this study. It also indicates that there is a shift within the dominant culture regarding same-sex marriage that radiates to a variety of cultural institutions, including the NFL and the Black church.

12. The Don't Ask, Don't Tell Act that prohibited openly gay men and lesbians from serving in the military exemplifies the exclusion of LGBTQ individuals from the accepted national identity. The dominant rhetoric was that gays in the military would undermine the armed forces because gay men possessed feminine traits (i.e., submissiveness, compassion, passivity, and weakness) that would be a direct threat to national security (Adam 2003). Debates about LGBTQ soldiers in the military were associated with other national projects that sought to link outsiders with imminent risk to national security. Gendered norms dictate that masculinity encompasses strength, dominance, aggression, and compulsory heterosexuality. Any deviance from these expectations results in a person being less "manly." Similarly, the integration of women and African Americans into the military was also directly associated with fears about America's national identity and undermining constructions of masculinity as embodied by the military (Adam 1998).

13. For example, the Colorado Supreme Court ruled that "gay and lesbian people are not to be excluded from the basic political and constitutional rights as a group, but neither are they to be protected as a group against systemic discrimination" (Donovan, Wenzel, and Bowler 2000, 172.)

14. While legal restrictions on miscegenation were primarily aimed at prohibiting Black–White relationships, they also banned Whites from marrying American Indians, Chinese, Ethiopians, Hindus, Koreans, Japanese, and Malayans (Sickels 1972). Framed as a White supremacist, heteropatriarchal, and nativist project, antimiscegenation laws were based on the right of individuals to marry, not racial groups. Over three hundred years-worth of antimiscegenation laws were struck down with *Loving vs. Virginia* (1967), which concluded that "under our Constitution, the freedom to marry, or not to marry, a person of another race resides with the individual and cannot be infringed by the State" (Gerstmann 2004, 80). The Supreme Court ruled that individuals could marry the person of their choice insofar as this person was of the opposite sex.

15. See for example, former Republican National Committee chairman Michael Steele's response to Lieutenant Dan Choi's comments on the February 7, 2012, airing of *Now with Alex Wagner*. Steele commented that interracial and same-sex marriage was not an equal comparison. Citing race as an immutable characteristic, Steele contended that "there are a significant number of African Americans— myself included—who do not appreciate that particular equation. Ok? Because, when you walk into a room, I don't know if you're gay or not. But when I walk into a room, you know I'm Black" (Cabrera 2012).

16. See Ferguson (2003) for a critique how the language of crisis masks the entrenchment of the heteropatriarchal Black family.

17. Yet African Americans have traditional views of family and strongly believe in the institution of family (Staples 1982).

18. Take for example, Eldridge Cleaver's denunciation of Black homosexuality as a racial death wish and the literal desire for Whiteness. Cleaver writes:

    The White man has deprived him of his masculinity, castrated him in the center of his burning skull, and when he submits to the change and takes the White man for his lover as well as Big Daddy, he focuses on "Whiteness" all the love in his pent up soul and turns the razor edge on hatred against "Blackness"— upon himself what he is, and all those who look like him, remind him of himself. He may even hate the darkness of night. (1968, 103)

    For Cleaver (1998), Black male homosexuality is not only to be condemned due to its sexual orientation but also characterizes Black masculinity in crisis. For him, the dissolution of the Black family is tied in heteropatriarchal terms to the disbanding of a Black nation. Similarly, Molefi Asante blames the disintegration of the Black nuclear family on the homosexuality of Black men, a legacy of European decadence (1992, 57). He urges Black men to "guard your minds and you shall save your bodies" (57); for Asante, the body represents the location of the Black nation.

19. As of 2009 U.S. Census Bureau estimates, Prince George's County had a population of 834,560 and was the wealthiest county in the nation with an African American majority. Prince George's County has become a stronghold for Democrats running in the state.

20. Montgomery County has the largest number of marriage bill supporters for a number of reasons. First, there are two openly gay and lesbian legislators (Senators Madaleno and Kaiser) from Montgomery, and this influences their colleagues to support them. Second, this jurisdiction is generally known as being more progressive, partially because it is right outside of Washington, DC. Long before the state, Montgomery County passed a smoking ban, a living wage law, a sexual orientation nondiscrimination law, and a domestic partner benefits measure. Montgomery County's state legislators are all Democrats, and Democrats tend to answer to constituencies that favor LGBTQ civil rights more frequently than Republicans. Finally, Montgomery County legislators view themselves as "adjunct" Washingtonians, and Washington, DC, is an LGBTQ-friendly jurisdiction. It may be that people in Montgomery County are more apt to be "out" than people in other areas of the state. It is noteworthy that Washington, DC, signed same-sex marriage into law on December 19, 2009 and that this bill was ushered into law by a Black mayor and a majority Black council.

21. Although earlier same-sex marriage bills were not passed, the general assembly did establish a weak form of domestic partnership in Maryland with the passage of two pieces of legislation, SB 566 and SB 597. SB 566 included eleven protections for domestic partners including hospital visitation and the making of

funeral arrangements; SB 597 allowed a domestic partner's name to be added or removed from the deed of a residence without incurring a tax liability, as with married spouses. According to the general assembly's summary of SB 597, domestic partners are defined in that state as adults (same sex or different sex) in "a relationship of mutual interdependence" who are not related by blood and who are not in a marriage, civil union, or domestic partnership with anyone else. The law did not establish a domestic partnership registry, and so couples may be required by officials or facilities to prove that their partnership exists by providing a sworn affidavit along with two other documents enumerated in the law, such as evidence of a joint mortgage, checking account, or insurance coverage, among others. The two bills were signed into law by Governor Martin O'Malley on May 22, and came into effect on July 1, 2008.

22. In the House of Delegates, the bill was co-sponsored by forty-four legislators during the 2009 legislative session. In the Senate the bill was co-sponsored by nine legislators during the 2009 legislative session.

23. However, research has shown that heterosexual representatives who are supportive of LGBTQ rights can represent gays and lesbians adequately. Nevertheless, openly gay legislators are the most supportive of domestic partner benefits (Haider-Markel, Joslyn, and Kniss 2000).

24. For example, see Dorian Warren's (2014) work on labor unions who have blocked the economic advance of Blacks, women, and other minorities after drawing upon the support of these marginalized groups.

CHAPTER 6

1. While there is one White man legislator who may be considered a caregiver for his elderly mother, I make a distinction between him and the Black women legislators who took or take physical care of their elderly relatives.

CHAPTER 7

1. Deliberative democracy is a conception of democratic politics in which decisions and policies are justified in a process of discussion among free and equal citizens or their accountable representatives.

2. While I did not focus on the two Asian American women and Latina legislators interviewed for this study, our interactions were similar to those with African American women legislators. Indeed, one of the Asian American women legislators was extremely warm and open. It was through her office that I was initially granted access to the Prince George's County Delegation Night. Her staffer also took me to lunch on my second day in the Maryland statehouse because she "want[ed] someone to look after her daughter in college the same way." This experience leads me to believe a study on other minority women conducted by women of color researchers may have similar outcomes.

3. In addition, the legislators were most likely calculated in what they shared with me. While our conversations were often candid and comfortable it cannot be assumed that they granted me full access into their world. For example, one delegate was under criminal investigation during the time of our feminist life history interview. She did not talk about the allegations and the impending criminal and civil lawsuits. I did not ask about the charges because I wanted her to feel at ease during our interactions.

APPENDIX

1. See Knoblauch (2005) for information on details of a focused ethnographic method.
2. I spent a lot of time interviewing members of the Judiciary Committee because the Religious Freedom and Civil Marriage Protection bill was before the committee. The Judiciary Committee held several hearings on the bill during the last week of my fieldwork.
3. This essay does not assume that social groups are homogenous. Indeed, each category of difference comprises internal diversity.

BIBLIOGRAPHY

Adam, Barry. 1998. "Theorizing Homophobia," *Sexualities* 1(4): 387–404.

Adam, Barry. 2003. "The Defense of Marriage Act and American Exceptionalism: The 'Gay Marriage' Panic in the United States." *Journal of the History of Sexuality* 12(2): 259–276.

Alarcón, Norma. 1990. "Chicana Feminism: In the Tracks of 'the' Native Woman." *Cultural Studies* 4(3): 248–256.

Alexander-Floyd, Nikol G. 2007. *Gender, Race, and Nationalism in Contemporary Black Politics*. New York: Palgrave McMillan.

Allard, Sharon Angella. 1991. "Rethinking Battered Woman Syndrome: A Black Feminist Perspective." *UCLA Women's Law Journal* 1: 191–207.

Allen, Katherine R., and Victoria Chin-Sang. 1990. "A Lifetime of Work: The Context and Meanings of Leisure for Aging Black Women." *Gerontologist* 30(6): 734–740.

Allen, Richard, Michael Dawson, and Ronald Brown. 1989. "A Schema-Based Approach to Modeling an African-American Racial Belief System." *American Political Science Review* 83(2):421–441.

Anderson, Kristin J., Melinda Kanner, and Nisreen Elsayegh. 2009. "Are Feminists Man Haters? Feminists' and Nonfeminists' Attitudes Toward Men." *Psychology of Women Quarterly* 33(2): 216–224.

Applegate, Jeffrey S., and Lenard W. Kaye. 1993. "Male Elder Caregivers." In *Men in Nontraditional Occupations*. ed. Christine L. Williams, 152–167. Newbury Park, CA: SAGE.

Appleton, Susan F. 2005. "Missing in Action? Searching for Gender Talk in the Same-Sex Marriage Debate." *Stanford Law and Policy Review* 16(98): 1–39.

Asante, Molefi K. 1992. *Afrocentricity*. Trenton, NJ: Africa World.

Asbury, Jo-Ellen. 1987. "African-American Women in Violent Relationships: An Exploration of Cultural Differences." In *Violence in the Black Family: Correlates and Consequences*. ed. R. L. Hampton, 89–105. Lexington, KY: Lexington Books.

Asbury, Jo-Ellen. 1999. "What Do We Know Now about Spouse Abuse and Child Sexual Abuse in Families of Color in the United States?" In *Family Violence: Prevention and Treatment*. Issues in Children's and Families' Lives. eds. Robert L. Hampton, Thomas P. Gullotta, and Gerald R. Adams, 148–167. New York: SAGE.

Ashforth, Blake E., and Fred Mael. 1989. "Social Identity Theory and the Organization." *Academy of Management Review* 14(1): 20–39.

Ashmore, Richard D., Kay Deaux, and Tracy McLaughlin-Volpe. 2004. "An Organizing Framework for Collective Identiy: Articulation and Significance of Multidimensionality." *Psychological Bulletin* 130(1): 80–114.

Baca Zinn, Maxine, and Bonnie Thornton Dill. 1996. "Theorizing Difference from Multicultural Feminisms." *Feminist Studies* 22(2): 321–331.

Bailey, Kimberly D. 2009. "Lost in Translation: Domestic Violence, 'The Personal Is Political,' and the Criminal Justice System." *Journal of Criminal Law and Criminology* 11(4): 1255–1302.

Ball, Carlos. 2006. "The Backlash Thesis and Same-Sex Massiage: Learning from *Brown v. Board of Education* and Its Aftermath." *William and Mary Bill of Rights Journal* 14(11): 1493–1540.

Barnes, S. Y. 1999. "Theories of Spouse Abuse: Relevance to African Americans." *Issues of Mental Health Nursing* 20(4): 357–371.

Barrett, Edith J. 1995. "The Policy Priorities of African American Women in State Legislatures." *Lesgislative Studies Quarterly* 20(2): 223–247.

Battle, Juan, Natalie Bennett, and Todd Shaw. 2004. "From the Closet to a Place at the Table: Past, Present, and Future Assesments of Social Science Research on Black, Lesbian, Gay, Bisexual, and Transgender Populations." *African American Research Perspectives* 10(1): 9–26.

Baxter, Sandra, and Marjorie Lansing. 1981. *Women and Politics: The Invisible Majority*. Ann Arbor: University of Michigan Press.

Beck, Allen J., and Christopher J. Mumola. 1999. "Prisoners in 1998." Special Report for the United States Department of Justice, Office of Justice Programs. Washington, DC: Bureau of Justice Statistics. http://www.bjs.gov/content/pub/pdf/p98.pdf

Belgrave, Linda L., May L. Wykle, and Jung M. Choi. 1993. "Health, Double Jeopardy, and Culture: The Use of Institutionalization by African Americans." *Gemntologist* 33(3): 379–385.

Bell, Derrick. 2004. *Silent Covenants*: Brown v. Board of Education *and the Unfulfilled Hopes for Racial Reform*. New York: Oxford University Press.

Bell, EdmondsonElla L. J., and Stella M. Nkomo. 2003. *Our Separate Ways: Black and White Women and the Struggle for Professional Identity*. Cambridge, MA: Harvard Business School Press.

Bell, T.R., Sr., and Bell, J. L. 1999. "Help-Seeking in the Black Church: An Important Connection for Social Work to Make." *Social Work and Christianity* 26: 144–154.

Bell-Scott, Patricia, and Beverly Guy-Sheftall, eds. 1991. *Double Stitch: Black Women Write about Mothers and Daughters*. Boston: Beacon.

Belsky, Jay. 1984. "The Determinants of Parenting: A Processmodel." *Child Development* 55(1): 83–96.

Beltran, Cristina. 2010. *The Trouble with Unity: Latino Politics and the Creation of Identity*. New York: Oxford University Press.

Bent-Goodley, Tricia B. 2001. "Eradicating Domestic Violence in the African American Community: A Literature Review and Action Agenda." *Trauma and Violence Abuse* 2(4): 316–330.

Bercovitch, Sacvan. 1993. *The Rites of Assent: Transformations in the Symbolic Construction of America*. New York: Routledge.

Berger, Michele Tracy. 2004. *Workable Sisterhood: The Political Journey of Stigmatized Women with HIV/AIDS*. Princeton, NJ: Princeton University Press.

Bhandari, Mohit, Sonia Dosanjh, Paul Tornetta III, and David Matthews. 2006. "Musculoskeletal Manifestations of Physical Abuse After Intimate Partner Violence." *Journal of Trauma-Injury Infection and Critical Care* 61(6): 1473–1479.

Billingsley, Andrew. 1968. *Black Families in White America*. Englewood Cliffs, NJ: Prentice Hall.

Black Star Project. 2010. "The Silent Genocide: Facts about the Deepening Plight of Black Men in America." Chicago: Black Star Project. http://www.blackstarproject. org/home/images/facts/deepeningplightblackmeninamerica.pdf

Blake, Wayne M., and Carol A. Darling. 1994. "The Dilemmas of the African American Male." *Journal of Black Studies* 24(4): 402–415.

Blaxton, Reginald G. 1998. "Jesus Wept: Reflections on HIV Disease and the Churches of Black Folk." In *Dangerous Liaisons: Blacks, Gays, and the Struggle for Equality*. ed. E. Brandt, 102–141. New York: New Press.

Bledsoe, Timothy, and Mary Herring. 1990. "Victims of Circumstances: Women in Pursuit of Political Office." *American Political Science Review* 84(1): 213–223.

Boaz, Rachel F., and Charlotte F. Muller. 1992. "Paid Work and Unpaid Help by Caregivers of the Disabled and Frail Elders." *Medical Care* 30(2): 149–158.

Boneham, Margaret, and Judith Sixsmith. 2006. "The Voices of Older Women in a Deprived Community: Issues of Health and Social Capital." *Social Science and Medicine* 62(2): 269–279.

Bositis, David. A. 2001. "Changing the Guard: Generational Differences among Black Elected Officials." Washington, DC: Joint Center for Political and Economic Studies.

Boykin, Keith. 1996. "Bearing Witness: Faith in the Lives of Black Lesbians and Gays." In *One More River to Cross: Black and Gay in America*. ed. Keith Boykin, 123–154. New York: Anchor Books.

Boykin, Keith. 1999. *Blacks and Gays in Conflict: An Interview with U.S. Representative Barney Frank*. New York: New Press.

Bradford, Fay W. 1993. "Understanding 'Generation X.'" *Marketing Research* 5(2): 54–55.

Brandt, Eric. 1999. *Dangerous Liaisons: Blacks, Gays, and the Struggle for Equality*. New York: New Press.

Bratton, Kathleen A., and Kerry Haynie. 1999. "Agenda Setting and Legislative Success in State Legislatures: The Effects of Gender and Race." *Journal of Politics* 61(3): 658–679.

Bratton, Kathleen A., Kerry L. Haynie, and Beth Reingold. 2006. "Agenda Setting and African-American Women in State Legislatures." *Journal of Women, Politics, and Policy* 28(3–4): 71–96.

Brewer Marilynn B., and Joseph G. Weber. 1994. "Self-Evaluation Effects of Interpersonal Versus Intergroup Social Comparison." *Journal of Personality and Social Psychology* 66(2): 268–275.

Brody, Elaine. 1991. "'Women in the Middle' and Family Help to Older People." *Gerontologist* 21(5): 471–480.

Brown, Ruth Nicole 2007. "Remembering Maleesa: Theorizing Black Girl Politics and the Politicizing of Socialization." *National Political Science Review* 11: 121–136.

Brown, Nadia. 2012. "Negotiating the Insider/Outsider Status: Black Feminist Ethnography and Legislative Studies." *Journal of Feminist Scholarship* 3: 19–39.

Brown-Dean, Khalilah 2007. "Felon Disenfranchisement and the Breakdown of Black Politics." In *The Expanding Boundaries of Black Politics*. ed. Georgia A. Persons, 43–64. New Brunswick, NJ: Transaction.

Browning, Rufus P., Dale R. Marshall, and David H. Tabb. 1984. *Protest Is Not Enough: The Struggle of Blacks and Hispanics for Equality in Urban Politics*. Berkeley: University of California Press.

Burden, Barry. 2007. *Personal Roots of Representation*. Princeton, NJ: Princeton University Press.

Bykowicz, Julie. 2009a. "Domestic Violence Bill Resurrected—General Assembly." *Baltimore Sun*, March 12.

Bykowicz, Julie. 2009b. "A Plea to Peers to Reject Legislation: House Votes Down Bill to Expunge Records after Delegate Tells of Being Victim of Abuse." *Baltimore Sun*, March 11.

Bykowicz, Julie. 2009c. "Under a Cloud—Lawmakers Debate Bill to Clear Records of Those Falsely Accused of Domestic Abuse." *Baltimore Sun*, March 13.

Cabrera, Claudio E. 2012. "Michael Steele: Don't Compare Gay Rights to Civil Rights." *The Root*, February 8. http://www.theroot.com/michael-steele-john-heilemann-gay-rights

Calhoun-Brown, Allison. 1996. "African American Churches and Political Mobilization: The Psychological Impact of Organizational Resources." *Journal of Politics* 58(4): 935–953.

Cannon, Justin. 2008. *The Bible, Christianity, and Homosexuality*. Lexington, KY: CreateSpace Independent Publishing.

Canon, David. 1999. *Race, Redistricting and Representation*. Chicago: University of Chicago Press.

Carmines, Edward G., and James A. Stimson. 1980. "The Two Faces of Issue Voting." *American Political Science Review* 74(1): 78–91.

Carroll, Susan J. 1994. *Women as Candidates in American Politics*. Indianapolis: Indiana University Press.

Casellas, Jason P. 2010. *Latino Representation in State Houses and Congress*. New York: Cambridge University Press.

Catholic African World Network, 2005. "Global Count of Catholics of African Decent: 270 Million." Baltimore: National Black Catholic Congress. http://www.nbccongress.org/black-catholics/worldwide-count-black-catholics-01.asp

Cazenave, Noel A., and Murray A. Straus. 1979. "Race, Class, Network Embeddedness and Family Violence: A Search for Potent Support Systems." *Journal of Comparative Family Studies* 10(3): 281–300.

Center for American Women and Politics. 2013. "Women of Color in Elective Office 2013: Congress, Statewide, and State Legislatures." New Brunswick, NJ: Center for American Women and Politics, Eagleton Institute of Politics, Rutgers Univesity.

Chambers, David L., and Nancy D. Polikoff. 1999. "Family Law and Gay and Lesbian Family Issues in the Twentieth Century." *Family Law Quarterly* 33(3): 523–542.

Chang, Robert S., and Jerome Culp. 2002. "After Intersectionality." *Kansas City Law Review* 71: 485–491.

Chappell, Kevin (November 2006). "America's Wealthiest Black County." *Ebony*. Retrieved 2012-08-27.

Clark, Kenneth B. 1965. *The Dark Ghetto: Dilemmas of Social Power*. New York: Harper and Row.

Clark, Jennifer Hayes and Veronica Caro. 2013. "Multi-member Districts and the Substantive Representation of Women: An Analysis of Legislative Cosponsorship Networks." *Politics and Gender* 9(1): 1–30.

Cleaver, Eldridge. 1968. *Soul on Ice*. New York: Dell.

Clifford, James. 1986. "On Ethnographic Allegory." In *Writing Culture: The Poetics and Politics of Ethnography*. eds. James Clifford and George E. Marcus, 98–121. Berkeley: Unversity of California Press.

Cohen, Cathy J. 1999. *The Boundaries of Blackness: AIDS and the Breakdown of Black Politics*. Chicago: University of Chicago Press.

Cohen, Cathy J. 2010. *Democracy Remixed: Black Youth and the Future of American Politics*. New York: Oxford University Press.

Cohen, Cathy J., and Micheal C. Dawson. 1993. "Neighborhood Poverty and African American Politics." *American Politial Science Review* 87(2): 286–302.

Cohen, Joshua, and Joel Rogers. 1995. *Associations and Democracy*. Real Utopias Project 1, ed. Erik Olin Wright. London: Verso.

Cole, Elizabeth R., and Abigail J. Stewart. 1999. "Meanings of Political Participation among Black and White Women: Political Identity and Social Responsibility." *Journal of Personality and Social Psychology* 71(1): 130–140.

Collins, Patricia H. 1990. *Black Feminist Thought: Knowledge, Consciousness and the Politics of Empowerment*. New York: Routledge.

Collins, Patricia H. 1993. "Black Feminism in the Twentieth Century." In *Black Women in the United States: An Historical Encyclopedia*. eds. Darlene Clarke Hine, Elisa Barkley Brown, and Rosalyn Terborg-Penn, 418–425. New York: Carlson.

Collins, Patricia H. 2000. *Black Feminist Thought: Knowledge, Consciousness, and the Politics of Empowerment*. 2d ed. New York: Routledge.

Collins, Patricia H. 2001. "What's in a Name? Womanism, Black Feminism, and Beyond." *Black Scholar* 26(1): 9–17.

Collins, Patricia H. 2004. *Black Sexual Politics: African Americans, Gender, and the New Racism*. New York: Routledge.

Combahee River Collective. 1983. "The Combahee River Collective Statement." In *Home Girls, A Black Feminist Anthology*. ed. Barbara Smith, 264–274. New Brunswick, NJ: Rutgers University Press.

Connell, R. 1995. *Masculinities*. Cambridge, UK: Polity Press.

Constantine-Simms, Delroy, ed. 2000. *The Greatest Taboo: Homosexuality in Black Communities*. Los Angeles: Alyson Books.

Coombs, Mary I. 1992. "Symposium: Gender and Law Essay and Article: Foreword: Gender and Justice." *University of Miami Law Review* 46: 503–510.

Crenshaw, Kimberle et al., eds. 1995. Critical Race Theory: The Key Writings that Formed the Movement. Edited by Kimberle Williams Crenshaw et al. New York: The New Press.

Crenshaw, Kimberle. 1989. "Demarginalizing the Intersection of Race and Sex: A Black Feminist Critique of Antidiscrimination Doctrine, Feminist Theory, and Antiracist Politics." In *Feminist Legal Theories*. ed. Karen J. Maschke, 23–52. New York: Rougledge.

Crenshaw, Kimberle. 1991. "Mapping the Margins: Intersectionality, Identity Politics, and Violence against Women of Color." *Stanford Law Review* 43(6): 1241–1299. [reprinted in *Critical Race Theory: The Key Writing That Formed the Movement*. 1995. eds. Kimberle Crenshaw, Neil Gotanda, Gary Peller, and Kendall Thomas, 357–383. New York: New Press].

Crichlow, Wesley E. A. 2004. *Buller Men and Batty Boys: Hidden Men in Toronto and Halifax Black Communities*. Toronto: University of Toronto Press.

Davis, Angela. 1981. *Women, Race and Class*. New York: Vintage Books.

Davis, Angela. 1989. *Women, Culture and Politics*. New York: Random House.

Dawson, Michael. 1994. *Behind the Mule: Race and Class in African-American Politics*. Princeton, NJ: Princeton University Press.

Dawson, Michael C. 2001. *Black Visions: The Roots of Contemporary African-American Political Ideologies*. Chicago: University of Chicago Press.

Dennis, Jack. 1986. "Preadult Learning of Political Independence: Media and Family Communication Effects." *Communication Research* 13(3): 401–433.

Dennis, R., Key, L., Kirk, A., & Smith, A. 1995. "Addressing domestic violence in the African American community." *Journal of Health Care for the Poor and Underserved* 6, 284–293.

Diamond, Irene. 1977. Sex Roles in the State House. New Haven, CT: Yale University Press.

Di Lorenzo Vincent. 1997. "Legislative Heart and Phase Transitions: An Exploratory Study of Congress and Minority Interests." *William and Mary Law Review* 38: 1729–1815.

Dill, Bonnie T. 1979. "The Dialectics of Black Womanhood." *Signs: Journal of Women in Culture and Society* 4(3): 543–555.

Dilworth-Anderson, Peggye, and Norman B. Anderson. 1994. "Dementia Caregiving in Backs: A Contextual Approach to Research." In *Stress Effects on Family Caregivers of Alzheimer's Patients: Research and Interventions*. eds. Enid Light, George Niederehe, and Barry Lebowitz, 185–202. New York: Springer.

Dodson, Debra L., and Susan J. Carroll. 1998. "Representing Women's Interests in the US House of Representatives." In *Women and Elective Office: Past, Present, and Future*. eds. Sue Thomas and Clyde Wilcox, 130–149. New York: Oxford University Press.

Donovan, Todd, Jim Wenzel, and Shaun Bowler. 2000. *Direct Democracy and Gay Rights Initiatives after Romer*. Chicago: University of Chicago Press.

Douglas, Kelly Brown. 1999. "Homophobia and Heterosexism in the Black Church and Community." In *Sexuality and the Black Church: A Womanist Perspective*. ed. Kelly Brown Douglas, 87–108. Maryknoll, NY: Orbis Books.

Douglas, Kelly Brown. 1999. *Sexuality and the Black Church: A Womanist Perspective*. Maryknoll, NY: Orbis Books.

Dovi, Suzanne. 2002. "Preferable Descriptive Representatives: Will Just Any Woman, Black or Latino Do?" *American Political Science Review* 96(2): 729–743.

Dowling, Colette. 2000. *The Frailty Myth: Redefining the Physical Potential of Women and Girls*. New York: Random House.

Drake, St. Clair, and Horace R. Clayton. 1945. *Black Metropolis: A Study of Negro Life in a Northern City*. New York: Harper and Row.

Easton, David and Jack Dennis. 1965. "The Child's Image of Government." *Annals of the American Academy of Political and Social Science* 361: 40–57.

Elazar, Daniel J. 1972. *American Federalism: A View from the States*. 2nd ed. New York: Thomas Y. Crowell.

Fagan, Jeffrey. 1996. "The Criminalization of Domestic Violence: Promise and Limits." Presentation at the 1995 Conference on Criminal Justice Research and Evaluation. United States Department of Justice. Office of Justice Programs, National Institute of Justice, Washington, DC, January. https://www.ncjrs.gov/pdffiles/crimdom.pdf.

Farajaje-Jones, Elias. 1998. "Breaking Silence: Toward an In the-Life Theology." In *Black Theology: A Documentary History*. Vol. 2, *1980–1992*. eds. James H. Cone and Gayraud Wilmore, 139–159. Maryknoll, NY: Orbis Books.

Fenno, Richard, Jr. 1973. *Congressmen in Committees*. Boston: Little and Brown.

Fenno, Richard, Jr. 1978. *Home Style: House Members in their Districts*. Boston: Little and Brown.

Fenno, Richard, Jr. 2003. *Going Home: Black Representatives and Their Constituents*. Chicago: University of Chicago Press.

Ferguson, Karen Jane. 2002. *Black Politics in New Deal Atlanta*. Chapel Hill: University of North Carolina Press.

Ferguson, Kathy. 1993. *The Man Question: Visions of Subjectivity in Feminist Theory*. Berkeley: University of California Press.

Ferguson, Roderick. 2003. *Aberrations in Black: Toward a Queer of Color Critique*. Minneapolis: University of Minnesota Press.

Fernandes, Leela. 1997. *Producing Workers: The Politics of Gender, Class, and Culture in the Calcutta Jute Mills*. Philedelphia: University of Pennsylvania.

Few, April L., Dionne P. Stephens, and Marlo Rouse-Arnett. 2003. "Sister-to-Sister Talk: Transcending Boundaries and Challenges in Qualitative Research with Black Women." *Family Relations* 52(3): 205–215.

Fivush, R., and Haden, C. A. (Eds.). 2003. *Autobiographical Memory and the Construction of a Narrative Self: Developmental and Cultural Perspectives*. Mahwah, NJ: Lawrence Erlbaum Associates.

Flammang, Janet A. 1997. *Women's Political Voice: How Women Are Transforing the Practice and Study of Politics*. Philadelphia: Temple University Press.

Fox, Richard L., and Jennifer. L. Lawless. 2004. "Entering the Arena? Gender and the Decision to Run for Office." *American Journal of Political Science* 48(2): 264–280.

Fox, Richard L., Jennifer L. Lawless, and Courtney Feeley. 2001. "Gender and the Decision to Run for Office." *Legislative Studies Quarterly* 26(3): 411–435.

Fraser, Nancy. 2008. *Scales of Justice: Reimagining Political Space in a Globalizing World*. New York: Columbia University Press.

Frasure-Yokely, Lorrie. in progress. *Politics Beyond the Urban Core: Immigrant and Ethnic Minority Settlement in Suburban America*.

Frazier, E. Franklin. 1939. *The Negro Family in the United States*. Chicago: University of Chicago Press.

Frazier, E. Franklin. 1963. *The Negro Church in America*. New York: Schocken Books.

Friedman, Alissa. 1987. "The Necessity for State Recognition of Same-Sex Marriage: Constitutional Requirements and Evolving Notions of Family." *Berkeley Women's Law Journal* 3: 134.

Fullilove, Mindy T., and Robert E. Fullilove. 1999. "Stigma as an Obstacle to AIDS Action." *American Behavioral Scientist* 42(7): 113–125.

Gamble, Katrina L. 2010. *Young, Gifted, Black, and Female: Why Aren't There More Yvette Clarkes in Congress?* New York: Routledge.

Gans, Herbert J. 2011. "The Moynihan Report and its Aftermaths: A Critical Analysis". *Du Bois Review*, 8:2, 315–327.

Garcia Bedolla Lisa, and Becki Scola. 2006. "Finding Intersection: Race, Class, and Gender in the California Recall Vote." *Politics and Gender* 2(1): 5–27.

Garcia Bedolla Lisa, Katherine Tate, and Janelle Wong. 2005. "Indelible Effects: The Impact of Women of Color in the U.S. Congress." In *Women and Elective Office: Past, Present, and Future*. eds. Thomas, Sue and Clyde Wilcox, 152–175. New York: Oxford University Press.

Gay, Claudine. 2001. "The Effect of Black Congressional Representation on Political Participation." *American Political Science Review* 95(3): 589–602.

Gay, Claudine. 2002. "Spirals of Trust: The Effect of Descriptive Representation on the Relationship between Citizens and Their Government." *American Journal of Political Science* 46(4): 717–732.

Gay, Claudine, and Katherine Tate. 1998. "Doubly Bound: The Impact of Gender and Race on the Politics of Black Women." *Political Psychology* 19(1): 169–184.

Geertz, Clifford. 1988. *Works and Lives: The Anthropologist as Author*. Stanford: Stanford University Press.

Gerstel, Naomi, and Sally K. Gallagher. 2001. "Men's Caregiving: Gender and the Contingent Character of Care." *Gender and Society* 15(2):197–217.

Gerstmann, Evan. 2004. *Same-Sex Marriage and the Constit*ution. New York: Cambridge University Press.

Giddings, Paula. 1984. *When and Where I Enter: The Impact of Black Women on Sex and Race in America*. New York: Morrow.

Gilgoff, Dan. 2012. "Across Country, Black Pastors Weigh In on Obama's Same-Sex Marriage Support." CNN.com, May 13. http://religion.blogs.cnn.com/2012/05/13/across-country-black-pastors-weigh-in-on-obamas-same-sex-marriage-support/

Gillespie, Andra. 2009. "The Third Wave: A Theoretica Introduction to the Post–Civil Rights Cohort of Black Elected Leadership." *National Political Science Review* 12(1): 139–161.

Gillespie, Andra, ed. 2010. *Whose Black Politics: Cases in Post-Racial Black Leadership*. New York: Routledge.

Gillespie, Andra. 2012. *The New Black Politician: Cory Booker, Newark and Post-Racial America*. New York: New York University Press.

Glaude, Eddie, Jr. 2007. *In a Shade of Blue: Pragmatism and the Politics of Black America*. Chicago: University of Chicago Press.

Glenn, Evelyn Nakano. 2002. *Unequal Freedom: How Race and Gender Shaped American Citizenship and Labor*. Cambridge, MA: Harvard University Press.

Goldstein, Joshua R., and Catherine T. Kennney. 2001. "Marriage Delayed or Marriage Forgone? New Cohort Forecasts of First Marriage for U.S. Women." *American Sociological Review* 66(4): 506–519.

Gomes, Peter J. 1996. "The Bible and Homosexuality: The Last Prejudice." In *The Good Book: Reading the Bible with Mind and Heart*. ed. Peter J. Gomes, 144–174. New York: Morrow.

Gooding-Willams, Robert. 2009. *In The Shadow of Du Bois: Afro-Modern Political Thought in America*. Cambridge, MA: Harvard University Press.

Green, Lorraine. 2005. "Theorizing Sexuality, Sexual Abuse and Residential Children's Homes: Adding Gender to the Equation." *British Journal of Social Work* 35: 453–481.

Greenberg, Edward S., ed. 1970. *Political Socialization*. New Brunswick, NJ: Aldine Transaction.

Greenstein, Fred I. 1970. "A Note on the Ambiguity of 'Political Socialization': Definitions, Criticisms, and Strategies of Inquiry." *Journal of Politics* 32(4): 959–978.

Greer, Christina. 2013 Black Ethnics: Race, Immigration, and the Pursut of the American Dream. New York, NY: Oxford University Press.

Griffin, Horace. 2000. "Their Own Received Them Not: African American Lesbians and Gays in Black Churches." In *The Greatest Taboo: Homosexuality in Black Communities*. ed. Delroy Constantine-Simms, 110–111. Los Angeles: Alyson Books.

Guinier, Lani, and Gerald Torres. 2003. *The Miner's Canary: Enlisting Race, Resisting Power, Transforming Democracy*. Nathan I. Huggins Lectures. Cambridge, MA: Harvard University Press.

Gurin, Patricia, Shirley Hatchett, and James Jackson. 1989. *Hope and Independence: Blacks' Reactions to Party and Electoral Politics*. New York: Russell Sage Foundation.

Guy-Sheftall, Beverly. 1991. "Breaking the Silence: A Black Feminist Response to the Thomas/Hill Hearings (for Audre Lorde)." *Black Scholar* 1/2: 35.

Guy-Sheftall, Beverly. 1992. "Black Women's Studies: The Interface of Women's Studies and Black Studies." *Phylon (1960–)* 49(1/2): 33–41.

Haider-Markel, Donald P., Mark R. Joslyn, and Chad J. Kniss. 2000. "Minority Group Interests and Political Representation: Gay Elected Officials in the Policy Process." *Journal of Politics* 62(2): 568–577.

Haider-Markel, Donald P., and Kenneth J. Meier. 1996. "The Politics of Gay and Lesbian Rights: Expanding the Scope of the Conflict." *Journal of Politics* 58(2): 332–349.

Haight, Wendy. 2002. *African American Children at Church: A Sociocultural Perspective.* New York: Cambridge University Press.

Haley, William E., David L. Roth, Marci I. Coleton et al. 1996. "Appraisal, Coping, and Social Support as Mediators of Well-Being in Black and White Family Caregivers of Patients with Alzheimer's Disease." *Journal of Consulting and Clinical Psychology* 64(1): 121–129.

Hall, S. A. 1989. "Cultural Identity and Cinematic Representation." *Framework* 36: 68–81.

Hallam, Julia and Annecka Marshall. 1993. "Layers of Difference: The Significance of a Self-Reflexive Research Practice for a Feminist Epsitemological Project." In *Making Connections: Women's Studies, Women's Movements, Women's Lives.* ed. Mary Kennedy, 64–78. Washington, DC: Taylor and Francis.

Hampton, Robert L., and Richard J. Gelles. 1994. "Violence Toward Black Women in a Nationally Representative Sample of Black Families." *Journal of Comparative Family Studies* 25(1): 105–119.

Hancock, Ange-Marie. 2003. *The Politics of Disgust: The Public Identity of the "Welfare Queen."* New York: New York University Press.

Hancock, Ange-Marie. 2004. *The Politics of Disgust: The Public Identity of the "Welfare Queen."* New York: New York University Press.

Hancock, Ange-Marie. 2007. "When Multiplication Doesn't Equal Quick Addition: Examining Intersectionality as a Research Paradigm." *Perspectives on Politics* 5(1): 63–79.

Hancock, Ange-Marie. 2011. *Solidarity Politics for Millennials: A Guide to Ending the Oppression Olympics.* New York: Palgrave MacMillan.

Haraway, Donna. 1988. "Situated Knowledges: The Science Question in Feminism and the Privilege of Partial Perspective." *Feminist Studies* 14(3): 575–599.

Haraway, Donna. 1991. *Simians: Cyborgs and Women: The Reinvention of Nature.* New York: Routeledge.

Harding, Sandra. 1991. *Whose Science? Whose Knowledge? Thinking from Women's Lives.* Ithaca, NY: Cornell University Press.

Hardy-Fanta, Carol, Christine M. Sierra, Pei-te Lien, Dianne Pinderhughes, and Wartyna Davis. 2005. "Race, Gender, and Descriptive Representation: An Exploratory View of Multicultural Elected Leadership in the United States". Paper presented at the Annual Meeting of the American Political Science Association. Washington, DC, September.

Hare, Nathan, and Julia Hare. 1984. *The Endangered Black Family.* San Francisco: Black Think Tank.

Harrell, Raker. 2007. "Court of Appeals of Maryland Opinion on *Frank Conaway, et al. v. Gitanjali Deane, et al.*, No. 44, Sept. Term 2006." Circuit Court, Baltimore City, September 18. http://mdcourts.gov/opinions/coa/2007/44a06.pdf

Harris, Angela. 1999. "Women of Color and the Law." In *Feminist Jurisprudence, Women, and the Law: Critical Essays, Research Agenda, and Bibliography*. eds. Betty Taylor, Sharon Rush, and Robert J. Munro, 283–290. Buffalo, NY: Rothman.

Harris, Angela. 2009. "Foreword: Economics of Color." In *Shades of Difference: Why Skin Color Matters*. ed. Evelyn Glenn, 1–6. Stanford, CA: Stanford University Press.

Harris, Craig G. 1986. "Cut Off from Among Their People." In *In the Life: A Black Gay Anthology*. ed. Joseph Beam, 63–67. Boston: Alyson.

Harris, Duchess. 2001. *From the Kennedy Commission to the Combahee Collective: Black Feminist Organizing, 1960–1980*. New York: New York University Press.

Harris, Fredrick C. 1994. "Something Within: Religion as a Mobilizer of African-American Political Activism". *Journal of Politics* 56(1): 42–68.

Harris, Frederick C. 1999. *Something Within: Religion in African American Political Activism*. New York: Oxford University Press.

Harris, Phyllis Braudy. 1998. "Listening to Caregiving Sons: Misunderstood Realities." *Gerontologist* 38(3): 342–352.

Hartsock, Nancy C. M. 2004. "The Feminist Standpoint: Developing the Ground for a Specifically Feminist Historical Materialism." In *The Feminist Standpoint Theory Reader: Intellectual and Political Controversies*. ed. Sandra Harding, 35–54. New York: Routledge.

Haslam, S. Alexander, , John C. Turner, Penelope J. Oakes, Craig McGarty, and Brett K. Hayes. 1992. "Context-Dependent Variation in Social Stereotyping: The Effects of Intergroup Relations as Mediated by Social Change and Frame of Reference." *European Journal of Social Psychology* 22(2): 3–20.

Hawkesworth, Mary. 2003. "Congressional Enectments of Race–Gender: Toward at Theory of Race–Gendered Institutions." *American Political Science Review* 97(4): 529–550.

Haynie, Kerry L. 2001. *African American Legislators in the American States*. New York: Columbia University Press.

Helderman, Rosiland S. 2009. "Abuse Bills Tug at Several Md. Lawmakers Personally." *Washington Post*, March 27.

Helminiak, Daniel A. 2000. What the Bible Really Says about Homosexuality. Tajique, NM: Alamo Square.

Herek, Gregory M. 2002. "Thinking About AIDS and Stigma: A Psychologist's Perspective." *Journal of Law, Medicine, and Ethics* 30(4): 594–607.

Herek, Gregory M. 2006. "Legal Recognition of Same-Sex Relationships in the United States: A Social Science Perspective." *American Psychologist* 61(6): 607–621.

Herek, Gregory M., and John P. Capitanio. 1995. "Black Heterosexual Attitudes toward Lesbians and Gay Men in the United States." *Journal of Sex Research* 32(2): 95–105.

Higginbotham, Evelyn Brooks. 1992. "African-American Women's History and the Metalanguage of Race." *Signs: Journal of Women in Culture and Society* 17(2): 251–274.

Higginbotham, Evelyn Brooks. 1993. *Righteous Discontent: The Women's Movement in the Black Baptist Church, 1880–1920*. Cambridge: Harvard University Press.

Hochschild, Jennifer L. 1995. *Facing Up to the American Dream: Race, Class and the Soul of the Nation*. Princeton, NJ: Princeton University Press.

Hochschild, Arlie, and Anne Machung. 1989. *The Second Shift*. New York: Avon Books.

hooks, bell. 1981. *Ain't I a Woman? Black Women and Feminism*. Boston: South End.

hooks, bell. 1984. *Feminist Theory: From Margin to Center*. Boston: South End.
hooks, bell. 1989. *Talking Back: Thinking Feminist, Thinking Black*. Toronto, ON: Between the Lines.
hooks, bell. 1990. *Yearning: Race, Gender, and Cultural Politics*. Boston: South End.
Hotaling, Gerald T., and David B. Sugarman. 1986. "An Analysis of Risk Markers in Husband to Wife Violence: The Current State of Knowledge." *Violence and Victims* 1(2): 101–124.
Howell, Tom Jr. 2006. "Census 2000 Special Report. *Maryland Newsline*, Census: Md. Economy Supports Black-Owned Businesses." University of Maryland. Philip Merrill College of Journalism.
Htun, Mala. 2004. "Is Gender Like Ethnicity? The Political Representation of Identity Groups." *Perspectives on Politics* 2(3): 439–458.
Huckfeldt, Robert, and Carol W. Kohfeld. 1989. *Race and the Decline of Class in American Politics*. Urbana: University of Illinois Press.
Huddy, Leonie. 2001. "From Social to Political Identity: A Critical Examination of Social Identity Theory." *Political Psychology* 22(1): 127–156.
Hudson, Walter W., and Wendell A. Ricketts. 1980. "A Strategy for the Measurement of Homophobia." *Journal of Homosexuality* 5(4): 356–371.
Hughes, Diane, and Lisa Chen. 1997. "When and What Parents Tell Children About Race: An Examination of Race-Related Socialization Among African American Families." *Applied Developmental Science* 1(4): 200–214.
Hull, Gloria T., Patricia Bell Scott, and Barbara Smith. 1982. *All the Women Are White and All the Blacks Are Men, But Some of Us Are Brave*. New York: Feminist Press.
Hyman, Herbert. 1959. *Political Socialization: A Study in the Psychology of Political Behavior*. Glencoe, IL: Free Press.
Ijames, Earl, and Michelle Lanier. 2009. "Uncovering a Person's Story: Edward R. 'Ned' Rawls." *Tar Heel Junior Historian* 48(2): 1–6.
Ingersoll-Dayton, Berit, Marjorie E. Starrels, and DavidDowler. 1996. "Caregiving for Parents and Parents-in-Law: Is Gender Important?" *Genrontologist* 36(4): 483–491.
Jenkins, Richard. 1996. *Social Identity*. New York: Taylor and Francis.
Johnson, Patrick. 2003. *Appropriating Blackness: Performance and the Politics of Authenticity*. Durham, NC: Duke University Press.
Jordan-Zachery, Julia S. 2007. "Am I a Black Woman or a Woman Who is Black? A Few Thoughts on the Meaning of Intersectionality." *Politics and Gender* 3(2): 254–263.
Jordan-Zachery, Julia S. 2012. "Blogging at the Intersections: Black Women, Identity, and Lesbianism." *Politics and Gender* 8(3): 405–141.
Kahn, Kim Fridkin. 1994. "Does Gender Make a Difference? An Experimental Examination of Sex Stereotypes and Press Patterns in Statewide Campaigns." *American Journal of Political Science* 38(1): 162–195.
Kahn, Kim Fridkin. 1996. *The Political Consequences of Being a Woman*. New York: Columbia University Press.
Karenga, Maulana. 1986. "Social Ethics and the Black Family." *Black Scholar* 17(5): 41–54.
Karp, Hank., Danilo Sirias, and Kristin Arnold. 1999. "Teams: Why Generation X Marks the Spot." *Journal for Quality and Participation* 22(4): 30–33.
Kessler, Laura T. 2001. "The Attachment Gap: Employment Discrimination Law, Women's Cultural Caregiving, and the Limits of Economic and Liberal Legal Theory." *University of Michigan Journal of Law Review* 34(3): 371–469.

Kimmel, Michael, and Matthew Mahler. 2003. "Adolescent Masculinity, Homophobia, and Violence Random School Shootings, 1982–2001." *American Behavioral Scientist* 46(10): 1439–1458.

King, Deborah. 1988. "Multiple Jeopardy, Multiple Consciousness: The Context of Black Feminist Ideology." *Signs: Journal of Women in Culture and Society* 14(1): 88–111.

King-Meadows, Tyson, and Thomas F. Schaller. 2006. *Devolution and Black State Legislators Challenges and Choices in the Twenty-first Century.* New York: State University of New York Press.

Kingdon, John. 1989. *Congressmen's Voting Decisions.* 3rd ed. Ann Arbor: University of Michigan Press.

Knoblauch, Hubert. 2005. Focused Ethnography. Forum: Qualitative Social Research 6(3): 44.

Koch, Jeffrey W. 2000. "Do Citizens Apply Gender Stereotypes to Infer Candidates' Ideological Orientation?" *Journal of Politics* 62(2): 414–429.

Kupenda, Angela Mae. 1998. "Law, Life, and Literature: A Critical Reflection of Life and Literature to Illuminate How Laws of Domestic Violence, Race, and Class Bind Black Women Based on Alice Walker's Book *The Third Life of Grange Copeland.*" *Howard Law Journal* 42(1): 1–26.

Kumar, Anugrah. 2012. "Polls Show Sudden Increase in Black Support for Gay Marriage." *The Christian Post.*

Kupperschmidt, Betty R. 2000. "Multigeneration Employees: Strategies for Effective Management." *Health Care Manager* 19(1): 65–76.

Ladner, Joyce. 1971. *Tomorrow's Tomorrow: The Black Woman.* New York: Doubleday.

Lawrence-Webb, Claudia, Melissa Littlefield, and Joshua N.Okundaye. 2004. "African American Intergender Relationships: A Theoretical Exploration of Roles, Patriarchy, and Love." *Journal of Black Studies* 34(5): 623–639.

Lawton M., Powell, Doris Rajagopal, Elaine Brody, and Morton H. Kleban. 1992. "The Dynamics of Caregiving for a Demented Elder Among Black and White Families." *Journal of Gerontology* 47(4): 156–164.

Lazarus, Richard S., and Susan Folkman. 1984. *Stress, Appraisal, and Coping.* New York: Springer.

Lemelle, Anthony J., Jr., and Juan Battle. 2004. "Black Masculinity Matters in Attitudes Toward Gay Males." *Journal of Homosexuality* 47(1): 39–51.

Lerner, Gerda. 1997. *Why History Matters: Life and Thought.* New York: Oxford University Press.

Levitt, Eugene E., and Albert D. Klassen, Jr. 1974. "Public Attitudes Toward Homosexuality: Part of the 1970 National Survey by the Institute for Sex Research." *Journal of Homosexuality* 1(1): 29–43.

Levy, Peter. 2003. *Civil War on Race Street: The Civil Rights Movement in Cambridge, Maryland (Southern Dissent).* Gainesville: University of Florida Press.

Lewis, Gregory B. 2003. "Black–White Differences in Attitudes Toward Homosexuality and Gay Rights." *Public Opinion Quarterly* 67(1): 59–78.

Lewis, Gregory B., and Charles Gossett. 2008. "Changing Public Opinion on Same-Sex Marriage: The Case of California." *Politics and Policy* 36(1): 4–30.

Lincoln, Eric C., and Lawrence H. Mamiya. 1990. *The Black Church in the African American Experience.* Durham, NC: Duke University Press.

Link, Bruce G., and Jo C. Phelan. 2001. "Conceptualizing Stigma." *Annual Review of Sociology* 27: 363–385.

Lockhart, Lettie, and Barbara W. White. 1989. "Understanding Marital Violence in the Black Community." *Journal of Interpersonal Violence* 4(4): 421–426.

Lorde, Audre. 1984. *Sister Outsider*. New York: Crossing Press.

Mansbridge, Jane. 1999. "Should Black Represent Blacks and Women Represent Women? A Contingent 'Yes'." *Journal of Politics* 61(3): 628–657.

Mansbridge, Jane. 2003. "Rethinking Representation." *American Political Science Review* 97(4): 515–528.

Mansbridge, Jane, and Katherine Tate. 1992. "Race Trumps Gender: The Thomas Nomination in the Black Community." *PS: Political Science and Politics* 25(3): 488–493.

Marable, Manning. 1983. *How Capitalism Underdeveloped Black America: Problems in Race, Political Economy, and Society*. Boston: South End.

Marsh, Clifton E. 1993. "Sexual Assault and Domestic Violence in the African American Community". *Western Journal of Black Studies* 17(3): 149–155.

Marshall, Sheree. 1995. "Ethnic Socialization of African American Children: Implications for Parenting, Identity Development, and Academic Achievement." *Journal of Youth and Adolescence* 24(4): 377–396.

Martinez, Elizabeth. 1993. "Beyond Black/White: The Racisms of our Times." *Social Justice* 20(1/2): 22–34.

Mayhew, David. 1974. *Congress: The Electoral Connection*. New Haven, CT: Yale University Press.

McAdoo, Harriette P., and Vanella Crawford. 1990. "The Black Church and Family Support Programs." *Prevention in Human Services* 9(1): 193–203.

McCall, Leslie. 2005. "The Complexity of Intersectionality." *Signs: Journal of Women in Culture and Society* 30(3): 1771–1800.

McClerking, Harwood. 2001. *We're In This Together: The Origins of Maintenance of African American Fate Perceptions*. Ann Arbor: University of Michigan Press.

McDaniel, Eric 2004. *Politics in the Pews: The Creation and Maintenance of Black Political Churches*. Urbana-Champaign: University of Illinois Press.

McKenna, Katelyn Y. A., and John A. Bargh 1998. "Coming Out in the Age of the Internet: Identity 'Demarginalization' Through Virtual Group Participation." *Journal of Personality and Social Psychology* 75(3): 681–694.

McNeil, John 1993. *The Church and the Homosexual*. Kansas City: Sheed, Andrews and McMeel.

MetLife Mature Market Institute. 2009. "Broken Trust: Elders, Family, and Finances." New York: MetLife Mature Market Institute https://www.metlife.com/assets/cao/mmi/publications/studies/mmi-study-broken-trust-elders-family-finances.pdf

Milkie, Melissa A., and Pia Peltola. 1999. "Playing All the Roles: Gender and the Work–Family Balancing Act." *Journal of Marriage and Family* 61(2): 476–490.

Miller, Robert L., Jr. 2007. "Legacy Denied: African American Gay Men, AIDS, and the Black Church." *Social Work* 52(1): 51–62.

Milner, H. Richard. 2007. "Race, Culture, and Researcher Personality: Working Through Dangers Seen, Unseen, and Unforeseen." *Educational Researcher* 36(7): 388–400.

Minta, Michael D. 2009. "Legislative Oversight and the Substantive Representation of Black and Latino Interests in Congress." *Legislative Studies Quarterly* 34(2): 193–218.

Mishler, Elliot G. 1999. *Storylines: Craftartists' Narratives of Identity*. Cambridge: Harvard University Press.

Moffatt, Michael. 1992. "Ethnographic Writing about American Culture."*Annual Review of Anthropology* 21: 205–29.

Morgan, Joan. 1999. *When Chickenheads Come Home to Roost: My Life as a Hip-Hop Feminist*. New York: Simon and Schuster.

Morris, Aldon. 1984. *The Origins of the Civil Rights Movement: Black Communitites Organizing for Change*. New York: Free Press.

Moynihan, Daniel Patrick. 1965. "The Negro Family: The Case for National Action." Report for the Office of Policy Planning and Research. Washington, DC: United States Department of Labor. http://www.dol.gov/oasam/programs/history/webid-meynihan.htm

Mui, Ada C. 1992. "Caregiver Strain Among Black and White Daughter Caregivers: A Role Theory Perspective." *Gerontologist* 32(2): 203–212.

Mutran, Elizabeth. 1985. "Intergenerational Family Support Among Blacks and Whites: Response to Culture or to Socioeconomic Differences." *Journal of Gerontology* 40(3): 382–389.

Naples, Nancy A., and Carolyn Sachs. 2000. "Standpoint Epistemology and the Uses of Self–Reflection in Feminist Ethnography: Lessons from Rural Sociology." *Rural Sociology* 65(2): 194–214.

Nash, Jennifer C. 2008. "Rethinking Intersectionality."*Feminist Review* 89: 1–15.

Nash, Jennifer C. 2011. "'Hometruths' on Intersectionality." *Yale Journal of Law and Feminism* 23(3): 455–470.

National Association for the Advancement of Colored People 2009. "Criminal Justice Fact Sheet." http://www.naacp.org/pages/criminal-justice-fact-sheet

Navaie-Waliser, Maryam, Aubrey Spriggs, and Penny H. Feldman. 2002. "Informal Caregiving: Differential Experiences by Gender." *Medical Care* 40(12): 1249–1259.

Nelson, Albert. 1991. *Emerging Influentials in State Legislatures*. New York: Praeger.

Norton, Noelle H. 2002. "Transforming Policy from the Inside: Participation in Committee." In *Women Transforming Congress*. ed. Cindy Simon Rosenthal, 316–340. Norman: University of Oklahoma Press.

O'Bannon, Gary. 2001. "Managing Our Future:The Generation X Factor." *Public Personnel Management* 30(1): 95–109.

Ochs, E. and Capps, L. 2001. *Living Narrative: Creating Lives in Everyday Storytelling*. Cambridge, MA: Harvard University Press.

Ogbu, John. 1985. "A Cultural Ecology of Competence Among Inner-City Blacks." In *Beginnings: The Social and Affective Development of Black Children*. eds. M. B. Spencer, G. K. Brookins, and W. R. Allen, 45–66. Hillsdale, NJ: Erlbaum.

Ongiri, Amy A. 1997. "We Are Family: Black Nationalism, Black Masculinity, and the Black Gay Cultural Imagination." *College Literature* 24(1): 280–294.

Orey, Bryon D'Andra, Wendy Smooth, Kimberly S.Adams, and Kisah Harris-Clark. 2006. "Race and Gender Matter: Refining Models of Legislative Policy Making in State Legislatures." *Journal of Women, Politics, and Policy* 28(314): 97–119.

Pateman, Carole. 1988. *The Sexual Contract*. Stanford, CA: Stanford University Press.

Paxton, Pamela, Sheri Kunovich, and Melanie M. Hughes. 2007. "Gender in Politics." *Annual Review of Sociology* 33: 263–284.

Pennock, James R., and John Chapman, eds. 1968. *Representation*. New York: Atherton.

Pew Forum on Religion & Public Life, 2010. "U.S. Religious Landscape Survey." http://religions.pewforum.org/.

Pew Research Center, 2012. "More Support for Gun Rights, Gay Marriage than in 2008 or 2004." Washington, DC: Pew Research Center. http://www.people-press.org/2012/04/25/more-support-for-gun-rights-gay-marriage-than-in-2008-or-2004/

Phillips, Anne. 1995. *Politics of Presence*. New York: Clarendon.

Phillips, Anne. 1998. "Democracy and Representation: Or, Why Should It Matter Who Our Representatives Are?" In *Feminism and Politics*. ed, Anne Phillips, 224–240. New York: Oxford University Press.

Phillips, Anne. 1999. "Why Does Local Democracy Matter?" In *Local Democracy and Local Government*. eds. Lawrence Pratchett and David Wilson, 20–37. New York: Macmillan.

Phinney, Jean S., Tanya Madden, and Lorena J. Santos. 1998. "Psychological Variables as Predictors of Perceived Ethnic Discrimination among Minority and Immigrant Adolescents." *Journal of Applied Social Psychology* 28(11): 937–953.

Pieterse, Jan Nederveen. 1992. *White on Black: Images of Africa and Blacks in Western Popular Culture*. New Haven, CT: Yale University Press.

Pinderhughes, Elaine. 1989. *Signs and Symbols: African Images in African American Quilts*. 2nd ed. Atlanta: Tinwood Books.

Pinquart, Martin, and Silvia Sorensen. 2005. "Ethnic Differences in Stressors, Resources, and Psychological Outcomes of Family Caregiving: A Meta-Analysis". *Gerontologist* 45(1): 90–106.

Pitkin, Hannah. 1967. *The Concept of Representation*. Berkeley: University of California Press.

Plass, Peggy S. 1993. "African American Family Homicide: Patterns in Partner, Parent, and Child Victimization, 1985–1987." *Journal of Black Studies* 23(4): 515–538.

Polikoff, Nancy D. 1993. "We Wil Get What We Ask For: Why Legalizing Gay and Lesbian Marriage Will Not 'Dismantle the Legal Structure of Gender in Ever Marriage'." *Virginia Law Review* 79(7): 1535–1550.

Prestage, Jewel Limar. 1977. "Black Women State Legislators: A Profile." In *A Portrait of Marginality: The Politial Behavior of the African American Woman*. eds. Marianne Githens and Jewel L. Prestage, 410–418. New York: McKay.

Price, Melanye T. 2009. *Dreaming Blackness: Black Nationalism and African American Public Opinion*. New York: New York University Press.

Reed, Adolph, Jr., 2000. *Class Notes: Posing as Politics and Other Thoughts on the American Scene*. New York: New Press.

Reingold, Beth. 2000. *Representing Women: Sex, Gender and Legislative Behavior in Arizona and California*. Chapel Hill: University of North Carolina Press.

Reingold, Beth. 2008. "Women as Officeholders: Linking Descriptive and Substantive Representation." In *Political Women and American Democracy*. eds. Christina Wolbrecht, Karen Beckwith, and Lisa Baldez, 128–147. New York: Cambridge University Press.

Rennison, Callie Marie. 2001. "Intimate Partner Violence and Age of Victim, 1993–99." Special Report for the United States Department of Justice, Office of Justice Programs. Washington, DC: Bureau of Justice Statistics. http://www.bjs.gov/content/pub/pdf/ipva99.pdf.

Rennison, Callie Marie, and Sarah Welchans. 2000. "Intimate Partner Violence." Special Report for the United States Department of Justice, Office of Justice Programs. Washingtn, DC: Bureau of Justice Statistics. http://www.bjs.gov/content/pub/pdf/ipv.pdf

Richie, Beth. 1996. *Compelled to Crime: The Gender Entrapment of Battered Black Women*. New York: Routledge.

Richie, Beth. 2000. "A Black Feminist Reflection on the Antiviolence Movement." *Signs: Journal of Women in Culture and Society* 25(4): 1133–1137.

Risman, Barbara J. 1998. *Gender Vertigo*. New Haven, CT: Yale University Press.

Rosenthal, Cindy Simon. 2000. "Gender Styles in State Legislative Committees: Raising Their Voices in Resolving Conflict." *Women and Politics* 21(2): 21–45.

Rosenwald, Michael. 2012. "Delegate Emmett Burns Blasts Ravens for Linebacker's Support of Gay Mmarriage." *Washington Post*, September 6.

Sanbonmatsu, Kira. 2002. "Gender Stereotypes and Vote Choice." *American Journal of Political Science* 46(1): 20–34.

Sanbonmatsu, Kira. 2005. "State Elelctions: Where Do Women Run: Where Do Women Win?" In *Gender and Elections in America: Shaping the Future of American Politics*. eds. Susan Carrol and Richard Fox, 189–214. New York: Cambridge University Press.

Sánchez, Rosaura. 2006. "On a Critical Realist Theory of Identity." In *Identity Politics Reconsidered*. eds. Linda MartínAlcoff, MicchaelHomes-García, Satya P. Mohanty, and Paula M.L. Moya, 31–52. New York: Palgrave Macmillan.

Sapiro, Virginia. 1981. "When Are Interests Insteresting? The Problem of Political Representation of Women." *American Political Science Review* 75(3): 701–716.

Schattschneider, Elmer E. 1960. *The Semi-Sovereign People: A Realist's View of Democracy*. New York: Holt, Rinehart and Winston.

Schiller, Wendy J. 2000. *Partners and Rivals: Representation in U.S. Senate Delegations*. Princeton, NJ: Princeton University Press.

Schneider, Anne. L., and Helen Ingram. 1993. "Social Construction of Target Populations." *American Political Science Review* 87(2): 334–347.

Schneider, William, and I. A. Lewis. 1984. "The Straight Story on Homosexuality and Gay Rights." *Public Opinion*7 (February/March): 16–60.

Schulte, Lisa, and Juan Battle. 2004. "The Relative Importance of Ethnicity and Religion in Predicting Attitudes Towards Gays and Lesbians." *Journal of Homosexuality* 47(2): 22–25.

Schwartz, Nancy. 1988. *The Blue Guitar: Political Representation and Community*. Chicago: Chicago University Press.

Scola, Beki. 2006. Women of Color in State Legislatures: Gender, Race, and Legislative Office Holding." *Journal of Women, Politics, and Policy* 28(3–4), 43–70.

Scott, Anne Firor. 1990. "Most Invisible of All: Black Women's Voluntary Associations." *The Journal of Southern History* 56(1): 3–22.

Scroggs, Robin. 1983. *The New Testament and Homosexuality*. Philadelphia: Fortress.

Shelby Rosette, Ashleigh, and Tracy L. Dumas. 2007. "The Hair Dilemma: Conform to Mainstream Expectations or Emphasize Racial Identity." *Duke Journal of Gender Law and Policy* 14(1): 407–422.

Shelby, Tommie. 2005. *We Who Are Dark: The Philosophical Foundations of Black Solidarity*. Cambridge, MA: Harvard University Press.

Sickels, Robert J. 1972. *Race, Marriage and the Law*. Albuquerque: University of New Mexico Press.

Siegel, Andrea F. 2012. "Maryland Court Recognizes Out-of-State, Same–Sex Marriages : Decision in Divorce Case Comes as State's Gay Marriage Law Is in Limbo." *Baltimore Sun*, May 18.

Simien, Evelyn M. 2005. "Race, Gender, and Linked Fate." *Journal of Black Studies* 35(5): 529–550.

Simien, Evelyn M. 2006. *Black Feminist Voices in Politics*. Albany: State University of New York Press.

Simien, Evelyn M. 2007. "Doing Intersectionality Research: From Conceptual Issues to Practical Examples." *Politics and Gender* 3(2). 264–271.

Simien, Evelyn M., and Rosalee Clawson. 2004. "The Intersection of Race and Gender: An Experimentation of Black Feminist Consciousness, and Policy Attitudes." *Social Science Quarterly* 85(3): 793–810.

Simons, Margaret A. 1979. "Racism and Feminism: A Schism in the Sisterhood." *Feminist Studies* 5(2): 384–401.

Simpson, Andrea Y. 1998. *The Tie That Binds: Identity and Political Attitudes in the Post-Civil Rights Generation*. New York: New York University Press.

Smith, Barbara. 1976. "Doing Research on Black American Women."*Women's Studies Newsletter* 4(2): 4–5, 7.

Smith, Barbara, ed. 1983. *Home Girls: A Black Feminist Anthology*. New York: Kitchen Table: Women of Color Press.

Smith, Barbara. 2000a. "Introduction." In *Home Girls: A Black Feminist Anthology*. ed. Barbara Smith, xxi–lviii. New York: Kitchen Table: Women of Color Press.

Smith, Barbara, ed. 2000b. *Home Girls: A Black Feminist Anthology*. New Brunswick: Rutgers University Press.

Smith, Dorothy E. 1974. "Women's Perspective as a Radical Critique of Sociology." *Sociological Inquiry* 44(1): 264–271.

Smith, Fraser C. 2008. *Here Lies Jim Crow: Civil Rights in Maryland*. Baltimore: Johns Hopkins University Press.

Smola, Karen W., and Charlottte D. Sutton. 2002. "Generational Differences: Revisiting Generational Work Values for the New Millennium". *Journal of Organizational Behavior* 23(4): 363–382.

Smooth, Wendy G. 2001. "Perceptions of Influence in State Legislatures: A Focus on the Experiences of African American Women in State Legislatures." PhD diss., University of Maryland, College Park.

Smooth, Wendy G. 2006. "Intersectionality in Electoral Politics: A Mess Worth Making." *Politics and Gender* 2(31): 400–414.

Smooth, Wendy, and Tamelyn Tucker. 1999. "Behind But Not Forgotten: Women and the Behind the Scenes Organizing of the Million Man March." In *Still Lifting, Still Climbing: Black Women's Contemporary Activism*. ed. Kimberly Springer, 241–258. New York: New York University Press.

Soule, Sarah A. 2004. "Going to the Chapel? Same-Sex Marriage Bans in the United States, 1973–2000." *Social Problems* 52(4): 453–477.

Spencer, Margaret Beale. 1983. "Children's Cultural Values and Parental Child Rearing Strategies." *Developmental Review* 3(4): 351–370.

Springer, Kimberly. 2002. "Third Wave Black Feminism?" *Signs: Journal of Women in Culture and Society* 27(4): 1059–1082.

Staples, Robert. 1982. *Black Masculinity: The Back Male's Role in American Society*. San Francisco: Black Scholar.

Straus, Murray A., and Richard J. Gelles. 1986. "Societal Change and Change in Family Violence from 1975 to 1985 as Revealed by Two National Surveys." *Journal of Marriage and Family* 48(3): 465–479.

Strolovitch, Dara. 2007. *Affirmative Advocacy: Race, Class, and Gender in Interest Group Politics*. Chicago: University of Chicago Press.

Stryker, Rachael. 2000. "Ethnographic Solutions to the Problems of Russian Adoptees." *Anthropology of Eastern Europe Review*. 18(2):79–84.

Swain, Carol M. 1993. *Black Faces, Black Interests: The Representation of African Americans in Congress*. Cambridge, MA: Harvard University Press.

Swers, Michele L. 2002. *The Difference Women Make*. Chicago: University of Chicago Press.

Tajfel, Henri. 1974. "Social Identity and Intergroup Behaviour." *Social Science Information* 13, 65–93.

Tate, Katherine. 1994. *From Protest to Politics: The New Black Voters in American Elections*. Cambridge, MA: Harvard University Press.

Tate, Katherine. 2003. *Black Faces in the Mirror: African Americans and Their Representatives in the U.S. Congress*. Princeton, NJ: Princeton University Press.

Taylor, Jill M., Carol Gilligan, and Amy M. Sullivan. 1995. *Between Voice and Silence: Women and Girls, Race and Relationship*. Cambridge, MA: Harvard University Press.

Thomas, Kendall. 1996. *Ain't Nothin' Like the Real Thing: Black Masculinity, Gay Sexuality, and the Jargon of Authenticity*. New York: Routledge.

Thompson, Lisa. 2010. *Beyond the Black Lady: Sexuality and the New African American Middle Class*. Chicago: University of Illinois Press.

Tiemeyer, Peter E. 1993. *Relevant Public Opinion Sexual Orientation and U.S. Military Personnel Policy: Options and Assessment*. Santa Monica, CA: National Defense Research Institute.

Tjaden, Patricia and Nancy Theonnes. 2006. "Extent, Nature, and Consequences of Rape Victimization: Findings from the National Violence Against Women Survey." Special Report for the United States Department of Justice, Office of Justice Programs. Washington, DC: National Institute of Justice. https://www.ncjrs.gov/pdffiles1/nij/210346.pdf.

Trosino, James. 1993. "American Wedding: Same-Sex Marriage and the Miscegenation Analogy ". *Boston University Law Review* 79: 93–120.

Trounstine, Jessica. 2009. "All Politics Is Local: The Reemergnce of the Study of City Politics." *Persepctive on Politics* 7(3): 611–618.

Truth, Sojourner. 1851. *Ain't I a Woman?* Akron, OH: Women's Convention.

Turner, John C., M. A. Hogg, P. J. Oakes, S. D. Reicher, and M. S. Wetherell. 1987. *Rediscovering the Social Group: A Self-Categorization Theory*. New York: Blackwell.

U.S. Census Bureau. 1995. Geography Division. Washington DC: US Census Bureau. http://www.census.gov/geo/

Uzzell, Odell, and Wilma Peebles-Wilkins. 1989. "Black Spouse Abuse: A Focus on Relational Factors and Intervention Strategies ". *Western Journal of Black Studies* 13(1): 10–16.

Vanderbeck, R. M. 2005. "Masculinities: Widening the Discussion."*Gender, Place, and Culture* 12: 387–402.

Verba, Sidney, and Norman Nie. 1972. *Participation in America: Political Democracy and Social Equality*. New York: Harper and Row.

Wadsworth, Nancy D. 2010. "Intersectionality in California's Same-Sex Marriage Battles: A Complex Proposition". *Political Research Quarterly* 64(1) 200–216.

Wagner, John, and Peyton M. Craighil. 2012. "Half of Maryland Residents Back Legalizing Same-Sex Marriage." *Washington Post*, January 30.

Wakabayashi, Chizuko, and Katharine Donato. 2005. "The Consequences of Caregiving: Effects on Women's Employment and Earnings." *Population Research and Policy Review* 24(5): 467–488.

Walby, Sylvia. 1990. *Theorizing Patriarchy*. Oxford: Basil Blackwell.

Walby, Sylvia. 1994. "Is Citizenship Gendered?" *Sociology* 28(2): 379–395.

Walby, Sylvia. 1997. *Gender Transformations*. New York: Routledge.

Walker, Alice. 1983. *In Search of Our Mothers' Gardens: Womanist Prose*. New York: Harcourt, Brace Jovanovich.

Wallace, Michele. 1978. *Black Macho and the Myth of the Superwoman*. New York: Dial Press.

Wallace, Michele. 1990. *Invisibility Blues: From Pop to Theory*. New York: Verso.

Walton, Hanes. 1985. *Invisible Politics, Black Political Behavior*. Albany: State University of New York.

Ward, Elijah G. 2005. "Homophobia, Hypermasculinity and the US Black Church." *Culture, Health, and Sexuality* 7(5): 493–504.

Warner, Michael. 1999. *The Trouble with Normal*. New York: New Press.

Warren, Dorian T. 2007. "A New Labor Movement? Race, Class, and the Missing Intersections Between Black and Labor Politics." In *The Expanding Boundaries of Black Politics*.ed. Georgia A. Persons, 43–64. New Brunswick, NJ: Transaction.

Warren, Dorian T. forthcoming. *The Three Faces of Unions: Inclusion and Democracy in the U.S. Labor Movement*. Oxford: Oxford University Press.

Weissert, Carol S. 2000. "Michigan's Welfare Reform: Generous But Tough." In *Learning from Leaders: Welfare Reform Politics and Policy in Five Midwestern States*. ed. Carol S. Weissert, 141–172. Albany, NY: Rockefeller Institute Press.

Weldon, S. Laurel. 2008. "Difference and Social Structure: Iris Young's Legacy of a Critical Social Theory of Gender." *Politics and Gender* 4(2): 311–317.

West, Cornell. 1984. "The Paradox of the Afro-American Rebellion." In *The Sixties Without Apology*. eds. Sohnya Stephanson, Anders Stephanson, Stanley Aronowtiz, and Fredric Jameson, 44–58. Minneapolis: University of Minnesota Press.

West, Traci. 1999. *Wounds of the Spirit: Black Women, Violence, and Resistance Ethics*. New York: New York University Press.

West, Carolyn M., and Suzanna Rose. 2000. "Dating Aggression among African Americans: An Examination of Gender Differences and Adversarial Beliefs ". *Violence Against Women* 6(5): 470–494.

Wharton, Carol S. 1994. "Finding Time for the 'Second Shift': The Impact of Flexible Work Schedules on Women's Double Days." *Gender and Society* 8(2): 189–205.

White, B. 2009. "Bill to Keep Protective Orders from Public Fails." Associated Press, March 10.

White, Evelyn C. 1994.*Chain, Chain, Change: For Bladk Women in Abusive Relationships*. Seattle, WA: Seal Press.

Williams, James H. 1999. *Responding to the Needs of the Gay Male Client*. Thousand Oaks, CA: SAGE.

Williams, Linda F. 2001. "The Civil Rights–Black Power Legacy: Black Women Elected Officials at the Local, State, and National Levels." In *Sisters in the Struggle: African-American Women in the Civil Rights–Black Power Movement*. eds. Bettye Collier-Thomas and V. P.Franklin, 306–331. New York: New York University Press.

Williams, Melissa. 1998. *Voice Trust and Memory: Marginalized Groups and the Failings of Liberal Representation*. Princeton, NJ: Princeton University Press.

Williams, Oliver J., and Lance Becker. 1994. "Partner Abuse Treatment Programs and Cultural Competence: The Results of a National Survey." *Violence and Victims* 9(3): 287–296.

Wilson, Erlene B. 2009. "Maryland: A Leader in Minority Business Enterprise." *Daily Record*, July, 3–5. http://thedailyrecord.com/wp-files/_pdf/publications/ minority%20business.pdf

Winddance Twine, France. 2000. "Racial Ideologies and Racial Methodologies." In *Racing Research, Researching Race: Methodological Dilemmas in Critical Race Studies*, eds. France Winddance Twine and Jonathan Warren, 1–34. New York: New York University Press.

Wilson, William J. 1978. *The Declining Significance of Race: Blacks and Changing American Institutions*. Chicago: University of Chicago Press.

Witko, Christopher, and Sally Friedman. 2008. "Business Backgrounds and Congressional Behavior ". *Congress and the Presidency* 35(1): 71–86.

Wyatt, Gail E., Julie Axelrod, Dorothy Chin, Jennifer VargasCarmona, and Tamra BurnsLoeb. 2000. "Examining Patterns of Vulnerability to Domestic Violence Among African American Women."*Violence Against Women* 3(5): 495–514.

Yanow, D. and Schwartz-Shea, P. 2006 "Doing social science in a humanistic manner," in D. Yanow and P. Schwartz-Shea (eds), *Interpretation and Method: Empirical Research Methods and the Interpretive Turn* Armonk. New York: M E Sharpe, 380–94.

Young, Iris Marion. 1997. *Intersecting Voices: Dilemmas of Gender, Political Philosophy and Policy*. Princeton, NJ: Princeton University Press.

Yuval-Davis, Nira. 2006. "Intersectionality and Feminist Politics." *European Journal of Women's Studies* 13(3): 193–209.

Yuval-Davis, Nira. 2012. *The Politics of Belonging: Intersectional Contestations*. London: Sage Publications.

INDEX

Note: "c" indicates material by chapter. "f" indicates material in figures. "n" indicates material in endnotes. "t" indicates material in tables.

rinted in the USA/Agawam, MA
arch 17, 2015

10746.014